W9-DAR-306

SLAVERY

GREAT
SPEECHES
IN
HISTORY

Karin Coddon, *Book Editor*

Daniel Leone, *President*

Bonnie Szumski, *Publisher*

Scott Barbour, *Managing Editor*

GREENHAVEN PRESS
SAN DIEGO, CALIFORNIA

GALE GROUP
™
THOMSON LEARNING

Detroit • New York • San Diego • San Francisco
Boston • New Haven, Conn. • Waterville, Maine
London • Munich

Every effort has been made to trace the owners of copyrighted material. The articles in this volume may have been edited for content, length, and/or reading level. The titles have been changed to enhance the editorial purpose.

No part of this book may be reproduced or used in any form or by any means, electrical, mechanical, or otherwise, including, but not limited to, photocopy, recording, or any information storage and retrieval system, without prior written permission from the publisher.

Library of Congress Cataloging-in-Publication Data

Slavery / Karin Coddon, book editor.
p. cm. — (Greenhaven Press's great speeches in history)
Includes bibliographical references and index.
ISBN 0-7377-0876-X (pbk. : alk. paper) — ISBN 0-7377-0877-8 (lib. : alk. paper)
1. Slavery—United States—History—19th century—Sources. 2. African Americans—Civil rights—History—19th century—Sources. 3. Antislavery movements—United States—History—19th century—Sources. 4. United States—History—Civil War, 1861–1865—Causes—Sources. 5. United States—History—1815–1861—Sources. I. Coddon, Karin. II. Greenhaven Press great speeches in history.

E449 .S624 2002
973.5—dc21

2001051234

Cover Photo: © CORBIS
Library of Congress, 33, 64, 127, 170
North Wind Picture Archives, 26, 154, 164, 180, 189

Copyright © 2002 by Greenhaven Press, an imprint of The Gale Group
10911 Technology Place, San Diego, CA 92127

Printed in the U.S.A.

Contents

Chapter 1: The Morality of Slavery

Chapter 2: Slavery and Antebellum Law

the federal Fugitive Slave Law by assisting escapes and distributing propaganda. Emancipation would have destructive social consequences on the nation.

Chapter 3: "A House Divided": Civil War

Chapter 4: Emancipation and Reconstruction

Foreword

I have a dream that one day this nation will rise up and live out the true meaning of its creed: "We hold these truths to be self-evident: that all men are created equal."

I have a dream that one day on the red hills of Georgia the sons of former slaves and the sons of former slave owners will be able to sit down together at the table of brotherhood.

I have a dream that one day even the state of Mississippi, a state sweltering with the heat of injustice, sweltering with the heat of oppression, will be transformed into an oasis of freedom and justice.

I have a dream that my four little children will one day live in a nation where they will not be judged by the color of their skin but by the content of their character.

Perhaps no speech in American history resonates as deeply as Martin Luther King Jr.'s "I Have a Dream," delivered in 1963 before a rapt audience of 250,000 on the steps of the Lincoln Memorial in Washington, D.C. Decades later, the speech still enthralls those who read or hear it, and stands as a philosophical guidepost for contemporary discourse on racism.

What distinguishes "I Have a Dream" from the hundreds of other speeches given during the civil rights era are King's eloquence, lyricism, and use of vivid metaphors to convey abstract ideas. Moreover, "I Have a Dream" serves not only as a record of history—a testimony to the racism that permeated American society during the 1960s—but it is also a historical event in its own right. King's speech, aired live on national television, marked the first time that the grave injustice of racism was fully articulated to a mass audience in a way that was both logical and evocative. Julian Bond, a fellow participant in the civil rights movement and student of King's, states that

> King's dramatic 1963 "I Have a Dream" speech before the Lincoln Memorial cemented his place as first among equals in civil rights leadership; from this first televised mass meeting, an American audience saw and heard the unedited oratory of America's finest preacher, and for the first time, a mass white audience heard the undeniable justice of black demands.

Moreover, by helping people to understand the justice of the civil rights movement's demands, King's speech helped to transform the nation. In 1964, a year after the speech was delivered, President Lyndon B. Johnson signed the Civil Rights Act, which outlawed segregation in public facilities and discrimination in employment. In 1965, Congress passed the Voting Rights Act, which forbids restrictions, such as literacy tests, that were commonly used in the South to prevent blacks from voting. King's impact on the country's laws illustrates the power of speech to bring about real change.

Greenhaven Press's Great Speeches in History series offers students an opportunity to read and study some of the greatest speeches ever delivered before an audience. Each volume traces a specific historical era, event, or theme through speeches— both famous and lesser known. An introductory essay sets the stage by presenting background and context. Then a collection of speeches follows, grouped in chapters based on chronology or theme. Each selection is preceded by a brief introduction that offers historical context, biographical information about the speaker, and analysis of the speech. A comprehensive index and an annotated table of contents help readers quickly locate material of interest, and a bibliography serves as a launching point for further research. Finally, an appendix of author biographies provides detailed background on each speaker's life and work. Taken together, the volumes in the Greenhaven Great Speeches in History series offer students vibrant illustrations of history and demonstrate the potency of the spoken word. By reading speeches in their historical context, students will be transported back in time and gain a deeper understanding of the issues that confronted people of the past.

Introduction

On May 17, 1838, Pennsylvania Hall, an impressive three-story structure in Philadelphia built for the express purpose of providing a meeting place for abolitionists, was burned to the ground by a mob incensed by the assembly of the First Annual Convention of Antislavery Women. Philadelphia's mayor and police did little to intervene, just as they had made no great attempt to control the angry throng's disruptive shouting and stone throwing over the previous three days, during which three thousand abolitionists had gathered to hear speeches by Maria Chapman, Angelina Grimké, and others. The mob's next target was the home of Lucretia Mott, the abolitionist, Quaker reformer, and founder of the Philadelphia Female Antislavery Society, but the vigilantes were misdirected and as a result Mott's home, and possibly her life, was spared.

The rioters harbored numerous grievances deeply rooted in the prejudices of the times. For example, in flagrant disregard of social boundaries, the convention had brought together both races and both sexes under one roof, on equal footing. Furthermore, white laborers feared that abolishing slavery would bring an influx of black workers to the industrial North, intensifying competition for jobs. Moreover, for many in the North, the attack on slavery was tantamount to an attack on the constitutionally guaranteed right to personal property, a category to which slaves were assigned.

Official accounts of the fire blamed the abolitionist group itself for inciting the riots because of its racially mixed assembly as well as the views of its members. But the destruction of Pennsylvania Hall did not silence the voices of those who had gathered to speak against slavery. In the decades before the Civil War, the battle over slavery was waged predominantly in public forums, the written and spoken word imbued with rhetoric designed to inflame passions and incite action. Politicians, preachers, and poets all weighed in on the debate over slavery as increasingly incendiary events shaped antebellum America—the Fugitive Slave Law, the Kansas-Nebraska Act, the *Dred Scott* decision, Harpers Ferry.

The chief antagonists in the slavery conflict used extreme rhetoric, casting their respective positions and that of their adversaries in terms of absolute good and absolute evil. Many of those in the political arena sought to defuse the incendiary rhetoric by espousing a "middle course," moderate measures designed to appease both sides by restricting slavery in the territories yet strengthening its legality in the South along with the rights of slaveholders to retrieve slaves who escaped to the North.

A Moral Conflict

Both pro- and antislavery advocates saw themselves as occupying the moral high ground. They commonly invoked the Bible, the Constitution, and the notion of "natural law" to bolster their arguments. The matter of "states' rights"—that is, the sovereignty of individual states over federal intervention—at times seemed to trump the particular issue of slavery. But much of the public discourse offers compelling evidence that the conflict was at heart over slavery: whether to extend it, abolish it, tolerate or denounce it. "States' rights" was in effect a smokescreen thrown up by slavery's apologists, defenders, and appeasers to obscure the essentially moral question of whether a just and democratic society should permit the enslavement of human beings.

Race, of course, played a major role in the debate. While some defenders of slavery sought to minimize the racial element, others emphasized the inferiority of the African to whites in what slavery's apologists called "natural order." Ironically, even many of those who called for emancipation similarly held that blacks were inherently unequal to whites;

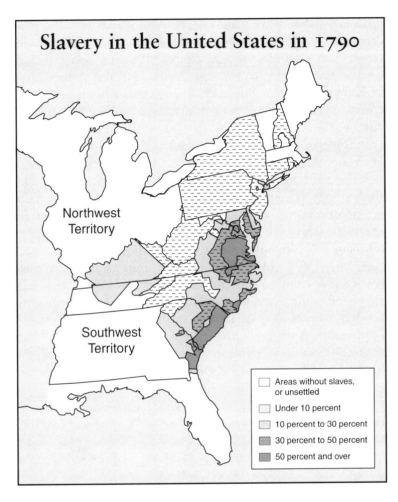

Slavery in the United States in 1790

Northwest Territory

Southwest Territory

Areas without slaves, or unsettled

Under 10 percent

10 percent to 30 percent

30 percent to 50 percent

50 percent and over

these individuals opposed the notion of an integrated society. Despite the prominence of educated, well-spoken, and well-dressed black men such as Frederick Douglass and William Wells Brown, the culturally prevalent image of the ignorant, alternately childlike and barbaric African suited only to subservience and manual labor permeated the slavery debate.

The Origins of Abolitionism

Abolitionism, philosophically rooted in Quaker pacifism and the ideals of New England Transcendentalism and Unitarianism, remained for many years a passionate but largely marginalized social movement. For many southerners and north-erners alike, the early abolitionists were smug moralists at-tempting to foist impractical, utopian ideas of egalitarianism on the rest of the nation. Not unlike several of the slave-holding constitutional framers (e.g., Jefferson), many Ameri-cans viewed slavery in pragmatic terms—abhorrent in prin-ciple but a necessary evil.

However, even in colonial America the debate over slav-ery was usually cast in terms of sectional interests. This sec-tionalism seemed to grow more dramatic with each decade. Eli Whitney's invention of the cotton gin in 1793 spurred the nation's economic dependence on the cotton industry and, by extension, slave labor, from southern plantations to northern textile mills. While it is true that the majority of southerners were not slaveholders, and that most of those who were owned fewer than twenty slaves, the economy and social fab-ric of the South became in the first decades of the nineteenth century increasingly dependent on slavery. Just as northern opposition to slavery came to represent broader views than those of the radical abolitionists, the South's fervent defense of its ostensible rights extended beyond the direct economic interests of wealthy slaveholders.

In the North, a handful of white Christians, many of them Quakers, had been calling for the abolition of slavery since colonial days. But the opposition to slavery increased and intensified due as much to the power of the written and spoken word as to economic change and political events. William Lloyd Garrison's antislavery newspaper the *Libera-tor* was a highly influential organ for the abolitionist move-ment from 1831 through 1865. First-person narratives about the travails of slaves' lives by such writers as Harriet Jacobs, Josiah Henson, and Frederick Douglass, among others, found a wide audience for their harrowing accounts of hu-man bondage, inhumane labor conditions, and destruction of families, as did Harriet Beecher Stowe's immensely popular novel *Uncle Tom's Cabin* (1852).

Middle-class white women formed a significant audience for antislavery popular literature, which drew them to the abolitionist cause. The overtly sentimental, domestic quali-ties of many slave narratives, stressing the grievous toll slavery exacted on religious development and familial bonds, appealed to the tastes and values of the mid-nineteenth-century female readership. Slavery was frequently characterized in contemporary literature as an affront to the sanctity of home, hearth, and Christian virtue. Although "voiceless" in terms of the ballot, blacks and women were key participants in the public discourse, forging an alliance (albeit sometimes an uneasy one) dedicated to the cause of universal suffrage. The presence of so many women in northern antislavery societies provoked internal debates over the propriety of public speaking by female abolitionists and fanned the animosity of slavery's proponents, who largely believed that women should confine their attention to domestic concerns.

The Defense of Slavery

Defenders attempted to counter the popular abolitionist image of slavery as a tyrannical and abusive institution by arguing that the atrocities depicted in abolitionist literature were exaggerated and sensationalized and represented the exception rather than the rule. The typical slaveholder, defenders claimed, was benevolent and paternal, looking after his charges in sickness and old age, regulating their work hours, providing them with food and shelter. The African, slavery's advocates argued, was childlike and incapable of self-determination; hence, slavery was both destiny and boon to blacks. The working conditions of slaves often were favorably compared to those of exploited free laborers in Europe and among the immigrant populace in the Northeast. According to the proslavery argument, the slaves' working hours were regulated; they received adequate food and housing and even medical treatment. It was in the slaveholder's economic interests, apologists argued, to ensure the overall well-being of his unpaid labor force. Some slaves were permitted by their masters to marry, although the unions had no legal standing.

While it is true that not all masters physically abused their slaves, a cursory glance at the copious advertisements for the recapture of runaways testifies to the matter-of-fact manner with which the mistreatment of slaves was regarded. Scars and other disfiguring injuries resulting from abuse are presented as mere distinguishing marks, no more or less remarkable than a fugitive's innate physical characteristics. Certainly as common as physical abuse was the psychological violence inflicted on black families. Healthy young slaves were valuable economic commodities in the domestic trade, and were apt to be sold regardless of their filial ties to other slaves.

Political Speech and Repression

Abolitionist newspapers and pamphlets helped to disseminate the eloquent speeches given at antislavery meetings, enabling the words of Douglass, Thoreau, and Theodore Weld, among others, to reach audiences beyond the particular auditorium where the oration was delivered. This proved especially incendiary when the antislavery literature found its way to the South. Southern politicians such as John C. Calhoun and northerners who sympathized with the slaveholders, such as President James Buchanan, roundly denounced the influx of antislavery literature to slaves (who were in many states officially prohibited from reading and writing) as abolitionist "agitation," designed to provoke escape and/or insurrection. Given the sporadic literacy among slaves, the attempts to repress abolitionist texts in the South were obviously also intended to stymie the spread of antislavery sentiment among nonslaveholding white southerners. In her pamphlet *An Appeal to the Christian Women of the South*, Angelina Grimké makes a particular appeal to her southern sisters to oppose slavery and free their slaves, suggesting that many pious southern ladies were unaware of the atrocities of the institution.

Abolitionist literature also took the controversy overseas, gathering support, especially in Great Britain, for the American antislavery movement. Frederick Douglass and William Wells Brown lobbied abroad for emancipation of American slaves, their speeches often pointing out the disparity between black liberty in Europe (the British Empire outlawed slavery in 1833) and legal bondage in the United States. The successful lecture tours of Douglass and Brown helped cement England's own antislavery sentiment, laying the groundwork for Britain's eventual resistance to the fervent diplomatic efforts of Confederate envoys in the first two years of the Civil War.

Stateside, the antislavery forces encountered their share of legislative obstacles. Congress had imposed on itself a gag rule in 1836 that served to table, or postpone indefinitely, hearing and acting on all antislavery petitions coming before the body. Previously, Congress had dealt in limited ways with the slavery issue, but the gag rule effectively stifled debate on the numerous abolitionist petitions sent to Congress, and thus on the issue of slavery itself. (The gag rule would be rescinded in 1844 under increasing pressure from former president John Quincy Adams and northern congressmen.) The international slave trade was abolished in 1808; the Missouri Compromise of 1821 established a somewhat arbitrary line (at 36" 30' north latitude) endorsing a balance between free and slave states. But if Congress sought to regard the matter as already settled, westward movement of white settlers forced the issue of slavery back into the political forefront. While the debate was frequently couched in the less incendiary terms of "Free-Soil" and "States' Rights," the underlying dispute was firmly over slavery. Representatives of the slaveholding South vigorously argued for the right of each new state admitted to the Union to choose whether or not to permit slavery, as expansion threatened to upset the tenuous balance of power struck in the Missouri Compromise. Free-Soilers, who would be instrumental in the formation of the Republican Party, defended their position just as heatedly.

The Fugitive Slave Law

The Compromise of 1850 admitted California as a free state, but in a conciliatory gesture to the South included a harsher Fugitive Slave Law requiring, among other proslavery measures, that citizens assist authorities in the apprehension of runaway slaves.[1] Although intended to appease both factions, the Compromise had the opposite effect. The Fugitive Slave Law was seen as too harsh by many white northerners

1. The Compromise of 1850 also granted the Utah and New Mexico territories the right to decide by popular vote the matter of slavery, and abolished the slave trade in the nation's capital, although slavery itself was not outlawed in Washington, D.C.

previously disinterested in the slavery controversy or even sympathetic to the concerns of their southern neighbors.

But the Fugitive Slave Law proved most catastrophic for black Americans. Those who had successfully escaped to the North and started new, free lives now lived in renewed danger of apprehension. Even blacks who had purchased or been given their freedom were in danger, since slave hunters rarely troubled to ascertain whether they had captured the right person and the Fugitive Slave Law denied the accused runaway the right to a jury trial. In 1854, public consciousness—and outrage—brought thousands of Bostonians to the streets in protest when federal officers transported escaped slave Anthony Burns to a harborside ship that would bear him back to captivity. In the popular northern imagination, the likes of Anthony Burns became the symbols of an inhumane institution perpetuated by venal southerners and craven, complicit northern politicians.

The conflict over slavery continued to widen throughout the 1850s. The Kansas-Nebraska Act of 1854 effectively negated the parameters set forth in the Missouri Compromise and sparked a series of bloody clashes in southern Kansas between pro- and antislavery settlers. However, the majority of Free-Soilers were not necessarily motivated by the moral aspect of the debate; rather, they were determined that slaveholders not gain what they perceived as an unfair advantage in the competition for land and political clout. These pragmatic Free-Soilers joined many idealistic abolitionists in forming the Republican Party as a loose coalition opposed to slavery's expansion.

In 1857 the Supreme Court handed slaveholders a resounding victory in ruling that Dred Scott, who had sued for his freedom ten years earlier based on the fact that his master had transported him to a free state, was, as one of African descent, not entitled to the rights of citizenship. The *Dred Scott* decision essentially invalidated all previous legislation designed to limit slavery, and became one of the key issues in the famed Lincoln-Douglas debates of 1858. Democrat Stephen Douglas, the U.S. senator from Illinois, was a seasoned proponent of popular sovereignty, instrumental in forging the Compromise of 1850 and the Kansas-Nebraska

Act. His challenger, an ambitious Springfield attorney named Abraham Lincoln, espoused the views of the fledgling Republican Party. Lincoln was a Free-Soiler rather than an abolitionist, firm in his conviction that the Constitution neither endorsed slavery nor prohibited Congress from imposing limitations on it. Douglas won reelection, but the 1858 senatorial contest served to establish Lincoln on the national political landscape as a masterful debater and a formidable opponent of the expansion of slavery.

Lincoln seemed to assume, with many others opposed to slavery, the inherent inferiority of the black race and the necessity of segregating whites and blacks, even toying with the idea of resolving the slavery crisis by sending blacks "back" to Africa. Nonetheless, Lincoln achieved heroic stature to Garrison, Douglass, and many other fervent abolitionists, just as he was viewed by the proslavery South as a radical scarcely less fanatical than John Brown. Both sides seemed to recognize Lincoln's essential aversion to slavery, evident throughout his writings and public addresses as well as in his acts as president.

The "Irrepressible Conflict"

The 1850s saw the conflict over slavery escalate; measures intended to be conciliatory only further polarized the adversaries. In 1859 John Brown, already a veteran of the more violent wing of the abolitionist movement, attempted to spark a widespread slave revolt by seizing the federal arsenal at Harpers Ferry, Virginia. By the time U.S. Marines, armed with bayonets and a battering ram, recaptured the arsenal, eighteen (mostly Brown's men) lay dead; Brown himself was summarily tried, convicted, and hanged. His swift execution did not appease the South, however, especially given the vocal support for Brown's failed mission among northern abolitionists, among them Garrison, Thoreau, and Ralph Waldo Emerson. The raid on Harpers Ferry worked to stoke southern fears about the ultimate aims of northern antislavery "agitators," and talk of secession grew. Proslavery southerners responded to Lincoln's election the next year as though it were an overt act of aggression on the part of the abolitionist North. In their view, Lincoln was not a pragmatic Illinois

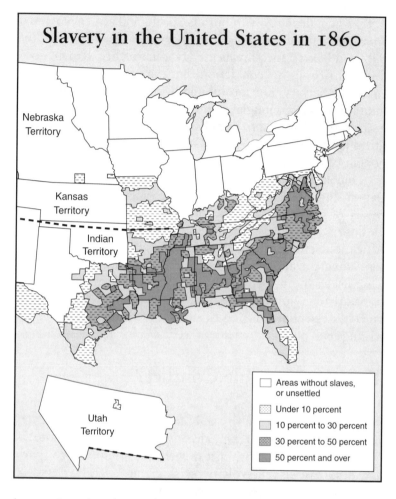

Slavery in the United States in 1860

Nebraska Territory

Kansas Territory

Indian Territory

Utah Territory

	Areas without slaves, or unsettled
	Under 10 percent
	10 percent to 30 percent
	30 percent to 50 percent
	50 percent and over

lawyer but the ghost of John Brown come to wreak destruction on the "peculiar institution" of slavery and hence the entire social and economic fabric of the South. On December 20, 1860, little more than a month after Lincoln's election, South Carolina became the first southern state to secede from the Union. Six months later the Confederacy would consist of eleven southern states in total.

War and Emancipation

At the outbreak of the Civil War Lincoln still defined the key issue as preservation of the Union by quelling the southern rebellion. The focal shift from secession to slavery, however, was not long in coming. In August 1861 Congress passed the First Confiscation Act, authorizing the seizure of any Confederate property (including slaves) that abetted the rebellion; the Second Confiscation Act of July 1862 expressly freed all Confederate slaves, and Lincoln began planning his Emancipation Proclamation, which was issued on September 22, 1862, to take effect the following January. Black troops were actively recruited to fight for the Union; by the end of the war over two hundred thousand black soldiers had served their country, thirty-eight thousand dying. The Civil War, initially characterized as a conflict over the abstract political ideologies of "popular sovereignty" and "preserving the Union," went into its third year as an all but explicit war over slavery. Lincoln's assertion in the opening of his Gettysburg Address that the equality of all men is a basic constitutional tenet identifies universal emancipation as the paramount cause of the conflict. The position once strictly aligned with radical abolitionism had become the driving force of a nation determined to reestablish unity but no longer at the expense of tolerating slavery. The abolitionists' goals were now the Union's stated goals.

The Thirteenth Amendment brought an official end to American slavery in 1865. With freedom came social, demographic, and political upheaval, as the nation strove to heal bitter divisions, mourn its dead, and define the social role and civil rights of the freed slaves. Some abolitionists, like Garrison, saw the long battle over and victory secured, while other veterans of the antislavery movement joined Douglass and J. Mercer Langston in working for black suffrage and all the other rights of full citizenship. Resistance to black equality still ran deep, and not just in the South. Attempts to educate, employ, and situate former slaves economically were derided by northern and southern Democrats as the mischief of "Radical Republicans" aiming to compound further the dire consequences of the Confederacy's fall. The assassination of Lincoln was the last desperate act of Confederate extremism, but it also violently ushered in a new, tumultuous chapter in American race relations. The passage of the Fourteenth and Fifteenth Amendments in 1867 granted black men full citi-

zenship and the right to vote, but less than a decade later Jim
Crow laws passed after the end of Reconstruction rendered
the free exercise of suffrage a principle rather than practice in
many parts of the country, especially the South, for nearly
one hundred years to come.

The Cultural Legacy of Slavery

The ordeal of American slavery affected the nation in countless ways and continues to do so in the early twenty-first century. Out of oppression African Americans forged a rich cul-
tural heritage: music, art, literature, religious practices.
Stereotypes of grinning, childlike slaves put forth in such popular culture classics as *Gone with the Wind* are giving way to
the complex, courageous protagonists created by such African
American writers as Toni Morrison, Richard Wright, and
Sherley Anne Williams. Alex Haley's chronicle *Roots*, detail-
ing the experiences of his slave ancestors, commanded a huge
popular readership and audience for the television miniseries
in the 1970s. Students of all races read the slave narratives
both as historical documents and as works of literature.

But the slavery chapter in American history is far from
closed. The controversies over the symbolism of the Confederate flag and the current debate over whether the descendants of slaves are owed reparations by the federal government suggest that the scars of slavery are not fully healed. It
is hoped that this collection of speeches, some measured,
some strident, some advocating halfway measures and others
fiercely uncompromising, will provide modern readers with a
broader historical perspective on the debate, and a reminder
that the words of the past still speak to our society and culture today. The values and beliefs that shape Americans'
views about race and shared assumptions about social justice
are touched by echoes from the war of words over slavery in
nineteenth century America.

CHAPTER
O N E

The
Morality
of Slavery

Slavery Is Just

George McDuffie

George McDuffie (1790–1851), like his fellow representative from South Carolina John C. Calhoun, was a
forceful advocate of nullification, the doctrine that a state
had the right to void its compact with the federal government should the latter violate the Constitution. McDuffie,
who served from 1821 to 1834 in the U.S. House of Representatives, also served brief terms as South Carolina
governor (1834–1836) and U.S. Senator (1842–1846).

In the following speech, delivered before the South
Carolina legislature in 1835, then-governor McDuffie
presents a justification for slavery based on scriptural as
well as republican principles. Slavery is divinely ordained,
since the "African Negro" is, by his physical, mental, and
moral inferiority, incapable of self-government. Given
their inherent aptitude only for servitude, McDuffie
claims, blacks enjoy a relatively secure and comfortable
existence as slaves, working fewer hours than free European laborers and looked after in old age by benevolent
masters. McDuffie calls slavery the "cornerstone" of truly
republican governments, the guarantor of a stable social
hierarchy. Almost as an afterthought McDuffie acknowledges the vast economic dependence of the South upon
slave labor.

Since your last adjournment, the public mind throughout
the slaveholding states has been intensely, indignantly,
and justly excited by the wanton, officious, and incendiary proceedings of certain societies and persons in some of
the nonslaveholding states, who have been actively employed

From George McDuffie's speech before the South Carolina legislature, 1835.

in attempting to circulate among us pamphlets, papers, and pictorial representations of the most offensive and inflammatory character, and eminently calculated to seduce our slaves from their fidelity and excite them to insurrection and massacre. These wicked monsters and deluded fanatics, overlooking the numerous objects in their own vicinity, who have a moral if not a legal claim upon their charitable regard, run abroad in the expansion of their hypocritical benevolence, muffled up in the saintly mantle of Christian meekness, to fulfill the fiendlike errand of mingling the blood of the master and the slave, to whose fate they are equally indifferent, with the smoldering ruins of our peaceful dwellings. . . .

For the institution of domestic slavery we hold ourselves responsible only to God, and it is utterly incompatible with the dignity and the safety of the state to permit any foreign authority to question our right to maintain it. It may nevertheless be appropriate, as a voluntary token of our respect for the opinions of our confederate brethren, to present some views to their consideration on this subject, calculated to disabuse their minds of false opinions and pernicious prejudices.

The Will of God

No human institution, in my opinion, is more manifestly consistent with the will of God than domestic slavery, and no one of His ordinances is written in more legible characters than that which consigns the African race to this condition, as more conducive to their own happiness, than any other of which they are susceptible. Whether we consult the sacred Scriptures or the lights of nature and reason, we shall find these truths as abundantly apparent as if written with a sunbeam in the heavens. Under both the Jewish and Christian dispensations of our religion, domestic slavery existed with the unequivocal sanction of its prophets, its apostles, and finally its great Author. The patriarchs themselves, those chosen instruments of God, were slaveholders. In fact, the divine sanction of this institution is so plainly written that "he who runs may read" it, and those overrighteous pretenders and Pharisees who affect to be scandalized by its existence among us would do well to inquire how much more nearly they walk in the ways of godliness than did Abraham, Isaac, and Jacob.

That the African Negro is destined by Providence to occupy this condition of servile dependence is not less manifest.
It is marked on the face, stamped on the skin, and evinced by
the intellectual inferiority and natural improvidence of this
race. They have all the qualities that fit them for slaves, and
not one of those that would fit them to be freemen. They are
utterly unqualified not only for rational freedom but for self-
government of any kind. They are, in all respects, physical,
moral, and political, inferior to millions of the human race
who have for consecutive ages dragged out a wretched existence under a grinding political despotism, and who are
doomed to this hopeless condition by the very qualities
which unfit them for a better. It is utterly astonishing that
any enlightened American, after contemplating all the manifold forms in which even the white race of mankind is
doomed to slavery and oppression, should suppose it possible to reclaim the African race from their destiny.

The Capacity to Enjoy Freedom

The capacity to enjoy freedom is an attribute not to be communicated by human power. It is an endowment of God,
and one of the rarest which it has pleased His inscrutable
wisdom to bestow upon the nations of the earth. It is conferred as the reward of merit, and only upon those who are
qualified to enjoy it. Until the "Ethiopian can change his
skin," it will be in vain to attempt, by any human power, to
make freemen of those whom God has doomed to be slaves
by all their attributes.

Let not, therefore, the misguided and designing inter-
meddlers who seek to destroy our peace imagine that they
are serving the cause of God by practically arraigning the decrees of His providence. Indeed, it would scarcely excite sur-
prise if, with the impious audacity of those who projected the
Tower of Babel, they should attempt to scale the battlements
of heaven and remonstrate with the God of wisdom for having put the mark of Cain and the curse of Ham upon the
African race instead of the European.

If the benevolent friends of the black race would compare the condition of that portion of them which we hold in servitude with that which still remains in Africa, totally unblessed by the sights of civilization or Christianity and groaning under a savage despotism, as utterly destitute of hope as of happiness, they would be able to form some tolerable estimate of what our blacks have lost by slavery in America and what they have gained by freedom in Africa. Greatly as their condition has been improved by their subjection to an enlightened and Christian people—the only mode under heaven by which it could have been accomplished—they are yet wholly unprepared for anything like a rational system of self-government. Emancipation would be a positive curse, depriving them of a guardianship essential to their happiness, and they may well say in the language of the Spanish proverb, "Save us from our friends and we will take care of our enemies."

If emancipated, where would they live and what would be their condition? The idea of their remaining among us is utterly visionary. Amalgamation is abhorrent to every sentiment of nature; and if they remain as a separate caste, whether endowed with equal privileges or not, they will become our masters, or we must resume the mastery over them. This state of political amalgamation and conflict, which the Abolitionists evidently aim to produce, would be the most horrible condition imaginable and would furnish Dante or Milton with the type for another chapter illustrating the horrors of the infernal regions. The only disposition, therefore, that could be made of our emancipated slaves would be their transportation to Africa, to exterminate the natives or be exterminated by them; contingencies either of which may well serve to illustrate the wisdom, if not the philanthropy, of these superserviceable madmen who in the name of humanity would desolate the fairest region of the earth and destroy the most perfect system of social and political happiness that ever has existed.

It is perfectly evident that the destiny of the Negro race is either the worst possible form of political slavery or else domestic servitude as it exists in the slaveholding states. The advantage of domestic slavery over the most favorable condition of political slavery does not admit of a question.

NORTHEAST WISCONSIN TECHNICAL COLLEGE
LEARNING RESOURCE CENTER
GREEN BAY WI 54307

The Conditions of Slaves

In all respects, the comforts of our slaves are greatly superior to those of the English operatives, or the Irish and continental peasantry, to say nothing of the millions of paupers crowded together in those loathsome receptacles of starving humanity, the public poorhouses. Besides the hardships of incessant toil, too much almost for human nature to endure, and the sufferings of actual want, driving them almost to despair, these miserable creatures are perpetually annoyed by the most distressing cares for the future condition of themselves and their children.

Some slave owners believed that because they provided for the slave's basic needs their slaves were far better off living in servitude.

From this excess of labor, this actual want, and these distressing cares, our slaves are entirely exempted. They habitually labor from two to four hours a day less than the operatives in other countries; and it has been truly remarked, by some writer, that a Negro cannot be made to injure himself by excessive labor. It may be safely affirmed that they usually eat as much wholesome and substantial food in one day as English operatives or Irish peasants eat in two. And as it regards concern for the future, their condition may well be envied even by their masters. There is not upon the face of the earth any class of people, high or low, so perfectly free from care and anxiety. They know that their masters will provide for them, under all circumstances, and that in the extremity of old age, instead of being driven to beggary or to seek public charity in a poorhouse, they will be comfortably accommodated and kindly treated among their relatives and associates. . . .

In a word, our slaves are cheerful, contented, and happy, much beyond the general condition of the human race, except where those foreign intruders and fatal ministers of mischief, the emancipationists, like their arch-prototype in the Garden of Eden and actuated by no less envy, have tempted them to aspire above the condition to which they have been assigned in the order of Providence. . . .

Reason and philosophy can easily explain what experience so clearly testifies. If we look into the elements of which all political communities are composed, it will be found that servitude, in some form, is one of the essential constituents. No community ever has existed without it, and we may confidently assert none ever will. In the very nature of things there must be classes of persons to discharge all the different offices of society, from the highest to the lowest. Some of those offices are regarded as degrading, though they must and will be performed; hence those manifold forms of dependent servitude which produce a sense of superiority in the masters or employers and of inferiority on the part of the servants. Where these offices are performed by members of the political community, a dangerous element is introduced into the body politic; hence the alarming tendency to violate the rights of property by agrarian legislation, which is beginning to be manifest in the older states, where universal suffrage prevails without domestic slavery, a tendency that will increase in the progress of society with the increasing inequality of wealth.

Slavery Preserves Social Order

No government is worthy of the name that does not protect the rights of property, and no enlightened people will long submit to such a mockery. Hence it is that, in older countries, different political orders are established to effect this indispensable object; and it will be fortunate for the nonslave-holding states if they are not, in less than a quarter of a century, driven to the adoption of a similar institution, or to take refuge from robbery and anarchy under a military despotism.

But where the menial offices and dependent employments of society are performed by domestic slaves, a class well defined by their color and entirely separated from the political body, the rights of property are perfectly secure without the establishment of artificial barriers. In a word, the institution of domestic slavery supersedes the necessity of an order of nobility and all the other appendages of a hereditary system of government. If our slaves were emancipated and admitted, bleached or unbleached, to an equal participation in our political privileges, what a commentary should we furnish upon the doctrines of the emancipationists, and what a revolting spectacle of republican equality should we exhibit to the mockery of the world! No rational man would consent to live in such a state of society if he could find a refuge in any other.

Domestic slavery, therefore, instead of being a political evil, is the cornerstone of our republican edifice. No patriot who justly estimates our privileges will tolerate the idea of emancipation, at any period, however remote, or on any conditions of pecuniary advantage, however favorable. I would as soon open a negotiation for selling the liberty of the state at once as for making any stipulations for the ultimate emancipation of our slaves. So deep is my conviction on this subject that, if I were doomed to die immediately after recording these sentiments, I could say in all sincerity and under all the sanctions of Christianity and patriotism, "God forbid that my descendants, in the remotest generations, should live in any other than a community having the institution of domestic slavery as it existed among the patriarchs of the primitive church and in all the free states of antiquity."

If the legislature should concur in these general views of this important element of our political and social system, our confederates should be distinctly informed, in any communications we may have occasion to make to them, that in claiming to be exempted from all foreign interference, we can recognize no distinction between ultimate and immediate emancipation. . . .

The Value of Cotton

And we have the less reason to look forward to this inauspicious result from considering the necessary consequences which would follow to the people of those states and of the whole commercial world from the general emancipation of our slaves. These consequences may be presented, as an irresistible appeal, to every rational philanthropist in Europe or America. It is clearly demonstrable that the production of cotton depends, not so much on soil and climate as on the existence of domestic slavery. In the relaxing latitudes where it grows, not one-half the quantity would be produced but for the existence of this institution; and every practical planter will concur in the opinion that if all the slaves in these states were now emancipated, the American crop would be reduced the very next year from 1,200,000 to 600,000 bales.

No great skill in political economy will be required to estimate how enormously the price of cotton would be increased by this change, and no one who will consider how largely this staple contributes to the wealth of manufacturing nations, and to the necessaries and comforts of the poorer classes all over the world, can fail to perceive the disastrous effects of so great a reduction in the quantity and so great an enhancement in the price of it. In Great Britain, France, and the United States, the catastrophe would be overwhelming, and it is not extravagant to say that for little more than 2 million Negro slaves, cut loose from their tranquil moorings and set adrift upon the untried ocean of at least a doubtful experiment, 10 million poor white people would be reduced to destitution, pauperism, and starvation.

An anxious desire to avoid the last sad alternative of an injured community prompts this final appeal to the interests and enlightened philanthropy of our confederate states. And we cannot permit ourselves to believe that our just demands, thus supported by every consideration of humanity and duty, will be rejected by states who are united to us by so many social and political ties, and who have so deep an interest in the preservation of that Union.

The North Must Fight Slavery

Angelina Grimké

Angelina Grimké (1803–1879) was, along with her sister
Sarah, a leading proponent of the abolition of slavery
and universal suffrage for blacks and women alike. The
daughter of a South Carolina slaveholder, Grimké
moved north to Philadelphia in 1819. Angelina and
Sarah Grimké were the first women lecturers for the
Anti-Slavery Society, inciting criticism from conservative
preachers who disapproved of women speaking publicly.
Angelina Grimké married abolitionist Theodore Weld in
1835. Throughout her life she continued to campaign for
civil rights and universal suffrage.

As an abolitionist Grimké seldom failed to make deft
use of her own heritage and her firsthand familiarity with
the customs and attitudes of many southern slaveholders.
In the following speech of May 16, 1838, while an un-
ruly mob demonstrated outside Pennsylvania Hall, she
chides Northerners for their general indifference to the
horrors of slavery, and firmly asserts that there may be
no such thing as "neutrality" for Christian men and
women of conscience. Grimké offers a program for fighting slavery: read about the horrors of human bondage;
circulate antislavery books and pamphlets; petition Congress. Even women, though deprived of the right to vote,
are invested with a degree of political influence. Accordingly, Grimké exhorts them especially to petition legislators. Grimké's ardent yet reasoned abolitionism demon-
strates the early affinity between the antislavery and
women's rights movements.

From Angelina Grimké's speech at Pennsylvania Hall, May 16, 1838.

Men, brethren and fathers—mothers, daughters and sisters, what came ye out to see? A reed shaken with the wind? Is it curiosity merely, or a deep sympathy with the perishing slave, that has brought this large audience together? [A yell from the mob without the building.] Those voices without ought to awaken and call out our warmest sympathies. Deluded beings! "they know not what they do." They know not that they are undermining their own rights and their own happiness, temporal and eternal. Do you ask, "what has the North to do with slavery?" Hear it—hear it. Those voices without tell us that the spirit of slavery is here, and has been roused to wrath by our abolition speeches and conventions: for surely liberty would not foam and tear herself with rage, because her friends are multiplied daily, and meetings are held in quick succession to set forth her virtues and extend her peaceful kingdom. This oppression shows that slavery has done its deadliest work in the hearts of our citizens. Do you ask, then, "What has the North to do?" I answer, cast out first the spirit of slavery from your own hearts, and then lend your aid to convert the South. Each one present has a work to do, be his or her situation what it may, however limited their means, or insignificant their supposed influence. The great men of this country will not do this work; the church will never do it. A desire to please the world, to keep favor of all parties and conditions, makes them dumb on this and every other unpopular subject. They have become worldly-wise, and therefore God, in his wisdom, employs them not to carry on his plans of reformation and salvation. He hath chosen the foolish things of this world to confound the wise, and the weak to overcome the mighty.

As a Southerner, I feel that it is my duty to stand up here tonight and bear testimony against slavery. I have seen it—I have seen it. I know it has horrors that can never be described. I was brought up under its wing: I witnessed for many years its demoralizing influences, and its destructiveness to human happiness. It is admitted by some that the slave is not happy under the worst forms of slavery. But I have never seen a happy slave. I have seen him dance in his chains, it is true; but he was not happy. There is a wide difference between happiness and mirth. Man cannot only [be] the former while his manhood is destroyed, and that part of the being which is necessary to the making, and to the enjoyment of happiness, is completely blotted out. The slaves, however, may be, and sometimes are, mirthful. When hope is extinguished, they say, "let us eat and drink, for tomorrow we die." [Just then stones were thrown at the windows,—a great noise without, and commotion within.] What is a mob? What would the breaking of every window be? What would the leveling of this Hall be? Any evidence that we are wrong, or that slavery is good and wholesome institution? What if the mob should now burst in upon us, break up our meeting and commit violence upon our persons—would this be anything compared to what the slaves endure? No, no: and we do not remember them "as bound with them," if we shrink in the time of peril, or feel unwilling to sacrifice ourselves, yet left life enough to feel the truth, even though it rages at it—that conscience is not so completely seared as to be removed by the truth of the living God.

Many persons go to the South for a season, and are hospitably entertained in the parlor and at the table of the slaveholder. They never enter the huts of the slaves; they know nothing of the dark side of the picture, and they return home with praises on their lips of the generous character of those with whom they tarried. Or if they have witnessed the cruelties of slavery, by remaining silent spectators they have naturally become callous—in sensibility has ensued which prepares them to apologize even for barbarity. Nothing but the corrupting influence of slavery on the hearts of the Northern people can induce them to apologize for it; and much will have been done for the destruction of Southern slavery when we have so reformed in [the] North that no one here will be willing to risk his reputation by advocating or even excusing the holding of men as property. The South know it, and acknowledge that as fast as our principle prevail, the hold of the master must be relaxed. [Another outbreak of mobocratic spirit, and some confusion in the house.]

How wonderfully constituted is the human mind! How it resists, as long as it can, all efforts made to reclaim [it] from error! I feel that all this disturbance is but an evidence that our efforts are the best that could have been adopted, or else the friends of slavery, would not care for what we say and do. The South knows what we do. I am thankful that they are reached by our efforts. Many times have I wept in the land of my birth over the system of slavery. I knew of none who sympathized in my feelings—I was unaware that any efforts were made to deliver the oppressed—no voice in the wilder-

Angelina Grimké

ness was heard calling on the people to repent and do works meet for repentance—and my heart sickened within me. Oh, how should I have rejoiced to know that such efforts as these were being made. I only wonder that I had such feelings. I wonder when I reflect under what influence I was brought up, that my heart is not harder than the nether millstone. But in the midst of temptation, I was preserved, and my sympathy grew warmer, and my hatred of slavery more inveterate, until at last I have exiled myself from my native land because I could no longer endure to hear the wailing of the slave. I fled to the land of Penn; for here, thought I, sympathy for the slave will surely be found. But I found it not. The people were kind and hospitable, but the slave had no place in their thoughts. Whenever questions were put to me as to his condition, I felt that they were dictated by an idle curiosity, rather than by that deep feeling which would lead to effort for his rescue. I therefore shut up my grief in my own heart. I remembered that I was a Carolinian, from a state which framed this iniquity by law. I know that throughout her territory was continued suffering, on the one part, and continual brutality and sin on the other. Every Southern breeze wafted to me the discordant tone of weeping and wailing, shrieks and groans, mingled with prayers and blasphemous curses. I thought there was no hope; that the wicked would go on [with] his wickedness, until he had destroyed both himself and his country. My heart sunk within me at the abominations in the midst of which I had been born and educated. What will it avail, cried I in bitterness of spirit, to expose to the gaze of strangers the horrors and pollutions of slavery, when there is no ear to hear nor heart to feel and pray for the slave. The language of my soul was, "Oh tell it not in Gath, publish it not in the streets of Askelon." But how different do I feel now! Animated with hope, nay, with an assurance of the triumph of liberty and good will to man, I will lift up my voice like a trumpet, and show this people their transgression, their sins of omission towards the slave and what they can do towards affecting Southern minds[s], and overthrowing Southern oppression.

No Neutral Ground

We may talk of occupying neutral ground, but on this subject, in its present attitude, there is no such thing as neutral ground. He that is not for us is against us, and he that gathereth not with us, scattereth abroad. If you are on what you suppose to be neutral ground, the South look upon you as an oppressor. And is there one who loves his country willing to give his influence, even indirectly, in favor of slavery—that curse of nations? God swept Egypt with the bosom of destruction, and punished Judea also with a sore punishment, because of slavery. And have we any reason to believe that he is less just now?—or that he will be more favorable to us than his own "peculiar people"? [Shoutings, stones thrown against the windows, &c.]

There is nothing to be feared from those who would stop our mouths, but they themselves should fear and tremble. The current is even now setting fast against them. If the arm of the North had not caused the great Bastille of slavery to totter to its foundations, you would not hear those cries. A few years ago, and the South felt secure, and with a contemptuous sneer asked, "Who are the abolitionists? The abolitionists are nothing"?—Ay, in one sense they were nothing, and they are nothing still. But in this we rejoice, that "God has chosen things that are not to bring to naught things that are." [Mob again disturbed the meeting.]

We often hear the question asked, "What shall we do?" Here is an opportunity for doing something now. Every man and every woman present may do something by showing that we fear not a mob, and, in the midst of threatenings and revilings, by opening our mouths for the dumb and pleading the cause of those who are ready to perish.

What Can Be Done to Fight Slavery

To work as we should in this cause, we must know what Slavery is. Let me urge you then to buy the books which have been written on this subject and read them, and then lend them to your neighbors. Give your money no longer for things which pander to pride and lust, but aid in scattering "the living coals of truth" upon the naked heart of the nation,—in circulating appeals to the sympathies of Christians in behalf of the outraged and suffering slave. But, it is said by some, our "books and papers do not speak the truth." Why, then, do they not contradict what we say? They cannot. Moreover the South has entreated, nay commanded us to be silent; and what greater evidence of the truth of our publications can be desired?

Women of Philadelphia! allow me as a Southern woman, with much attachment to the land of my birth, to entreat to you to come up to this work. Especially let me urge you to petition. Men may settle this and other questions at the ballot-box, but you have no such right; it is only through petitions that you can reach the Legislature. It is therefore peculiarly your duty to petition. Do you say, "It does no good?" The South already turns pale at the number sent. They have read the reports of the proceedings of Congress, and there have seen that among other petitions were very many from the women of the North on the subject of slavery. This fact has called the attention of the South on the subject. How could we expect to have done more as yet? Men who hold the rod over slaves, rule in the councils of the nation: and they deny our right to petition and to remonstrate against abuses of our sex and of our kind. We have these rights, however, from God. Only let us exercise them: and though of ten turned away unanswered, let us remember the influence of importunity upon the unjust judge, and act accordingly. The fact that the South look with jealousy upon our measures shows that they are effectual. There is, therefore, no cause for doubting or despair, but rather for rejoicing.

It was remarked in England that women did much to abolish Slavery in her colonies. Nor are they now idle. Numerous petitions from them have recently been presented to the Queen, to abolish the apprenticeship with its cruelties nearly equal to those of the old system whose place it supplies. One petition two miles and a quarter long has been presented. And do you think these labors will be in vain? Let the history of the past answer. When the women of these States send up to Congress such a petition, our legislators will arise as did those of England, and say, "When all the maids and matrons of the land are knocking at our doors we must legislate." Let the zeal and love, the faith and works of our English sisters quicken ours—that while the slaves continue to suffer, and when they shout deliverance, we may feel that satisfaction of having done what we could.

A Call to Resistance

Henry Highland Garnet

Henry Highland Garnet (1815–1882), along with his parents, escaped from slavery in 1824 and grew up to become a leading spokesman for the abolitionist movement. As a Presbyterian minister, Garnet became active in the Anti-Slavery Society for which he lectured extensively. Garnet aroused controversy when in a speech at the Free Colored People Convention of 1843 in Buffalo, New York, he explicitly called upon slaves to openly resist their bondage, even if violent revolution were the upshot. Even the ardent black abolitionist Frederick Douglass was taken aback by the forthrightness of Garnet's message, and recessed the proceedings. Garnet would be disowned by the Anti-Slavery Society for his advocacy of armed resistance. Garnet continued to speak on behalf of blacks throughout and after the Civil War, becoming the first African American to give a sermon before the House of Representatives.

Garnet, like Douglass, draws an ironic contrast between the American revolutionists' fight for freedom and the continued enslavement of blacks. Alluding to Patrick Henry's noted ultimatum "Give me liberty or give me death," Garnet characterizes the struggle for emancipation in like terms. He points to the prosperity in the British West Indies after slavery was abolished as an example North American blacks might employ to persuade their oppressors to free them. However, should attempts at rational persuasion fail, Garnet reminds his listeners of a host of heroes and martyrs they may emulate in the fight,

From Henry Highland Garnet's address to the slaves of the United States of America, Buffalo, New York, August 16, 1843.

invoking the spirits of Denmark Vesey, Joseph Cinque, and
Nat Turner, among others, in the struggle against bondage.
In a rousing conclusion, Garnet decries passivity and urges
"your motto be resistance! resistance! resistance!"

Brethren and Fellow-Citizens: Your brethren of the
North, East, and West have been accustomed to meet
together in National Conventions, to sympathize with
each other, and to weep over your unhappy condition. In
these meetings we have addressed all classes of the free, but
we have never, until this time, sent a word of consolation and
advice to you. We have been contented in sitting still and
mourning over your sorrows, earnestly hoping that before
this day your sacred liberties would have been restored. But,
we have hoped in vain. Years have rolled on, and tens of
thousands have been borne on streams of blood and tears, to
the shores of eternity. While you have been oppressed, we
have also been partakers with you; nor can we be free while
you are enslaved. We, therefore, write to you as being bound
with you.

Many of you are bound to us, not only by the ties of a
common humanity, but we are connected by the more tender relations of parents, wives, husbands, children, brothers, and sisters, and friends. As such we most affectionately
address you.

Slavery has fixed a deep gulf between you and us, and while
it shuts out from you the relief and consolation which your
friends would willingly render, it afflicts and persecutes you
with a fierceness which we might not expect to see in the fiends
of hell. But still the Almighty Father of mercies has left to us a
glimmering ray of hope, which shines out like a lone star in a
cloudy sky. Mankind are becoming wiser, and better—the oppressor's power is fading, and you, every day, are becoming
better informed, and more numerous. Your grievances,
brethren, are many. We shall not attempt, in this short address, to present to the world all the dark catalogue of this
nation's sins, which have been committed upon an innocent
people. Nor is it indeed necessary, for you feel them from day

to day, and all the civilized world look upon them with amazement. Two hundred and twenty-seven years ago, the first of our injured race were brought to the shores of America. They came not with glad spirits to select their homes in the New World. They came not with their own consent, to find an unmolested enjoyment of the blessings of this fruitful soil. The first dealings they had with men calling themselves Christians, exhibited to them the worst features of corrupt and sordid hearts: and convinced them that no cruelty is too great, no villainy and no robbery too abhorrent for even enlightened men to perform, when influenced by avarice and lust. Neither did they come flying upon the wings of Liberty, to a land of freedom. But they came with broken hearts, from their beloved native land, and were doomed to unrequited toil and deep degradation. Nor did the evil of their bondage end at their emancipation by death. Succeeding generations inherited their chains, and millions have come from eternity into time, and have returned again to the world of spirits, cursed and ruined by American slavery.

The Consequences of Enslavement

The propagators of the system, or their immediate ancestors, very soon discovered its growing evil, and its tremendous wickedness, and secret promises were made to destroy it. The gross inconsistency of a people holding slaves, who had themselves "ferried o'er the wave" for freedom's sake, was too apparent to be entirely overlooked. The voice of Freedom cried, "Emancipate your slaves." Humanity supplicated with tears for the deliverance of their children of Africa. Wisdom urged her solemn plea. The bleeding captive pleaded his innocence, and pointed to Christianity who stood weeping at the cross. Jehovah frowned upon the nefarious institution, and thunderbolts—red with vengeance, struggled to leap forth to blast the guilty wretches who maintained it. But all was vain. Slavery had stretched its dark wings of death over the land, the Church stood silently by—the priests prophesied falsely, and the people loved to have it so. Its throne is established, and now it reigns triumphant. Nearly three millions of your fellow-citizens are prohibited by law and public opinion (which in this country is stronger than law) from reading the Book of Life. Your intellect has been destroyed as much as possible, and every ray of light they have attempted to shut out from your minds. The oppressors themselves have become involved in the ruin. They have become weak, sensual, and rapacious—they have cursed you—they have cursed themselves—they have cursed the earth which they have trod. The colonists threw the blame upon England. They said that the mother country entailed the evil upon them, and that they would rid themselves of it if they could. The world thought they were sincere, and the philanthropic pitied them. But time soon tested their sincerity. In a few years the colonists grew strong, and severed themselves from the British Government. Their independence was declared, and they took their station among the sovereign powers of the earth. The declaration was a glorious document. Sages admired it, and the patriotic of every nation reverenced the God-like sentiments which it contained. When the power of Government returned to their hands, did they emancipate the slaves? No; they rather added new links to our chains. Were they ignorant of the principles of Liberty? Certainly they were not. The sentiments of their revolutionary orators fell in burning eloquence upon their hearts, and with one voice they cried, Liberty or Death. Oh what a sentence was that. It ran from soul to soul like electric fire, and nerved the arm of thousands to fight in the holy cause of Freedom. Among the diversity of opinions that are entertained in regard to physical resistance, there are but a few found to gainsay that stern declaration. We are among those who do not. Slavery! How much misery is comprehended in that single word. What mind is there that does not shrink from its direful effects? Unless the image of God be obliterated from the soul, all men cherish the love of Liberty. The nice discerning political economist does not regard the sacred right more than the untutored African who roams in the wilds of Congo. Nor has the one more right to the full enjoyment of his freedom than the other. In every man's mind the good seeds of liberty are planted, and he who brings his fellow down so low, as to make him contented with a condition of slavery, commits the highest crime against God and man. Brethren, your oppressors aim to do this. They endeavor to make you as much like brutes as possible. When they have blinded the eyes of your mind—when they have embittered the sweet waters of life—when they have shut out the light which shines from the word of God—then, and not till then, has American slavery done its perfect work.

To such Degradation it is sinful in the Extreme for you to make voluntary Submission. The divine commandments you are in duty bound to reverence and obey. If you do not obey them, you will surely meet with the displeasure of the Almighty. He requires you to love him supremely, and your neighbor as yourself—to keep the Sabbath day holy—to search the Scriptures—and bring up your children with respect for His laws, and to worship no other God but Him. But slavery sets all these at naught, and hurls defiance in the face of Jehovah. The forlorn condition in which you are placed does not destroy your moral obligation to God. You are not certain of heaven, because you suffer yourselves to remain in a state of slavery, where you cannot obey the commandments of the Sovereign of the universe. If the ignorance of slavery is a passport to heaven, then it is a blessing, and no curse, and you should rather desire its perpetuity than its abolition. God will not receive slavery, nor ignorance, nor any other state of mind, for love and obedience to him. Your condition does not absolve you from your moral obligation. The diabolical injustice by which your liberties are cloven down, neither God, nor angels, or just men, command you to suffer for a single moment. Therefore it is your solemn and imperative duty to use every means, both moral, intellectual, and physical, that promises success. If a band of heathen men should attempt to enslave a race of Christians, and to place their children under the influence of some false religion, surely, Heaven would frown upon the men who would not resist such aggression, even to death. If, on the other hand, a band of Christians should attempt to enslave a race of heathen men, and to entail slavery upon them, and to keep them in heathenism in the midst of Christianity, the God of heaven would smile upon every effort which the injured might make to disenthral themselves.

Brethren, it is as wrong for your lordly oppressors to

keep you in slavery, as it was for the man thief to steal our ancestors from the coast of Africa. You should therefore now use the same manner of resistance, as would have been just in our ancestors, when the bloody foot-prints of the first remorseless soul-thief was placed upon the shores of our fatherland. The humblest peasant is as free in the sight of God as the proudest monarch that ever swayed a sceptre. Liberty is a spirit sent out from God, and like its great Author, is no respecter of persons.

A Call to Action: Liberty or Death

Brethren, the time has come when you must act for yourselves. It is an old and true saying that, "if hereditary bondmen would be free, they must themselves strike the blow." You can plead your own cause, and do the work of emancipation better than any others. The nations of the old world are moving in the great cause of universal freedom, and some of them at least will, ere long, do you justice. The combined powers of Europe have placed their broad seal of disapprobation upon the African slave-trade. But in the slave-holding parts of the United States, the trade is as brisk as ever. They buy and sell you as though you were brute beasts. The North has done much—her opinion of slavery in the abstract is known. But in regard to the South, we adopt the opinion of the New York Evangelist—"We have advanced so far, that the cause apparently waits for a more effectual door to be thrown open than has been yet." We are about to point you to that more effectual door.

Look around you, and behold the bosoms of your loving wives heaving with untold agonies! Hear the cries of your poor children! Remember the stripes your fathers bore. Think of the torture and disgrace of your noble mothers. Think of your wretched sisters, loving virtue and purity, as they are driven into concubinage and are exposed to the unbridled lusts of incarnate devils. Think of the undying glory that hangs around the ancient name of Africa:—and forget not that you are native-born American citizens, and as such, you are justly entitled to all the rights that are granted to the freest. Think how many tears you have poured out upon the soil which you have cultivated with unrequited toil and enriched with your blood; and then go to your lordly enslavers and tell them plainly, that you are determined to be free. Appeal to their sense of justice, and tell them that they have no more right to oppress you, than you have to enslave them. Entreat them to remove the grievous burdens which they have imposed upon you, and to remunerate you for your labor. Promise them renewed diligence in the cultivation of the soil, if they will render to you an equivalent for your services. Point them to the increase of happiness and prosperity in the British West-Indies since the Act of Emancipation. Tell them in language which they cannot misunderstand, of the exceeding sinfulness of slavery, and of a future judgment, and of the righteous retributions of an indignant God. Inform them that all you desire is freedom, and that nothing else will suffice. Do this, and for ever after cease to toil for the heartless tyrants, who give you no other reward but stripes and abuse. If they then commence the work of death, they, and not you, will be responsible for the sequences. You had far better all die—die immediately, than live slaves, and entail your wretchedness upon your posterity. If you would be free in this generation, here is your only hope. However much you and all of us may desire it, there is not much hope of redemption without the shedding of blood. If you must bleed, let it all come at once—rather die freemen than live to be the slaves. It is impossible, like the children of Israel to make a grand exodus from the land of bondage. The Pharaohs are on both sides of the blood-red waters! You cannot move en masse, to the dominions of the British Queen—nor can you pass through Florida and overrun Texas, and at last find peace in Mexico. The propagators of American slavery are spending their blood and treasure, that they may plant the black flag in the heart of Mexico and riot in the halls of the Montezumas. In the language of the Rev. Robert Hall, when addressing the volunteers of Bristol, who were rushing forth to repel the invasion of Napoleon, who threatened to lay waste the fair homes of England, "Religion is too much interested in your behalf, not to shed over you her most gracious influences."

You will not be compelled to spend much time in order

to become inured to hardships. From the first moment that you breathed the air of heaven, you have been accustomed to nothing else but hardships. The heroes of the American Revolution were never put upon harder fare than a peck of corn and a few herrings per week. You have not become enervated by the luxuries of life. Your sternest energies have been beaten out upon the anvil of severe trial. Slavery has done this, to make you subservient to its own purposes; but it has done more than this, it has prepared you for an emergency. If you receive good treatment, it is what you could hardly expect; if you meet with pain, sorrow, and even death, these are the common lot of the slaves.

Fellow-men! patient sufferers! behold your dearest rights crushed to the earth! See your sons murdered, and your wives, mothers and sisters doomed to prostitution. In the name of the merciful God, and by all that life is worth let it no longer be a debatable question, whether it is better to choose Liberty or death.

The "Bright Stars of Freedom"

In 1822, Denmark Veazie, of South Carolina, formed a plan for the liberation of his fellow-men. In the whole history of human efforts to overthrow slavery, a more complicated and tremendous plan was never formed. He was betrayed by the treachery of his own people, and died a martyr to freedom. Many a brave hero fell, but history, faithful to her high trust, will transcribe his name on the same monument with Moses, Hampden, Tell, Bruce and Wallace, Toussaint L'Ouverture, Lafayette and Washington. That tremendous movement shook the whole empire of slavery. The guilty soul-thieves were overwhelmed with fear. It is a matter of fact, that at that time, and in consequence of the threatened revolution, the slave States talked strongly of emancipation. But they blew but one blast of the trumpet of freedom, and then laid it aside. As these men became quiet, the slaveholders ceased to talk about emancipation: and now behold your condition to-day! Angels sigh over it, and humanity has long since exhausted her tears in weeping on your account!

The patriotic Nathaniel Turner followed Denmark Veazie.

He was goaded to desperation by wrong and injustice. By despotism, his name has been recorded on the list of infamy, and future generations will remember him among the noble and brave.

Next arose the immortal Joseph Cinque, the hero of the Amistad. He was a native African, and by the help of God he emancipated a whole ship-load of his fellow-men on the high seas. And he now sings of liberty on the sunny hills of Africa and beneath his native palm-trees, where he hears the lion roar and feels himself as free as that king of the forest.

Next arose Madison Washington, that bright star of freedom, and took his station in the constellation of true heroism. He was a slave on board the brig Creole, of Richmond, bound to New Orleans, that great slave mart, with a hundred and four others. Nineteen struck for liberty or death. But one life was taken, and the whole were emancipated, and the vessel was carried into Nassau, New Providence. Noble men! Those who have fallen in freedom's conflict, their memories will be cherished by the true-hearted and the God-fearing in all future generations; those who are living, their names are surrounded by a halo of glory.

Brethren, arise, arise! Strike for your lives and liberties. Now is the day and the hour. Let every slave throughout the land do this, and the days of slavery are numbered. You cannot be more oppressed than you have been—you cannot suffer greater cruelties than you have already. Rather die freemen than live to be slaves. Remember that you are four millions!

It is in your power so to torment the God-cursed slaveholders, that they will be glad to let you go free. If the scale was turned, and black men were the masters and white men the slaves, every destructive agent and element would be employed to lay the oppressor low. Danger and death would hang over their heads day and night. Yes, the tyrants would meet with plagues more terrible than those of Pharaoh. But you are a patient people. You act as though you were made for the special use of these devils. You act as though your daughters were born to pamper the lusts of your masters and overseers. And worse than all, you tamely submit while your lords tear your wives from your embraces and defile them before your eyes. In the name of God, we ask, are you men?

Where is the blood of your fathers? Has it all run out of your veins? Awake, awake; millions of voices are calling you! Your dead fathers speak to you from their graves. Heaven, as with a voice of thunder, calls on you to arise from the dust.

Let your motto be resistance! resistance! resistance! No oppressed people have ever secured their liberty without resistance. What kind of resistance you had better make, you must decide by the circumstances that surround you, and according to the suggestion of expediency. Brethren, adieu! Trust in the living God. Labor for the peace of the human race, and remember that you are four millions.

Slavery: A National Guilt

William Wells Brown

William Wells Brown (ca. 1814–1884) was a leading black abolitionist writer and orator. His work *Clotel* was the first novel by an African American writer to be published. Born a slave in Kentucky to a black mother and white father (a relative of his owner), Brown escaped to the North in 1834 and began his career of assisting fugitive slaves to a safe haven in Canada. In 1836 Brown moved to Buffalo, New York, where he became active in the abolitionist movement. He befriended other black abolitionists such as Frederick Douglass, whose views about the inadvisability of violent resistance Brown shared.

Brown's literary career was blossoming as well with his increased political involvement. In 1847 he published his autobiography, followed over the years by numerous works of fiction, history, and personal narrative. In 1849 he embarked upon a lecture tour of Great Britain, addressing the evils of American slavery. Brown would not return to the United States until 1854, in part because the 1850 Fugitive Slave Law exposed him to the possibility of recapture by his former owner. In fact, British abolitionists effectively bought Brown's freedom in 1854, allowing his safe return to America.

In this speech to a London audience, Brown assails American hypocrisy in excusing slavery as ill imposed upon the New World by England yet refusing to emulate the British in abolishing it. He reminds his audience that even as he speaks as a free man in England, as an escaped slave, his freedom is at risk the moment he sets foot again

From William Wells Brown's speech at the Concert Rooms, Store Street, London, England, September 27, 1849.

in America. Unlike many others in the abolitionist movement, Brown characterizes the institution of slavery as
constitutionally sanctioned.

S ir, I wish to make a remark or two in seconding the resolution which is now before the meeting. I am really
glad that this meeting has produced this discussion, for
I think it will all do good; in fact, I know it will, for the cause
of truth. Reference has been made to slavery having been carried to America by the sanction of this country. Now, that is
an argument generally used in America by slaveholders themselves. (Hear, hear.) Go to the United States; talk to slaveholders about the disgrace of slavery being found in a pro-
fessedly Christian republic, and they will immediately reply,
"England imposed it upon us; Great Britain was the cause of
it, for she established slavery in America, and we are only
reaping the fruits of her act." Now, gentlemen, I would reply
to our friend here, as I have replied to Americans again and
again—If you have followed England in the bad example of
the institution of slavery, now follow her in the good example of the abolition of slavery. (Cheers.) Some remarks were
also made by that gentleman respecting the Americans having abolished the slave trade. It is true that they did pass a
law, but not in 1808, that the slave trade should be abolished: they passed a law in 1788 that they would only continue the slave trade for twenty years longer, and at the end
of that period there should not be any more slaves imported
into the United States. They said, "We will rob Africa of her
sons and daughters for twenty years longer, and then stop."
(Hear and laughter.) But why did they determine that the
slave trade should be put an end to? The honorable gentleman has not told you that. Why, it was to give to Virginia,
Kentucky and Maryland a monopoly in the trade of raising
slaves to supply the Southern market. (Cheers.) That was the
reason, and the only reason, why they abolished the foreign
slave trade in America. They allowed the foreign slave trade
to be carried on for twenty years from that time, and during
the whole of that period made those who were engaged in the

internal slave traffic pay a duty of ten dollars for every slave brought into the country, the whole of the money going into the exchequer of the United States. The Government said, "We will have a tariff of so much per head upon God's children that are stolen from Africa, and the revenue derived therefrom shall be the support of the republican institutions of the United States." (Hear, hear.) Do the Americans claim credit for an act like that? Claim credit for abolishing the foreign slave trade, in order that they might make a lucrative domestic slave trade! (Cheers.) Why, ladies and gentlemen, only a few years since, 40,000 slaves were carried out of the single State of Virginia, in one year, and driven off to the far South, to supply the market there. Claim credit for abolishing the slave trade! Claim credit for husbands torn from their wives, and children from their parents! Claim credit for herds of human beings carried off in coffle gangs, and to be worked to death in the rice and cotton fields! That is the character of the domestic slave trade now carried on, even in the capital of America. No, no; the people of the United States can claim no credit on that score. They can find no apology in the fact of slavery being a domestic institution. A pretty "domestic institution," truly! (Hear, hear.) Why, in 1847, only two years since, a woman and her daughter were sold in the very capital of America, in the very city of Washington, by the U.S. marshal, on the 3d day of July, the day before the national anniversary of the glorious Declaration of Independence, by which all men were declared free and equal, and the product of the sale of these immortal beings was put into the treasury of the United States. That is one specimen among many of the working of the "domestic institution" of America. (Cheers.) It dooms me, for example, to be a slave as soon as I shall touch any part of the United States. (Hear, hear.) Yes, Sir, it is indeed domestic enough; it is domesticated all over the country; it extends from one end of America to the other, and is as domesticated as is the Constitution of the United States itself; it is just as domesticated as is the territory over which the United States Government have jurisdiction. Wherever the Constitution proclaims a bit of soil to belong to the United States, there it dooms me to be a slave the moment I set my foot upon it; and all the 20,000 or 30,000

of my brethren who have made their escape from the Southern States, and taken refuge in Canada or the Northern
States, are in the same condition. And yet this American slavery is apologized for as a "domestic institution"! I am glad
that our eloquent friend, Mr. [English abolitionist George]
Thompson, has impressed the fact upon your minds, that
slavery is a *national institution*, and that the guilt of maintaining it is *national guilt*. I am anxious that that circumstance should be understood, and that Englishmen should
know, that the slave is just as much a slave in the city of
Boston; of which this gentleman is just as much a citizen as
he is in Charleston, South Carolina: he is just as much a slave
in any of the Eastern States as he is in the Southern States. If
I am protected in my person in the city of Boston, and if I
have been protected there for the last two or three years, and
the slaveholder has not been able to catch me and carry me
back again into slavery, I am not at all indebted for that privilege to the Constitution of the United States, but I owe it entirely to that public sentiment which my friend Mr. Thompson, at the peril of his life, so nobly helped to create in
America. (Loud cheers.) I am indebted to the anti-slavery
sentiment, and that alone, when I am in Boston itself, for the
personal protection I enjoy. I cannot look at the Constitution
or laws of America as a protection to me; in fact, I have no
Constitution, and no country. I cannot, like the eloquent gentleman who last addressed you, say—"I am bound to stand
up in favor of America." (Hear.) I would to God that I could;
but how can I! America has disfranchised me, driven me off,
and declared that I am not a citizen, and never shall be, upon
the soil of the United States. Can I, then, gentlemen, stand up
for such a country as that? Can I have any thing to say in favor of a country that makes me a chattel, that renders me a
saleable commodity, that converts me into a piece of property? Can I say any thing in favor of a country, or its institutions, that will give me up to the slaveholder, if he can only
find out where I am, in any part of America? Why I am more
free here tonight, in monarchical England, than I should be
in my own republican country! Whatever our friend from
Boston may do, I would that I could say with him, "I must,
in honor, stand up in favor of America." And yet I love

America as much as he does. I admire her enterprising and industrious people quite as ardently as he can; but I hate her hideous institution, which has robbed me of a dear mother, which has plundered me of a beloved sister and three dear brothers, and which institution has doomed them to suffer, as they are now suffering, in chains and slavery. Whatever else there may be to admire in the condition of America, at all events, I hate that portion of her Constitution. I hate, I fervently hate, those laws and institutions of America, which consign three millions of my brethren and sisters to chains for life. Talk about going to the slaveholders with money! Talk about recognizing their right to property in human beings! What! property in man! property in God's children! I will not acknowledge that any man has a right to hold me as property, till he can show his right to supersede the prerogative of that Creator whose alone I am. (Cheers.) Just read the letter which you will find in the preface to my narrative, where my own master has very kindly offered to sell me to myself for half price. (Laughter.) He imagines that the anti-slavery movement has depreciated his property in me, and therefore he offers to take half price for his runaway property. (Renewed laughter.) My answer to him was, that he should never receive a single dollar from me, or any one else in my behalf, with my consent. (Cheers.) I said so, because I am not willing to acknowledge the right of property in man under any circumstances. I believe that the same God who made the slaveholder made the slave (hear, hear) and that the one is just as free as the other.

On White Hypocrisy

Before resuming my seat, I would say to our friend from Boston, as I said to another gentleman a short time before I left America, who talked in a similar manner about the slave States, and the good treatment the slaves received, and so forth. At the close of a meeting, that gentleman rose, and requested permission to ask me some simple questions, which were as follows: Had I not enough to eat when I was in slavery? Was I not well clothed while in the Southern States? Was I ever whipped? and so forth. I saw that he only wanted a peg on which to hang a pro-slavery speech, but I answered his questions in the affirmative. He immediately rose and made a speech, in which he endeavored to make his audience believe that I had run away from a very good place indeed. (Laughter.) He asked them if they did not know hundreds and thousands of poor people in America and England, who would be willing to go into the State of Missouri and there fill the situation I had run away from. (Cries of Oh, Oh!) A portion of the assembly for a moment really thought his plea for slavery was a good one. I saw that the meeting was anxious to break up, in consequence of the lateness of the hour, and therefore that it would not do for me to reply at any length, and I accordingly rose and made a single remark in answer to this pro-slavery speech. I said, the gentleman has praised up the situation I left, and made it appear quite another thing to what it ever appeared to me when I was there; but however that may be, I have to inform him that that situation is still vacant, and as far as [I] have any thing voluntary to do with it, it shall remain so; but, nevertheless, if that gentleman likes to go into Missouri and fill it, I will give him a recommendation to my old master, and I doubt not that he would receive him with open arms, and give him enough to eat, enough to wear, and flog him when ever he thought he required it. (Loud cheers and laughter.) So I say to our friend from Boston, tonight, if he is so charmed with slavery, he shall have the same recommendation to my old master. (Loud cheers.)

GREAT
SPEECHES
IN
HISTORY

Slavery and Antebellum Law

The South Must Preserve the Institution of Slavery

John C. Calhoun

John Caldwell Calhoun (1782–1850), Yale-educated statesman from South Carolina, spent much of his adult life in public office, including the U.S. Senate (1842–43, 1845–50). Elected vice president in 1824 (under John Quincy Adams) and 1828 (under Andrew Jackson), Calhoun resigned from that office in 1832 due to his opposition to Jackson's Tariff of 1828. He subsequently was reelected to the Senate, where he remained steadfast on such issues as states' rights and slavery.

In "The South Must Preserve the Institution of Slavery," Calhoun speaks to Congress on behalf of a body of Southern legislators in arguing that the Constitution supports the rights of slaveholders, and that the Northern attempts to foil the Fugitive Slave Law are illegal. Moreover, he contends that many in the North strive to violate the law indirectly by enticing slaves to escape and then abetting them secretly (via the Underground Railroad, though Calhoun does not use the term) in the safe passage to Canada. Calhoun decries the "subversive" activities of the abolitionists, whose newspapers, pamphlets, lectures, and entreaties to Congress all seek to undermine the South and its Constitutionally sanctioned slaveholding rights.

From John C. Calhoun's speech "The Southern Address," before the U.S. Congress, 1849.

We, whose names are hereunto annexed, address you in discharge of what we believe to be a solemn duty, on the most important subject ever presented for your consideration. We allude to the conflict between the two great sections of the Union, growing out of a difference of feeling and opinion in reference to the relation existing between the two races, the European and the African, which inhabit the southern section, and the acts of aggression and encroachment to which it has led.

The conflict commenced not long after the acknowledgment of our independence, and has gradually increased until it has arrayed the great body of the North against the South on this most vital subject. In the progress of this conflict, aggression has followed aggression, and encroachment encroachment, until they have reached a point when a regard for your peace and safety will not permit us to remain longer silent. The object of this address is to give you a clear, correct, but brief account of the whole series of aggression and encroachments on your rights, with a statement of the dangers to which they expose you. Our object in making it is not to cause excitement, but to put you in full possession of all the facts and circumstances necessary to a full and just conception of a deep-seated disease, which threatens great danger to you and the whole body politic. We act on the impression, that in a popular government like ours, a true conception of the actual character and state of a disease is indispensable to effecting a cure.

We have made it a joint address, because we believe that the magnitude of the subject required that it should assume the most impressive and solemn form.

Not to go further back, the difference of opinion and feeling in reference to the relation between the two races, disclosed itself in the Convention that framed the Constitution, and constituted one of the greatest difficulties in forming it. After many efforts, it was overcome by a compromise, which provided in the first place, that representative and direct taxes shall be apportioned among the States according to their respective numbers; and that, in ascertaining the number of each, five slaves shall be estimated as three. In the next, that slaves escaping into States where slavery does not exist, shall not be discharged from servitude, but shall be delivered up on claim of the party to whom their labor or service is due. In the third place, that Congress shall not prohibit the importation of slaves before the year 1808; but a tax not exceeding ten dollars may be imposed on each imported. And finally, that no capitation or direct tax shall be laid, but in proportion to federal numbers; and that no amendment of the Constitution, prior to 1808, shall affect this provision, nor that relating to the importation of slaves.

So satisfactory were these provisions, that the second, relating to the delivering up of fugitive slaves, was adopted unanimously, and all the rest, except the third, relative to the importation of slaves until 1808, with almost equal unanimity. They recognize the existence of slavery, and make a specific provision for its protection where it was supposed to be the most exposed. They go further, and incorporate it, as an important element, in determining the relative weight of the several States in the Government of the Union, and the respective burden they should bear in laying capitation and direct taxes. It was well understood at the time, that without them the Constitution would not have been adopted by the Southern States, and of course that they constituted elements so essential to the system that it never would have existed without them. The Northern States, knowing all this, ratified the Constitution, thereby pledging their faith, in the most solemn manner, sacredly to observe them. How that faith has been kept and that pledge redeemed we shall next proceed to show.

With few exceptions of no great importance, the South had no cause to complain prior to the year 1819—a year, it is to be feared, destined to mark a train of events, bringing with them many, and great, and fatal disasters, on the country and its institutions. With it commenced the agitating debate on the question of the admission of Missouri into the Union. We shall pass by for the present this question, and others of the same kind, directly growing out of it, and shall proceed to consider the effects of that spirit of discord, which it roused up between the two sections. It first disclosed itself in the North, by hostility to that portion of the Constitution which provides for the delivering up of fugitive slaves. In its progress it led to the adoption of hostile acts, intended to render it of non-effect, and with so much success that it may be regarded now as practically expunged from the Constitution. How this has been effected will be next explained.

After a careful examination, truth constrains us to say, that it has been by a clear and palpable evasion of the Constitution. It is impossible for any provision to be more free from ambiguity or doubt. It is in the following words: "No person held to service, or labor, in one State, under the laws thereof, escaping into another State, shall, in consequence of any law or regulation therein, be discharged from such service or labor, but shall be delivered up on claim of the party to whom such service or labor may be due." All is clear. There is not an uncertain or equivocal word to be found in the whole provision. What shall not be done, and what shall be done, are fully and explicitly set forth. The former provides that the fugitive slave shall not be discharged from his servitude by any law or regulation of the State wherein he is found; and the latter, that he shall be delivered up on claim of his owner.

The Northern Evasion of Law

We do not deem it necessary to undertake to refute the sophistry and subterfuges by which so plain a provision of the Constitution has been evaded, and, in effect, annulled. It constitutes an essential part of the constitutional compact, and of course the supreme law of the land. As such it is binding on all, the Federal and State Governments, the States and the individuals composing them. The sacred obligation of compact, and the solemn injunction of the supreme law, which legislators and judges, both Federal and State, are bound by oath to support, all unite to enforce its fulfilment, according to its plain meaning and true intent. What that meaning and intent are, there was no diversity of opinion in the better days of the Republic, prior to 1819. Congress, State Legislatures, State and Federal Judges and Magistrates, and people, all spontaneously placed the same interpretation on it. During that period none interposed impediments in the way of the owner seeking to recover his fugitive slave; nor did any deny his right to have every proper facility to enforce his claim to have him delivered up. It was then nearly as easy to recover one found in a Northern State, as one found in a neighboring Southern State. But this has passed away, and the provision is defunct, except perhaps in two States [Indiana and Illinois].

When we take into consideration the importance and clearness of this provision, the evasion by which it has been set aside may fairly be regarded as one of the most fatal blows ever received by the South and the Union. This cannot be more concisely and correctly stated, than it has been by two of the learned judges of the Supreme Court of the United States. In one of his decisions [the case of Prigg *vs.* the Commonwealth of Pennsylvania] Judge [Joseph] Story said: "Historically it is well known that the object of this clause was to secure to the citizens of the slaveholding States the complete right and title of ownership in their slaves, as property, in every State of the Union, into which they might escape, from the State wherein they were held in servitude. The full recognition of this right and title was indispensable to the security of this species of this property, in all the slaveholding States, and, indeed, was so vital to the preservation of their interests and institutions, that it cannot be doubted, that it constituted a fundamental article without the adoption of which the Union would not have been formed. Its true design was to guard against the doctrines and principles prevalent in the non-slaveholding States, by preventing them from intermeddling with, or restricting, or abolishing the rights of the owners of slaves."

Again: "The clause was therefore of the last importance to the safety and security of the Southern States, and could not be surrendered by them without endangering their whole property in slaves. The clause was accordingly adopted in the Constitution by the unanimous consent of the framers of it— a proof at once of its intrinsic and practical necessity."

Again: "The clause manifestly contemplates the existence of a positive unqualified right on the part of the owner of the slave, which no State law or regulation can in any way regulate, control, qualify, or restrain."

The opinion of the other learned judges was not less emphatic as to the importance to this provision and the unquestionable right of the South under it. Judge [Henry] Baldwin, in charging the jury, said: [the case of Johnson *vs.* Tompkins and others] "If there are any rights of property which can be enforced, if one citizen have any rights of property which are inviolable under the protection of the supreme law of the State, and the Union, they are those which have been set at nought by some of these defendants. As the owner of property, which he had a perfect right to possess, protect, and take away—as a citizen of a sister State, entitled to all the privileges and immunities of citizens of any other States—Mr. Johnson stands before you on ground which cannot be taken from under him—it is the same ground on which the Government itself is based. If the defendants can be justified, we have no longer law or government." Again, after referring more particularly to the provision for delivering up fugitive slaves, he said: "Thus you see, that the foundations of the Government are laid, and rest on the right of property in slaves. The whole structure must fall by disturbing the corner-stone."

These are grave and solemn and admonitory words, from a high source. They confirm all for which the South has ever contended, as to the clearness, importance, and fundamental character of this provision, and the disastrous consequences which would inevitably follow from its violation. But in spite of these solemn warnings, the violation, then commenced, and which they were intended to rebuke, has been full and perfectly consummated. The citizens of the South, in their attempt to recover their slaves, now meet, instead of aid and co-operation, resistance in every form; resistance from hostile acts of legislation, intended to baffle and defeat their claims by all sorts of devices, and by interposing every description of impediment—resistance from judges and magistrates—and finally, when all these fail, from mobs, composed of whites and blacks, which, by threats or force, rescue the fugitive slave from the possession of his rightful owner. The attempt to recover a slave, in most of the Northern States, cannot now be made without the hazard of insult, heavy pecuniary loss, imprisonment, and even of life itself. Already has a worthy citizen of Maryland lost his life [Mr. Kennedy, of Hagerstown, Maryland] in making an attempt to enforce his claim to a fugitive slave under this provision.

The Northern Enticement of Slaves

But a provision of the Constitution may be violated indirectly as well as directly; by doing an act in its nature inconsistent with that which is enjoined to be done. Of the form of violation, there is a striking instance connected with the provision under consideration. We allude to secret combinations which are believed to exist in many of the Northern States, whose object is to entice, decoy, entrap, inveigle, and seduce slaves to escape from their owners, and to pass them secretly and rapidly, by means organized for the purpose, into Canada, where they will be beyond the reach of the provision. That to entice a slave, by whatever artifice, to abscond from his owner, into a non-slaveholding State, with the intention to place him beyond the reach of the provision, or prevent his recovery, by concealment or otherwise, is as completely repugnant to it, as its open violation would be, is too clear to admit of doubt or to require illustration. And yet, as repugnant as these combinations are to the true intent of the provision, it is believed, that, with the above exception, not one of the States, within whose limits they exist, has adopted any measure to suppress them, or to punish those by whose agency the object for which they were formed is carried into execution. On the contrary, they have looked on, and witnessed with indifference, if not with secret approbation, a great number of slaves enticed from their owners, and placed beyond the possibility of recovery, to the great annoyance and heavy pecuniary loss of the bordering Southern States.

When we take into consideration the great importance of this provision, the absence of all uncertainty as to its true meaning and intent, the many guards by which it is surrounded to protect and enforce it, and then reflect how completely the object for which it was inserted in the Constitution is defeated by these two-fold infractions, we doubt, taking all together, whether a more flagrant breach of faith is to be found on record. We know the language we have used is strong, but it is not less true than strong.

There remains to be noticed another class of aggressive acts of a kindred character, but which instead of striking at an express and specific provision of the Constitution, aims directly at destroying the relation between the two races at the South, by means subversive in their tendency of one of the ends for which the Constitution was established. We refer to the systematic agitation of the question by the Abolitionists, which, commencing about 1835, is still continued in all possible forms. Their avowed intention is to bring about a state of things that will force emancipation on the South. To unite the North in fixed hostility to slavery in the South, and to excite discontent among the slaves with their condition, are among the means employed to effect it. With a view to bring about the former, every means are resorted to in order to render the South, and the relation between the two races there, odious and hateful to the North. For this purpose societies and newspapers are everywhere established, debating clubs opened, lecturers employed, pamphlets and other publications, pictures and petitions to Congress, resorted to, and directed to that single point, regardless of truth or decency; while the circulation of incendiary publications in the South, the agitation of the subject of abolition in Congress, and the employment of emissaries are relied on to excite discontent among the slaves. This agitation, and the use of these means, have been continued with more or less activity for a series of years, not without doing much towards effecting the object intended. We regard both object and means to be aggressive and dangerous to the rights of the South, and subversive, as stated, of one of the ends for which the Constitution was established. Slavery is a domestic institution. It belongs to the States, each for itself to decide, whether it shall be established or not; and if it be established, whether it should be abolished or not. Such being the clear and unquestionable right of the States, it follows necessarily that it would be a flagrant act of aggression on a State, destructive of its rights, and subversive of its independence, for the Federal Government, or one or more States, or their people, to undertake to force on it the emancipation of its slaves. But it is a sound maxim in politics, as well as law and morals, that no one has a right to do that indirectly what he cannot do directly, and it may be added with equal truth, to aid, abet, or countenance another in doing it. And yet the Abolitionists of the North, openly avowing their intention, and resorting to the most efficient means for the purpose, have been attempting to bring about a state of things to force the Southern States to emancipate their slaves, without any act on the part of any Northern State to arrest or suppress the means by which they propose to accomplish it. They have been permitted to pursue their object, and to use whatever means they please, if without aid or countenance, also without resistance or disapprobation. What gives a deeper shade to the whole affair, is the fact, that one of the means to effect their object, that of exciting discontent among our slaves, tends directly to subvert what its preamble declares to be one of the ends for which the Constitution was ordained and established: "to ensure domestic tranquillity," and that in the only way in which domestic tranquillity is likely ever to be disturbed in the South. Certain it is, that an agitation so systematic—having such an object in view, and sought to be carried into execution by such means—would, between independent nations, constitute just cause of remonstrance by the party against which the aggression was directed, and if not heeded, an appeal to arms for redress. Such being the case where an aggression of the kind takes place among independent nations, how much more aggravated must it be between confederated States, where the Union precludes an appeal to arms, while it affords a medium through which it can operate with vastly increased force and effect? That it would be perverted to such a use, never entered into the imagination of the generation which formed and adopted the Constitution, and, if it had been supposed it would, it is certain that the South never would have adopted it. . . .

Slavery and Territories

For many years the subject of slavery in reference to the territories ceased to agitate the country. Indications, however, connected with question of annexing Texas, showed clearly that it was ready to break out again, with redoubled violence, on some future occasion. The difference in the case of

Texas was adjusted by extending the Missouri compromise line of 36° 30', from its terminus, on the western boundary of the Louisiana purchase, to the western boundary of Texas. The agitation again ceased for a short period.

The war with Mexico soon followed, and that terminated in the acquisition of New Mexico and Upper California, embracing an area equal to about one half of the entire valley of the Mississippi. If to this we add the portion of Oregon acknowledged to be ours by the recent treaty with England, our whole territory on the Pacific and west of the Rocky Mountains will be found to be in extent but little less than that vast valley. The near prospect of so great an addition rekindled the excitement between the North and South in reference to slavery in its connection with the territories, which has become, since those on the Pacific were acquired, more universal and intense than ever.

The effects have been to widen the difference between the two sections, and give a more determined and hostile character to their conflict. The North no longer respects the Missouri compromise line, although adopted by their almost unanimous vote. Instead of compromise, they avow that their determination is to exclude slavery from all the territories of the United States, acquired, or to be acquired; and, of course, to prevent the citizens of the Southern States from emigrating with their property in slaves into any of them. Their object, they allege, is to prevent the extension of slavery, and ours to extend it, thus making the issue between them and us to be the naked question, shall slavery be extended or not? We do not deem it necessary, looking to the object of this address, to examine the question so fully discussed at the last session, whether Congress has the right to exclude the citizens of the South from immigrating with their property into territories belonging to the confederated States of the Union. What we propose in this connection is, to make a few remarks on what the North alleges, erroneously, to be the issue between us and them.

So far from maintaining the doctrine, which the issue implies, we hold that the Federal Government has no right to extend or restrict slavery, no more than to establish or abolish it; nor has it any right whatever to distinguish between the domestic institutions of one State, or section, and another, in order to favor one and discourage the other. As the federal representative of each and all the States, it is bound to deal out, within the sphere of its powers, equal and exact justice and favor to all. To act otherwise, to undertake to discriminate between the domestic institutions of one and another, would be to act in total subversion of the end for which it was established—to be the common protection and guardian of all. Entertaining these opinions, we ask not, as the North alleges we do, for the extension of slavery. That would make a discrimination in our favor, as unjust and unconstitutional as the discrimination they ask against us in their favor. It is not for them, nor for the Federal Govern-

Slaves prepare cotton for the gin on a plantation near Beaufort, South Carolina.

ment to determine, whether our domestic institution is good or bad; or whether it should be repressed or preserved. It belongs to us, and us only, to decide such questions. What then we do insist on, is, not to extend slavery, but that we shall not be prohibited from immigrating with our property, into the Territories of the United States, because we are slaveholders; or, in other words, that we shall not on that account be disfranchised of a privilege possessed by all others, citizens and foreigners, without discrimination as to character, profession, or color. All, whether savage, barbarian, or civilized, may freely enter and remain, we only being excluded.

We rest our claim, not only on the high grounds above stated, but also on the solid foundation of right, justice, and equality. The territories immediately in controversy—New Mexico and California—were acquired by the common sacrifice and efforts of all the States, towards which the South contributed far more than her full share of men . . .

To say nothing of money, and is, of course, on every principle of right, justice, fairness and equality, entitled to participate fully in the benefits to be derived from their acquisition. But as impregnable as is this ground, there is another not less so. Ours is a Federal Government—a Government in which not individuals, but States as distinct sovereign communities, are the constituents. To them, as members of the Federal Union, the territories belong; and they are hence declared to be territories belonging to the United States. The States, then, are the joint owners. Now it is conceded by all writers on the subject, that in all such Governments their members are all equal—equal in rights and equal in dignity. They also concede that this equality constitutes the basis of such Government, and that it cannot be destroyed without changing their nature and character. To deprive, then, the Southern States and their citizens of their full share in territories declared to belong to them, in common with the other States, would be in derogation of the equality belonging to them as members of a Federal Union, and sink them, from being equals, into a subordinate and dependent condition. Such are the solid and impregnable grounds on which we rest our demand to an equal participation in the territories.

But as solid and impregnable as they are in the eyes of

justice and reason, they oppose a feeble resistance to a majority, determined to engross the whole. At the last session of Congress, a bill was passed, establishing a territorial government for Oregon, excluding slavery therefrom. The President gave his sanction to the bill, and sent a special message to Congress assigning his reasons for doing so. These reasons presupposed that the Missouri compromise was to be, and would be, extended west of the Rocky Mountains, to the Pacific Ocean, and the President intimated his intention in his message to veto any future bill that should restrict slavery south of the line of that compromise. Assuming it to have been the purpose and intention of the North to extend the Missouri compromise line as above indicated, the passage of the Oregon bill could only be regarded as evincing the acquiescence of the South in that line. But the developments of the present session of Congress have made it manifest to all, that no such purpose or intention now exists with the North to any considerable extent. Of the truth of this, we have ample evidence in what has occurred already in the House of Representatives, where the popular feelings are soonest and most intensely felt.

Congressional Aggression Toward Slavery

Although Congress has been in session but little more than one month, a greater number of measures of an aggressive character have been introduced, and they are more aggravated and dangerous, than have been for years before. And what clearly discloses whence they take their origin, is the fact, that they all relate to the territorial aspect of the subject of slavery, or some other of a nature and character intimately connected with it.

The first of this series of aggressions is a resolution introduced by a member from Massachusetts, the object of which is to repeal all acts which recognize the existence of slavery, or authorize the selling or disposing of slaves in this District [the District of Columbia]. On question of leave to bring in a bill, the votes stood 69 for and 82 against leave. The next was a resolution offered by a member from Ohio, instructing the Committee on Territories to report forthwith bills for excluding slavery from California and New Mexico. It passed by a vote of 107 to 80. That was followed by a bill introduced by another member from Ohio, to take the votes of the inhabitants of this District, on the question whether slavery within its limits should be abolished.

The bill provided, according to the admission of the mover, that free negroes and slaves should vote. On the question to lay the bill on the table, the votes stood, for 106, against 79. To this succeeded the resolution of a member from New York, in the following words: "Whereas the traffic now prosecuted in this metropolis of the Republic in human beings, as chattels, is contrary to natural justice and the fundamental principles of our political system, and is notoriously a reproach to our country, throughout Christendom, and a serious hindrance to the progress of republican liberty among the nations of the earth. Therefore,

"*Resolved*, That the Committee for the District of Columbia be instructed to report a bill, as soon as practicable, prohibiting the slave trade in said District." On the question of adopting the resolution, the votes stood 98 for, and 88 against. He was followed by a member from Illinois, who offered a resolution for abolishing slavery in the Territories, and all places where Congress has exclusive powers of legislation, that is, in all forts, magazines, arsenals, dockyards, and other needful buildings, purchased by Congress with the consent of the Legislature of the State.

This resolution was passed over under the rules of the House without being put to vote.

The votes in favor of all these measures were confined to the members from the Northern States. True, there are some patriotic members from that section who voted against all of them, and whose high sense of justice is duly appreciated; who in the progress of the aggressions upon the South have, by their votes, sustained the guaranties of the Constitution, and of whom we regret to say many have been sacrificed at home by their patriotic course.

We have now brought to close a narrative of the series of acts of aggression and encroachment, connected with the subject of this address, including those that are consummated and those still in progress. They are numerous, great, and dangerous, and threaten with destruction the greatest and most vital of all the interests and institutions of the South. Indeed, it may be doubted whether there is a single provision, stipulation, or guaranty of the Constitution, intended for the security of the South, that has not been rendered almost perfectly nugatory. It may even be made a serious question, whether the encroachments already made, without the aid of any other, would not, if permitted to operate unchecked, end in emancipation, and that at no distant day. But be that as it may, it hardly admits of a doubt that, if the aggressions already commenced in the House, and now in progress, should be consummated, such in the end would certainly be the consequence.

Little, in truth, would be left to be done after we have been excluded from all the territories, including those to be hereafter acquired; after slavery is abolished in this District and in the numerous places dispersed all over the South, where Congress has the exclusive right of legislation, and after the other measures proposed are consummated. Every outpost and barrier would be carried, and nothing would be left but to finish the work of abolition at pleasure in the States themselves. This District, and all places over which Congress has exclusive power of legislation, would be asylums for fugitive slaves, where, as soon as they placed their feet, they would become, according to the doctrines of our Northern assailants, free, unless there should be some positive enactments to prevent it.

The Dangers of Emancipation

Under such a state of things the probability is, that emancipation would soon follow, without any final act to abolish slavery. The depressing effects of such measures on the white race at the South, and the hope they would create in the black of a speedy emancipation, would produce a state of feeling inconsistent with the much longer continuance of the existing relations between the two. But be that as it may, it is certain, if emancipation did not follow, as a matter of course, the final act in the States would not be long delayed. The want of constitutional power would oppose a feeble resistance. The great body of the North is united against our peculiar institution. Many believe it to be sinful, and the residue, with inconsiderable exceptions, believe it to be wrong. Such being the case, it would indicate a very superficial knowledge of human nature, to think that, after aiming at abolition, systematically, for so many years, and pursuing it with such unscrupulous disregard of law and Constitution, that the fanatics who have led the way and forced the great body of the North to follow them, would, when the finishing stroke only remained to be given, voluntarily suspend it, or permit any constitutional scruples or considerations of justice to arrest it. To these may be added an aggression, though not yet commenced, long meditated and threatened: to prohibit what the abolitionists call the internal slave trade, meaning thereby the transfer of slaves from one State to another, from whatever motive done, or however effected. Their object would seem to be to render them worthless by crowding them together where they are, and thus hasten the work of emancipation. There is reason for believing that it will soon follow those now in progress, unless, indeed, some decisive step should be taken in the mean time to arrest the whole.

The question then is, Will the measures of aggression proposed in the House be adopted?

They may not, and probably will not be this session. But when we take into consideration, that there is a majority now in favor of one of them, and a strong minority in favor of the other, so far as the sense of the House has been taken; that there will be in all probability a considerable increase in the next Congress of the vote in favor of them, and that it will be largely increased in the next succeeding Congress under the census to be taken next year, it amounts almost to a certainty that they will be adopted, unless some decisive measure is taken in advance to prevent it.

But, even if these conclusions should prove erroneous—if fanaticism and the love of power should, contrary to their nature, for once respect constitutional barriers, or if the calculations of policy should retard the adoption of these measures, or even defeat them altogether, there would still be left one certain way to accomplish their object, if the determination avowed by the North to monopolize all the territories, to the exclusion of the South, should be carried into effect. That of itself would, at no distant day, add to the North a sufficient number of States to give her three fourths of the whole; when, under the color of an amendment to the Constitution, she would emancipate our slaves, however opposed it might be to its true intent.

Thus, under every aspect, the result is certain, if aggression be not promptly and decidedly met. How is it to be met, is for you to decide.

Such then being the case, it would be to insult you to suppose you could hesitate. To destroy the existing relation between the free and servile races at the South would lead to consequences unparalleled in history. They cannot be separated, and cannot live together in peace, or harmony, or to their mutual advantage, except in their present relation. Under any other, wretchedness, and misery, and desolation would overspread the whole South. The example of the British West Indies, as blighting as emancipation has proved to them, furnishes a very faint picture of the calamities it would bring on the South. The circumstances under which it would take place with us, would be entirely different from those which took place with them, and calculated to lead to far more disastrous results. There the Government of the parent country emancipated slaves in her colonial possessions— a Government rich and powerful, and actuated by views of policy (mistaken as they turned out to be), rather than fanaticism. It was besides, disposed to act justly towards the owners, even in the act of emancipating their slaves, and protect and foster them afterwards. It accordingly appropriated nearly $100,000,000 as a compensation to them for their losses under the act, which sum, although it turned out to be far short of the amount, was thought at the time to be liberal. Since the emancipation, it has kept up a sufficient military and naval force to keep the blacks in awe, and a number of magistrates, and constables, and other civil officers, to keep order in the towns and on plantations, and enforce respect to their former owners. To a considerable extent these have served as a substitute for the police formerly kept on the plantations by the owners and their overseers, and to preserve the social and political superiority of the white race. But, notwithstanding all this, the British West India possessions are ruined, impoverished, miserable, wretched, and destined probably to be abandoned to the black race.

Very different would be the circumstances under which emancipation would take place with us. If it ever should be effected, it will be through the agency of the Federal Government, controlled by the dominant power of the Northern States of the Confederacy, against the resistance and struggle of the Southern. It can then only be effected by the prostration of the white race; and that would necessarily engender the bitterest feelings of hostility between them and the North. But the reverse would be the case between the blacks of the South and the people of the North. Owing their emancipation to them, they would regard them as friends, guardians, and patrons, and centre, accordingly, all their sympathy in them. The people of the North would not fail to reciprocate and to favor them, instead of the whites. Under the influence of such feelings, and impelled by fanaticism and love of power, they would not stop at emancipation. Another step would be taken—to raise them to a political and social equality with their former owners, by giving them the right of voting and holding public offices under the Federal Government. We see the first step toward it in the bill already alluded to—to vest the free blacks and slaves with the right to vote on the question of emancipation in this District. But when once raised to an equality, they would become the fast political associates of the North, acting and voting with them on all questions, and by this political union between them, holding the white race at the South in complete subjection. The blacks, and the profligate whites that might unite with them, would become the principal recipients of federal offices and patronage, and would, in consequence, be raised above the whites of the South in the political and social scale. We would, in a word, change conditions with them—a degradation greater than has ever yet fallen to the lot of a free and enlightened people, and one from which we could not escape, should emancipation take place (which it certainly will if not prevented), but by fleeing the homes of ourselves and ancestors, and by abandoning our country to our former slaves, to become the permanent abode of disorder, anarchy, poverty, misery, and wretchedness.

A Plea for Unanimity

With such a prospect before us, the gravest and most solemn question that ever claimed the attention of a people is presented for your consideration: What is to be done to prevent it? It is a question belonging to you to decide. All we propose is, to give you our opinion.

We, then, are of the opinion that the first and indispensable step, without which nothing can be done, and with which every thing may be, is to be united among yourselves, on this great and most vital question. The want of Union and concert in reference to it has brought the South, the Union, and our system of government to their present perilous condition. Instead of placing it above all others, it has been made subordinate, not only to mere questions of policy, but to the preservation of party ties and ensuring of party success. As high as we hold a due respect for these, we hold them subordinate to that and other questions involving our safety and happiness. Until they are so held by the South, the North will not believe that you are in earnest in opposition to their encroachments, and they will continue to follow, one after another, until the work of abolition is finished. To convince them that you are, you must prove by your acts that you hold all other questions subordinate to it. If you become united, and prove yourselves in earnest, the North will be brought to a pause, and to a calculation of consequences; and that may lead to a change of measures, and the adoption of a course of policy that may quietly and peaceably terminate this long conflict between the two sections. If it should not, nothing would remain for you but to stand up immovably in defence of rights, involving your all—your property, prosperity, equality, liberty, and safety.

As the assailed, you would stand justified by all laws, human and divine, in repelling a blow so dangerous, without looking to consequences, and to resort to all means necessary for that purpose. Your assailants, and not you, would be responsible for consequences.

Entertaining these opinions, we earnestly entreat you *to be united,* and for that purpose adopt all necessary measures. Beyond this, we think it would not be proper to go at present.

We hope, if you should unite with any thing like unanimity, it may of itself apply a remedy to this deep-seated and dangerous disease; but, if such should not be the case, the time will then have come for you to decide what course to adopt.

Will the Union Be Dissolved?

Daniel Webster

Daniel Webster (1782–1852) was among the most notable statesmen, orators, and lawyers of his time. The New Hampshire–born Webster represented both his home state and Massachusetts in the U.S. Congress (1812–1815; 1829–1850). Webster served as Secretary of State first under William Henry Harrison (1841–1843) and again under Millard Fillmore (1850–1852). During his second, brief tenure as Secretary of State, he rigorously supervised the implementation of the Fugitive Slave Law, much to the disapproval of the abolitionists.

Webster opposed the expansion of slavery, but supported appeasing the South by helping owners recover fugitive slaves. In his famed "March 7th Speech" Webster urges the North to cooperate with the seizure of escaped slaves for the sake of preserving the Union. While conceding that each side has legitimate grievances, Webster also seems to assign more gravity to the complaints of the South regarding Northern obstruction of the Fugitive Slave Law. He dismisses the efforts of abolitionists as well-intentioned but not especially "useful." What most appalls Webster, however, is the notion of Southern secession over the slavery conflict, a possibility he regards as impossible to achieve peacefully. He concludes on an explicitly patriotic note, as if to remind the antagonists of the common ideals that bind Americans despite the current sectional divisions.

From Daniel Webster's address before the U.S. Congress, March 7, 1850.

Mr. President,—I wish to speak to-day, not as a Massachusetts man, nor as a Northern man, but as an American, and a member of the Senate of the United States. It is fortunate that there is a Senate of the United States; a body not yet moved from its propriety, not lost to a just sense of its own dignity and its own high responsibilities, and a body to which the country looks, with confidence, for wise, moderate, patriotic, and healing counsels. It is not to be denied that we live in the midst of strong agitations, and are surrounded by very considerable dangers to our institutions and our government. The imprisoned winds are let loose. The East, the North, and the stormy South combine to throw the whole sea into commotion, to toss its billows to the skies, and disclose its profoundest depths. I do not affect to regard myself, Mr. President, as holding, or as fit to hold, the helm in this combat with the political elements; but I have a duty to perform, and I mean to perform it with fidelity, not without a sense of existing dangers, but not without hope. I have a part to act, not for my own security or safety, for I am looking out for no fragment upon which to float away from the wreck, if wreck there must be, but for the good of the whole, and the preservation of all; and there is that which will keep me to my duty during this struggle, whether the sun and the stars shall appear, or shall not appear for many days. I speak to-day for the preservation of the Union. "Hear me for my cause." I speak to-day, out of a solicitous and anxious heart for the restoration to the country of that quiet and harmonious harmony which make the blessings of this Union so rich, and so dear to us all. These are the topics I propose to myself to discuss; these are the motives, and the sole motives, that influence me in the wish to communicate my opinions to the Senate and the country; and if I can do any thing, however little, for the promotion of these ends, I shall have accomplished all that I expect. . . .

Now, Sir, upon the general nature and influence of slavery there exists a wide difference of opinion between the northern portion of this country and the southern. It is said on the one side, that, although not the subject of any injunction or direct prohibition in the New Testament, slavery is a wrong; that it is founded merely in the right of the strongest; and that is an oppression, like unjust wars, like all those conflicts by which a powerful nation subjects a weaker to its will; and that, in its nature, whatever may be said of it in the modifications which have taken place, it is not according to the meek spirit of the Gospel. It is not "kindly affectioned"; it does not "seek another's, and not its own"; it does not "let the oppressed go free". These are the sentiments that are cherished, and of late with greatly augmented force, among the people of the Northern States. They have taken hold of the religious sentiment of that part of the country, as they have, more or less, taken hold of the religious feeling of a considerable portion of mankind. The South, upon the other side, having been accustomed to this relation between two races all their lives, from their birth, having been taught, in general, to treat the subjects of this bondage with care and kindness, and I believe, in general, feeling great kindness for them, have not taken the view of the subject which I have mentioned. There are thousands of religious men, with consciences as tender as any of their brethren at the North, who do not see the unlawfulness of slavery; and there are more thousands, perhaps, that whatsoever they may think of it in its origin, and as a matter depending upon natural right, yet take things as they are, and, finding slavery to be an established relation of the society in which they live, can see no way in which, let their opinions on the abstract question be what they may, it is in the power of the present generation to relieve themselves from this relation. And candor obliges me to say, that I believe they are just as conscientious, many of them, and the religious people, all of them, as they are at the North who hold different opinions.

The honorable Senator from South Carolina [John C. Calhoun] the other day alluded to the separation of that great religious community, the Methodist Episcopal Church. That separation was brought about by differences of opinion upon this particular subject of slavery. I felt great concern, as that dispute went on, about the result. I was in hopes that the difference of opinion might be adjusted, because I looked upon that religious denomination as one of the great props of religion and morals throughout the whole country, from Maine to Georgia, and westward to our utmost boundary. The result was against my wishes and against my hopes. I have read all their proceedings and all their arguments; but I have never yet been able to come to the conclusion that there was any real ground for that separation; in other words, that any good could be produced by that separation. I must say I think there was some want of candor or charity. Sir, when a question of this kind seizes on the religious sentiments of mankind, and comes to be discussed in religious assemblies of the clergy and laity, there is always to be expected, or always to be feared, a great degree of excitement. It is in the nature of man, manifested in his whole history, that religious disputes are apt to become warm in proportion to the strength of the convictions which men entertain of the magnitude of the questions at issue. In all such disputes, there will sometimes be found men with whom every thing is absolute; absolutely wrong, or absolutely right. They see the right clearly; they think others ought so to see it, and they are disposed to establish a broad line of distinction between what is right and what is wrong. They are not seldom willing to establish that line upon their own convictions of truth or justice; and are ready to mark and guard it by placing along it a series of dogmas, as lines of boundary on the earth's surface are marked by posts and stones. There are men who, with clear perception, as they think, of their own duty, do not see how too eager a pursuit of one duty may involve them in the violation of others, or how too warm an embracement of one truth may lead to a disregard of other truths equally important. As I heard it stated strongly, not many days ago, these persons are disposed to mount upon some particular duty, as upon a war-horse, and to drive furiously on and upon and over all other duties that may stand in the way. There are men who, in reference to disputes of that sort, are of the opinion that human duties may be ascertained with the exactness of mathematics. They deal with morals as with mathematics; and they think what is right may be distinguished from what is wrong with the precision of an algebraic equation. They have, therefore, none too much charity towards others who differ from them. They are apt, too, to think that nothing is good but what is perfect, and that there are no compromises or modifications to be made in consideration of difference of opinion or in deference to other men's judgment. If their perspicacious vision enables them to detect a spot on the face of the sun, they think that a good reason why the sun should be struck down from heaven. They prefer the chance of running into utter darkness to living in heavenly light, if that heavenly light be not absolutely without any imperfection. There are impatient men; too impatient always to give heed to the admonition of St. Paul, that we are not to "do evil that good may come"; too impatient to wait for the slow progress of moral causes in the improvement of mankind. . . .

Southern Grievances Against the North

Mr. President, in the excited times in which we live, there is found to exist a state of crimination and recrimination between the North and South. There are lists of grievances produced by each; and those grievances, real or supposed, alienate the minds of one portion of the country from the other, exasperate the feelings, and subdue the sense of fraternal affection, patriotic love, and mutual regard. I shall bestow a little attention, Sir, upon these various grievances existing on the one side and on the other. I begin with complaints of the South. I will not answer, further than I have, the general statements of the honorable Senator from South Carolina [Calhoun], that the North has prospered at the expense of the South in consequence of the manner of administering this government, in the collecting of its revenues, and so forth. These are disputed topics, and I have no inclination to enter into them. But I will allude to the other complaints of the South, and especially to one which has in my opinion just foundation; and that is, that there has been found at the North, among individuals and among legislators, a disinclination to perform fully their constitutional duties in regard to the return of persons bound to service who have escaped into the free States. In that respect, the South, in my judgment, is right, and the North is wrong. Every member of every Northern legislature is bound by oath, like every other officer in the country, to support the Constitution of the United States; and the article of the Constitution which says to these States that they shall deliver up fugitives from service is as binding in honor and conscience as any other article. No man fulfills his duty in any legislature who sets himself to find excuses, evasions, escapes from this constitutional obligation. I have always thought that the Constitution addressed itself to the legislatures of the States or to the States themselves. It says that those persons escaping to other States "shall be delivered up," and I confess I have always been of the opinion that it was an injunction upon the States themselves. When it is said that a person escaping into another State, and coming therefore within the jurisdiction of that State, shall be delivered up, it seems to me the import of the clause is, that the State itself, in obedience to the Constitution, shall cause him to be delivered up. That is my judgment. I have always entertained that opinion, and I entertain it now. But when the subject, some years ago, was before the Supreme Court of the United States, the majority of the judges held that the power to cause fugitives from service to be delivered up was a power to be exercised under the authority of this government. I do not know, on the whole, that it may not have been a fortunate decision. My habit is to respect the result of judicial deliberations and the solemnity of judicial decisions. As it now stands, the business of seeing that these fugitives are delivered up resides in the power of Congress and the national judicature, and my friend at the head of the Judiciary Committee [James M. Mason] has a bill on the subject now before the Senate, which, with some amendments tot [to it], I propose to support, with all its provisions, to the fullest extent. And I desire to call the attention of all sober-minded men at the North, of all conscientious men, of all men who are not carried away by some fanatical idea or some false impression, to their constitutional obligations. I put it to all the sober and sound minds at the North as a question of morals and a question of conscience. What right have they, in their legislative capacity or any other capacity, to endeavor to get round this Constitution, or to embarrass the free exercise of the rights secured by the Constitution to the persons whose slaves escape from them? None at all; none at all. Neither in the forum of conscience, nor before the face of the Constitution, are they, in my opinion, justified in such an attempt. Of course it is a matter for their consideration. They probably, in the excitement of the times, have not stopped to consider of this. They have followed what seemed to be the current of thought and of motives, as the occasion arose, and they have neglected to investigate fully the real question, and to consider their constitutional obligations; which, I am sure, if they did consider, they would fulfill with alacrity. I repeat, therefore, Sir, that here is a well-founded ground of complaint against the North, which ought to be removed, which it is now in the power of the different departments of this government to remove; which calls for the enactment of proper laws authorizing the judicature of this government, in the several States, to do all that is necessary for the recapture of fugitive slaves and for their restoration to those who claim them. Wherever I go, and whenever I speak on the subject, and when I speak here I desire to speak to the whole North, I say that the South has been injured in this respect, and has a right to complain; and the North has been too careless of what I think the Constitution peremptorily and emphatically enjoins upon her as a duty. . . .

Then, Sir, there are the Abolition societies, of which I am unwilling to speak, but in regard to which I have very clear notions and opinions. I do not think them useful. I think their operations for the last twenty years have produced nothing good or valuable. At the same time, I believe thousands of their members to be honest and good men, perfectly well-meaning men. They have excited feelings; they think they must do something for the cause of liberty; and, in their sphere of action, they do not see what else they can do than to contribute to an Abolition press, or an Abolition society, or to pay an Abolition lecturer. I do not mean to impute gross motives even to the leaders of these societies, but I am not blind to the consequences of their proceedings. I cannot but see what mischiefs their interference with the South has produced. And is it not plain to every man? Let any gentleman who entertains doubts on this point recur to the debates in the Virginia House of Delegates in 1832, and he will see with what freedom a proposition made by Mr. [Thomas] Jefferson Randolph for the gradual abolition of slavery was discussed in that body. Every one spoke of slavery as he thought; very ignominious and disparaging names and epithets were applied to it. The debates in the House of Delegates on that occasion, I believe, were all published. They were read by every colored man who could read, and to those who could not read, those debates were read by others. At that time Virginia was not unwilling or unafraid to discuss this question, and to let that part of her population know as much of the discussion as they could learn. That was in 1832. As has been said by the honorable member from South Carolina [Calhoun], these Abolition societies commenced their course of action in 1835. It is said, I do not know how true it may be, that they sent incendiary publications into the slave States; at any rate, they attempted to arouse, and did arouse, a very strong feeling; in other words, they created great agitation in the North against Southern slavery. Well, what was the result? The bonds of the slave were bound more firmly than before, their rivets were more strongly fastened. Public opinion, which in Virginia had begun to be exhibited against slavery, and was opening out for the discussion of the question, drew back and shut itself up in its castle. I wish to know whether any body in Virginia can now talk openly as Mr. Randolph, Governor [James] McDowell, and others talked in 1832 and sent their remarks to the press? We all know the fact, and we all know the cause; and every thing that these agitating people have done has been, not to enlarge, but to restrain, not to set free, but to bind faster the slave population of the South. . . .

The Impossibility of Peaceable Secession

Mr. President, I should much prefer to have heard from every member on this floor declarations of opinion that this Union could never be dissolved, than the declaration of opinion by any body, that, in any case, under the pressure of any circumstances, such a dissolution was possible. I hear with distress and anguish the word "secession," especially when it falls from the lips of those who are patriotic, and known to the country, and known all over the world, for their political services. Secession! Peaceable secession! Sir, your eyes and mine are never destined to see that miracle. The dismemberment of this vast country without convulsion! The breaking up of the fountains of the great deep without ruffling the surface! Who is so foolish, I beg every body's pardon, as to expect to see any such thing? Sir, he who sees these States, now revolving in harmony around a common centre, and expects to see them quit their places and fly off without convulsion, may look the next hour to see heavenly bodies rush from their spheres, and jostle against each other in the realms of space, without causing the wreck of the universe. There can be no such thing as peaceable secession. Peaceable secession is an utter impossibility. Is the great Constitution under which we live, covering this whole country, is it to be thawed and melted away by secession, as the snows on the mountain melt under the influence of a vernal sun, disappear almost unobserved, and run off? No, Sir! No, Sir! I will not state what might produce the disruption of the Union; but, Sir, I see as plainly as I see the sun in heaven what that disruption itself must produce; I see that it must produce war, and such a war as I will not describe, *in its twofold character.*

Peaceable secession! Peaceable secession! The concurrent agreement of all the members of this great republic to separate! A voluntary separation, with alimony on one side and on the other. Why, what would be the result? Where is the line to be drawn? What States are to secede? What is to remain American? What am I toe [to be]? An American no longer? Am I to become a sectional man, a local man, a separatist, with no country in common with the gentlemen who sit around me here, or who fill the other house of Congress? Heaven forbid! Where is the flag of the republic to remain? Where is the eagle still to tower? or is he to cower, and shrink, and fall to the ground? Why, Sir, our ancestors, our fathers and our grandfathers, those of them that are yet living amongst us with prolonged lives, would rebuke and reproach us; and our children and our grandchildren would cry out shame upon us, if we of this generation should dishonor these ensigns of the power of the government and the harmony of that Union which is every day felt among us with so much joy and gratitude. What is to become of the army? What is to become of the navy? What is to become of the public lands? How is each of the thirty States to defend itself? I know, although the idea has not been stated distinctly, there is to be, or it is supposed possible that there will be, a Southern Confederacy. I do not mean, when I allude to this statement, that any one seriously contemplates such a state of things. I do not mean to say that it is true, but I have heard it suggested elsewhere, that the idea has been entertained, that, after the dissolution of this Union, a Southern Confederacy might be formed. I am sorry, Sir, that it has ever been thought of, talked of, or dreamed of, in the wildest flights of human imagination. But the idea, so far as it exists, must be of a separation, assigning the slave States to one side and the free States to the other. Sir, I may express myself too strongly, perhaps, but there are impossibilities in the natural as well as in the physical world, and I hold the idea of a separation of these States, those that are free to form one government, and those that are slave-holding to form another, as such an impossibility. We could not separate the States by any such line, if we were to draw it. We could not sit down here to-day and draw a line of separation that would satisfy any five men in the country. There are natural causes that would keep and tie us together, and there are social and domestic relations which we could not break if we would, and which we should not if we could.

Sir, nobody can look over the face of this country at the present moment, nobody can see where its population is the most dense and growing, without being ready to admit, and compelled to admit, that ere long the strength of America will be in the Valley of the Mississippi. Well, now, Sir, I beg to inquire what the wildest enthusiast has to say about the possibility of cutting that river in two, and leaving free States at its source and on its branches, and slave States down near its mouth, each forming a separate government? Pray, Sir, let me say to the people of this country, that these things are worthy of their pondering and of their consideration. Here, Sir, are five millions of freemen in the free States north of the river of Ohio. Can any body suppose that this population can be severed, by a line that divides them from the territory of a foreign and alien government, down somewhere, the Lord knows where, upon the lower banks of the Mississippi? What would become of Missouri? Will she join the *arrondissement* of the slave States? Shall the man from the Yellow Stone and the Platte be connected, in the new republic, with the man who lives on the southern extremity of the

Cape of Florida? Sir, I am ashamed to pursue this line of remark. I dislike it, I have an utter disgust for it. I would rather
hear of natural blasts and mildews, war, pestilence, and
famine, than to hear gentlemen talk of secession. To break up
this great government! to dismember this glorious country!
to astonish Europe with an act of folly such as Europe for
two centuries has never beheld in any government or any
people! No, Sir! no, Sir! There will be no secession! Gentlemen are not serious when they talk of secession. . . .

The Glories of the Union

And now, Mr. President, I draw these observations to a close.
I have spoken freely, and I meant to do so. I have sought to
make no display. I have sought to enliven the occasion by no
animated discussion, nor have I attempted any train of elaborate argument. I have wished only to speak my sentiments,
fully and at length, being desirous, once and for all, to let the
Senate know, and to let the country know, the opinions and
sentiments which I entertain on all these subjects. These
opinions are not likely to be suddenly changed. If there be
any future service that I can render to the country, consis-
tently with these sentiments and opinions, I shall cheerfully
render it. If there be not, I shall still be glad to have had an
opportunity to disburden myself from the bottom of my
heart, and to make known every political sentiment that
therein exists.

And now, Mr. President, instead of speaking of the possibility or utility of secession, instead of dwelling in those cav-
erns of darkness, instead of groping with those ideas so full
of all that is horrid and horrible, let us come out into the light
of day; let us enjoy the fresh air of Liberty and Union; let us
cherish those hopes which belong to us; let us devote ourselves to those great objects that are fit for our consideration
and action; let us raise our conceptions to the magnitude and
the importance of the duties that devolve upon us; let our
comprehension be as broad as the country for which we act,
our aspirations as high as its certain destiny; let us not be pig-
mies in a case that calls for men. Never did there devolve on
any generation of men higher trusts than now devolve upon

us, for the preservation of this Constitution and the harmony and peace of all who are destined to live under it. Let us make our generation one of the strongest and brightest links in that golden chain which is destined, I fondly believe, to grapple the people of all the States to this Constitution for ages to come. We have a great, popular, constitutional government, guarded by law and by judicature, and defended by the affections of the whole people. No monarchical throne presses these States together, no iron chain of military power encircles them; they live and stand under a government popular in its form, representative in its character, founded upon principles of equality, and so constructed, we hope, as to last for ever. In all its history it has been beneficent; it has trodden down no man's liberty; it has crushed no State. Its daily respiration is liberty and patriotism; its yet youthful veins are full of enterprise, courage, and honorable love of glory and renown. Large before, the country has now, by recent events, become vastly larger. This republic now extends, with a vast breadth, across the whole continent. The two great seas of the world wash the one and the other shore. We realize, on a mighty scale, the beautiful description of the ornamental border of the buckler of Achilles:—

"Now, the broad shield completed, the artist crowned
With his last hand, and poured the ocean round;
In living silver seemed the waves to roll,
And beat the bucklers verge, and bound the whole."

Slavery in Massachusetts

Henry David Thoreau

American philosopher and essayist, Henry David
Thoreau (1817–1862) is perhaps best known today for
his works *Walden* (1854) and "On The Duty of Civil
Disobedience" (1849). Thoreau's deep concern with matters of social justice extended to slavery, especially in the
aftermath of the Fugitive Slave Law of 1850. He was also
a vehement defender of the fervent abolitionist John
Brown, whom Thoreau met in 1857.

In his speech "Slavery in Massachusetts," Thoreau
takes his home state to task over the 1854 return of fugitive slave Anthony Burns, who had escaped from Virginia
only to be apprehended in Boston by U.S. marshals and
ultimately returned to his owner. Thoreau was not alone
in his outrage. An estimated 20,000 Bostonians took to
the streets to watch as hundreds of federal troops es-
corted Burns to the Central Wharf and a ship waiting to
return him to slavery. Despite the enactment of the Fugitive Slave Law in 1850, Boston had seen no runaway returned to captivity since seventeen-year-old Thomas Sims
in 1851, but the Burns incident demonstrated the federal
and state authorities' renewed determination to enforce
the statute. As in "On Civil Disobedience," Thoreau
urges his fellow citizens to adhere to principles of humanity before the law of the land.

From Henry David Thoreau's speech "Slavery In Massachusetts," delivered before
an Anti-Slavery Celebration, Framingham, Massachusetts, July 3, 1854.

I lately attended a meeting of the citizens of Concord, expecting, as one among many, to speak on the subject of slavery in Massachusetts; but I was surprised and disappointed to find that what had called my townsmen together was the destiny of Nebraska, and not of Massachusetts, and that what I had to say would be entirely out of order. I had thought that the house was on fire, and not the prairie; but though several of the citizens of Massachusetts are now in prison for attempting to rescue a slave from her own clutches, not one of the speakers at that meeting expressed regret for it, not one even referred to it. It was only the disposition of some wild lands a thousand miles off which appeared to concern them. The inhabitants of Concord are not prepared to stand by one of their own bridges, but talk only of taking up a position on the highlands beyond the Yellowstone River. Our Buttricks and Davises and Hosmers [heroes of the Battle of Concord] are retreating thither, and I fear that they will leave no Lexington Common between them and the enemy. There is not one slave in Nebraska; there are perhaps a million slaves in Massachusetts.

They who have been bred in the school of politics fail now and always to face the facts. Their measures are half measures and makeshifts merely. They put off the day of settlement indefinitely, and meanwhile the debt accumulates. Though the Fugitive Slave Law had not been the subject of discussion on that occasion, it was at length faintly resolved by my townsmen, at an adjourned meeting, as I learn, that the compromise compact of 1820 having been repudiated by one of the parties, "Therefore, . . . the Fugitive Slave Law of 1850 must be repealed." But this is not the reason why an iniquitous law should be repealed. The fact which the politician faces is merely that there is less honor among thieves than was supposed, and not the fact that they are thieves.

As I had no opportunity to express my thoughts at that meeting, will you allow me to do so here?

Again it happens that the Boston Court-House is full of armed men, holding prisoner and trying a MAN, to find out if he is not really a SLAVE. Does any one think that justice or God awaits Mr. [Judge Edward G.] Loring's decision? For him to sit there deciding still, when this question is already decided from eternity to eternity, and the unlettered slave himself and the multitude around have long since heard and assented to the decision, is simply to make himself ridiculous. We may be tempted to ask from whom he received his commission, and who he is that received it; what novel statutes he obeys, and what precedents are to him of authority. Such an arbiter's very existence is an impertinence. We do not ask him to make up his mind, but to make up his pack. [Judge Loring ruled that Burns be returned to his master.]

I listen to hear the voice of a Governor, Commander-in-Chief of the forces of Massachusetts. I hear only the creaking of crickets and the hum of insects which now fill the summer air. The Governor's exploit is to review the troops on muster days. I have seen him on horseback, with his hat off, listening to a chaplain's prayer. It chances that that is all I have ever seen of a Governor. I think that I could manage to get along without one. If *he* is not of the least use to prevent my being kidnapped, pray of what important use is he likely to be to me? When freedom is most endangered, he dwells in the deepest obscurity. A distinguished clergyman told me that he chose the profession of a clergyman because it afforded the most leisure for literary pursuits. I would recommend to him the profession of a Governor.

Three years ago, also, when the [Thomas; a runaway slave] Sims tragedy was acted, I said to myself, There is such an officer, if not such a man, as the Governor of Massachusetts—what has he been about the last fortnight? Has he had as much as he could do to keep on the fence during this moral earthquake? It seemed to me that no keener satire could have been aimed at, no more cutting insult have been offered to that man, than just what happened—the absence of all inquiry after him in that crisis. The worst and the most I chance to know of him is that he did not improve that opportunity to make himself known, and worthily known. He could at least have *resigned* himself into fame. It appeared to be forgotten that there was such a man or such an office. Yet no doubt he was endeavoring to fill the gubernatorial chair all the while. He was no Governor of mine. He did not govern me.

But at last, in the present case, the Governor was heard from. After he and the United States government had perfectly succeeded in robbing a poor innocent black man of his liberty for life, and, as far as they could, of his Creator's likeness in his breast, he made a speech to his accomplices, at a congratulatory supper!

The Injustice of the Fugitive Slave Law

I have read a recent law of this State, making it penal for any officer of the "Commonwealth" to "detain or aid in the . . . detention," anywhere within its limits, "of any person, for the reason that he is claimed as a fugitive slave." Also, it was a matter of notoriety that a writ of replevin to take the fugitive out of the custody of the United States Marshal could not be served for want of sufficient force to aid the officer.

I had thought that the Governor was, in some sense, the executive officer of the State; that it was his business, as a Governor, to see that the laws of the State were executed; while, as a man, he took care that he did not, by so doing, break the laws of humanity; but when there is any special important use for him, he is useless, or worse than useless, and permits the laws of the State to go unexecuted. Perhaps I do not know what are the duties of a Governor; but if to be a Governor requires to subject one's self to so much ignominy without remedy, if it is to put a restraint upon my manhood, I shall take care never to be Governor of Massachusetts. I have not read far in the statutes of this Commonwealth. It is not profitable reading. They do not always say what is true; and they do not always mean what they say. What I am concerned to know is, that that man's influence and authority were on the side of the slaveholder, and not of the slave—of the guilty, and not of the innocent—of injustice, and not of justice. I never saw him of whom I speak; indeed, I did not know that he was Governor until this event occurred. I heard of him and Anthony Burns at the same time, and thus, undoubtedly, most will hear of him. So far am I from being governed by him. I do not mean that it was anything to his discredit that I had not heard of him, only that I heard what I did. The worst I shall say of him is, that he proved no better than the majority of his constituents would be likely to prove. In my opinion, he was not equal to the occasion.

The whole military force of the State is at the service of a Mr. Suttle, a slaveholder from Virginia, to enable him to catch a man whom he calls his property; but not a soldier is offered to save a citizen of Massachusetts from being kidnapped! Is this what all these soldiers, all this *training*, have been for these seventy-nine years past? Have they been trained merely to rob Mexico and carry back fugitive slaves to their masters?

These very nights I heard the sound of a drum in our streets. There were men *training* still; and for what? I could with an effort pardon the cockerels of Concord for crowing still, for they, perchance, had not been beaten that morning; but I could not excuse this rub-a-dub of the "trainers." The slave was carried back by exactly such as these; i.e., by the soldier, of whom the best you can say in this connection is that he is a fool made conspicuous by a painted coat.

Three years ago, also, just a week after the authorities of Boston assembled to carry back a perfectly innocent man, and one whom they knew to be innocent, into slavery, the inhabitants of Concord caused the bells to be rung and the cannons to be fired, to celebrate their liberty—and the courage and love of liberty of their ancestors who fought at the bridge. As if *those* three millions had fought for the right to be free themselves, but to hold in slavery three million others. Nowadays, men wear a fool's-cap, and call it a liberty-cap. I do not know but there are some who, if they were tied to a whipping-post, and could but get one hand free, would use it to ring the bells and fire the cannons to celebrate *their* liberty. So some of my townsmen took the liberty to ring and fire. That was the extent of their freedom; and when the sound of the bells died away, their liberty died away also; when the powder was all expended, their liberty went off with the smoke.

The joke could be no broader if the inmates of the prisons were to subscribe for all the powder to be used in such salutes, and hire the jailers to do the firing and ringing for them, while they enjoyed it through the grating.

This is what I thought about my neighbors.

Every humane and intelligent inhabitant of Concord, when he or she heard those bells and those cannons, thought not with pride of the events of the 19th of April, 1775, but with shame of the events of the 12th of April, 1851. But now we have half buried that old shame under a new one.

Massachusetts sat waiting Mr. Loring's decision, as if it could in any way affect her own criminality. Her crime, the most conspicuous and fatal crime of all, was permitting him to be the umpire in such a case. It was really the trial of Massachusetts. Every moment that she hesitated to set this man free—every moment that she now hesitates to atone for her crime, she is convicted. The Commissioner on her case is God; not Edward G. God, but simply God.

I wish my countrymen to consider, that whatever the human law may be, neither an individual nor a nation can ever commit the least act of injustice against the obscurest individual without having to pay the penalty for it. A government which deliberately enacts injustice, and persists in it, will at length even become the laughing-stock of the world.

Men Must Make the Law Free

Much has been said about American slavery, but I think that we do not even yet realize what slavery is. If I were seriously to propose to Congress to make mankind into sausages, I have no doubt that most of the members would smile at my proposition, and if any believed me to be in earnest, they would think that I proposed something much worse than Congress had ever done. But if any of them will tell me that to make a man into a sausage would be much worse—would be any worse—than to make him into a slave—than it was to enact the Fugitive Slave Law, I will accuse him of foolishness, of intellectual incapacity, of making a distinction without a difference. The one is just as sensible a proposition as the other.

I hear a good deal said about trampling this law under foot. Why, one need not go out of his way to do that. This law rises not to the level of the head or the reason; its natural habitat is in the dirt. It was born and bred, and has its life, only in the dust and mire, on a level with the feet; and he who walks with freedom, and does not with Hindoo mercy avoid treading on every venomous reptile, will inevitably tread on it, and so trample it under foot—and Webster, its maker, with it, like the dirt-bug and its ball.

Recent events will be valuable as a criticism on the administration of justice in our midst, or, rather, as showing
what are the true resources of justice in any community. It
has come to this, that the friends of liberty, the friends of the
slave, have shuddered when they have understood that his
fate was left to the legal tribunals of the country to be decided. Free men have no faith that justice will be awarded in
such a case. The judge may decide this way or that; it is a
kind of accident, at best. It is evident that he is not a compe-
tent authority in so important a case. It is no time, then, to
be judging according to his precedents, but to establish a
precedent for the future. I would much rather trust to the
sentiment of the people. In their vote you would get something of some value, at least, however small; but in the other
case, only the trammeled judgment of an individual, of no
significance, be it which way it might.

It is to some extent fatal to the courts, when the people
are compelled to go behind them. I do not wish to believe
that the courts were made for fair weather, and for very civil
cases merely; but think of leaving it to any court in the land
to decide whether more than three millions of people, in this
case a sixth part of a nation, have a right to be freemen or
not! But it has been left to the courts of *justice*, so called—to
the Supreme Court of the land—and, as you all know, recognizing no authority but the Constitution, it has decided
that the three millions are and shall continue to be slaves.
Such judges as these are merely the inspectors of a pick-lock
and murderer's tools, to tell him whether they are in working
order or not, and there they think that their responsibility
ends. There was a prior case on the docket, which they, as
judges appointed by God, had no right to skip; which having
been justly settled, they would have been saved from this hu-
miliation. It was the case of the murderer himself.

The law will never make men free; it is men who have got
to make the law free. They are the lovers of law and order
who observe the law when the government breaks it.

Among human beings, the judge whose words seal the
fate of a man furthest into eternity is not he who merely pro-
nounces the verdict of the law, but he, whoever he may be,

who, from a love of truth, and unprejudiced by any custom or enactment of men, utters a true opinion or *sentence* concerning him. He it is that *sentences* him. Whoever can discern truth has received his commission from a higher source than the chiefest justice in the world who can discern only law. He finds himself constituted judge of the judge. Strange that it should be necessary to state such simple truths!

The City and the Country

I am more and more convinced that, with reference to any public question, it is more important to know what the country thinks of it than what the city thinks. The city does not *think* much. On any moral question, I would rather have the opinion of Boxboro' than of Boston and New York put together. When the former speaks, I feel as if somebody *had* spoken, as if *humanity* was yet, and a reasonable being had asserted its rights—as if some unprejudiced men among the country's hills had at length turned their attention to the subject, and by a few sensible words redeemed the reputation of the race. When, in some obscure country town, the farmers come together to a special town-meeting, to express their opinion on some subject which is vexing the land, that, I think, is the true Congress, and the most respectable one that is ever assembled in the United States.

It is evident that there are, in this Commonwealth at least, two parties, becoming more and more distinct—the party of the city, and the party of the country. I know that the country is mean enough, but I am glad to believe that there is a slight difference in her favor. But as yet she has few, if any organs, through which to express herself. The editorials which she reads, like the news, come from the seaboard. Let us, the inhabitants of the country, cultivate self-respect. Let us not send to the city for aught more essential than our broadcloths and groceries; or, if we read the opinions of the city, let us entertain opinions of our own.

Among measures to be adopted, I would suggest to make as earnest and vigorous an assault on the press as has already been made, and with effect, on the church. The church has much improved within a few years; but the press is, almost without exception, corrupt. I believe that in this country the press exerts a greater and a more pernicious influence than the church did in its worst period. We are not a religious people, but we are a nation of politicians. We do not care for the Bible, but we do care for the newspaper. At any meeting of politicians—like that at Concord the other evening, for instance—how impertinent it would be to quote from the Bible! how pertinent to quote from a newspaper or from the Constitution! The newspaper is a Bible which we read every morning and every afternoon, standing and sitting, riding and walking. It is a Bible which every man carries in his pocket, which lies on every table and counter, and which the mail, and thousands of missionaries, are continually dispersing. It is, in short, the only book which America has printed and which America reads. So wide is its influence. The editor is a preacher whom you voluntarily support. Your tax is commonly one cent daily, and it costs nothing for pew hire. But how many of these preachers preach the truth? I repeat the testimony of many an intelligent foreigner, as well as my own convictions, when I say, that probably no country was ever rubled by so mean a class of tyrants as, with a few noble exceptions, are the editors of the periodical press in *this* country. And as they live and rule only by their servility, and appealing to the worse, and not the better, nature of man, the people who read them are in the condition of the dog that returns to his vomit.

The *Liberator* and the *Commonwealth* were the only papers in Boston, as far as I know, which made themselves heard in condemnation of the cowardice and meanness of the authorities of that city, as exhibited in '51. The other journals, almost without exception, by their manner of referring to and speaking of the Fugitive Slave Law, and the carrying back of the slave Sims, insulted the common sense of the country, at least. And, for the most part, they did this, one would say, because they thought so to secure the approbation of their patrons, not being aware that a sounder sentiment prevailed to any extent in the heart of the Commonwealth. I am told that some of them have improved of late; but they are still eminently time-serving. Such is the character they have won.

But, thank fortune, this preacher can be even more easily reached by the weapons of the reformer than could the recreant priest. The free men of New England have only to refrain from purchasing and reading these sheets, have only to withhold their cents, to kill a score of them at once. One whom I respect told me that he purchased Mitchell's *Citizen* in the cars, and then threw it out the window. But would not his contempt have been more fatally expressed if he had not bought it?

Are they Americans? are they New Englanders? are they inhabitants of Lexington and Concord and Framingham, who read and support the Boston *Post*, *Mail*, *Journal*, *Advertiser*, *Courier*, and *Times*? Are these the Flags of our Union? I am not a newspaper reader, and may omit to name the worst.

Could slavery suggest a more complete servility than some of these journals exhibit? Is there any dust which their conduct does not lick, and make fouler still with its slime? I do not know whether the Boston *Herald* is still in existence, but I remember to have seen it about the streets when Sims was carried off. Did it not act its part well-serve its master faithfully! How could it have gone lower on its belly? How can a man stoop lower than he is low? do more than put his extremities in the place of the head he has? than make his head his lower extremity? When I have taken up this paper with my cuffs turned up, I have heard the gurgling of the sewer through every column. I have felt that I was handling a paper picked out of the public gutters, a leaf from the gospel of the gambling-house, the groggery, and the brothel, harmonizing with the gospel of the Merchants' Exchange.

Be Men First, Americans Later

The majority of the men of the North, and of the South and East and West, are not men of principle. If they vote, they do not send men to Congress on errands of humanity; but while their brothers and sisters are being scourged and hung for loving liberty, while—I might here insert all that slavery implies and is—it is the mismanagement of wood and iron and stone and gold which concerns them. Do what you will, O

Government, with my wife and children, my mother and brother, my father and sister, I will obey your commands to the letter. It will indeed grieve me if you hurt them, if you deliver them to overseers to be hunted by bounds or to be whipped to death; but, nevertheless, I will peaceably pursue my chosen calling on this fair earth, until perchance, one day, when I have put on mourning for them dead, I shall have persuaded you to relent. Such is the attitude, such are the words of Massachusetts.

Rather than do thus, I need not say what match I would touch, what system endeavor to blow up; but as I love my life, I would side with the light, and let the dark earth roll from under me, calling my mother and my brother to follow.

I would remind my countrymen that they are to be men first, and Americans only at a late and convenient hour. No matter how valuable law may be to protect your property, even to keep soul and body together, if it do not keep you and humanity together.

I am sorry to say that I doubt if there is a judge in Massachusetts who is prepared to resign his office, and get his living innocently, whenever it is required of him to pass sentence under a law which is merely contrary to the law of God. I am compelled to see that they put themselves, or rather are by character, in this respect, exactly on a level with the marine who discharges his musket in any direction he is ordered to. They are just as much tools, and as little men. Certainly, they are not the more to be respected, because their master enslaves their understandings and consciences, instead of their bodies.

The judges and lawyers—simply as such, I mean—and all men of expediency, try this case by a very low and incompetent standard. They consider, not whether the Fugitive Slave Law is right, but whether it is what they call *constitutional*. Is virtue constitutional, or vice? Is equity constitutional, or iniquity? In important moral and vital questions, like this, it is just as impertinent to ask whether a law is constitutional or not, as to ask whether it is profitable or not. They persist in being the servants of the worst of men, and not the servants of humanity. The question is, not whether you or your grandfather, seventy years ago, did not enter into an agreement to serve the Devil, and that service is not accordingly now due; but whether you will not now, for once and at last, serve God—in spite of your own past recreancy, or that of your ancestor—by obeying that eternal and only just CON-STITUTION, which He, and not any Jefferson or Adams, has written in your being.

The amount of it is, if the majority vote the Devil to be God, the minority will live and behave accordingly—and obey the successful candidate, trusting that, some time or other, by some Speaker's casting-vote, perhaps, they may re-instate God. This is the highest principle I can get out or in-vent for my neighbors. These men act as if they believed that they could safely slide down a hill a little way—or a good way—and would surely come to a place, by and by, where they could begin to slide up again. This is expediency, or choosing that course which offers the slightest obstacles to the feet, that is, a downhill one. But there is no such thing as accomplishing a righteous reform by the use of "expedi-ency." There is no such thing as sliding up hill. In morals the only sliders are backsliders.

Thus we steadily worship Mammon, both school and state and church, and on the seventh day curse God with a tintamar from one end of the Union to the other.

Will mankind never learn that policy is not morality—that it never secures any moral right, but considers merely what is expedient? chooses the available candidate—who is invariably the Devil—and what right have his constituents to be sur-prised, because the Devil does not behave like an angel of light? What is wanted is men, not of policy, but of probity—who recognize a higher law than the Constitution, or the de-cision of the majority. The fate of the country does not de-pend on how you vote at the polls—the worst man is as strong as the best at that game; it does not depend on what kind of paper you drop into the ballot-box once a year, but on what kind of man you drop from your chamber into the street every morning.

What should concern Massachusetts is not the Nebraska Bill, nor the Fugitive Slave Bill, but her own slaveholding and servility. Let the State dissolve her union with the slaveholder. She may wriggle and hesitate, and ask leave to read the Constitution once more; but she can find no respectable law or precedent which sanctions the continuance of such a union for an instant.

Let each inhabitant of the State dissolve his union with her, as long as she delays to do her duty.

The events of the past month teach me to distrust Fame. I see that she does not finely discriminate, but coarsely hurrahs. She considers not the simple heroism of an action, but only as it is connected with its apparent consequences. She praises till she is hoarse the easy exploit of the Boston tea party, but will be comparatively silent about the braver and more disinterestedly heroic attack on the Boston Court-House, simply because it was unsuccessful!

Covered with disgrace, the State has sat down coolly to try for their lives and liberties the men who attempted to do its duty for it. And this is called *justice*! They who have shown that they can behave particularly well may perchance be put under bonds for *their good behavior*. They whom truth requires at present to plead guilty are, of all the inhabitants of the State, preeminently innocent. While the Governor, and the Mayor, and countless officers of the Commonwealth are at large, the champions of liberty are imprisoned.

Only they are guiltless who commit the crime of contempt of such a court. It behooves every man to see that his influence is on the side of justice, and let the courts make their own characters. My sympathies in this case are wholly with the accused, and wholly against their accusers and judges. Justice is sweet and musical; but injustice is harsh and discordant. The judge still sits grinding at his organ, but it yields no music, and we hear only the sound of the handle. He believes that all the music resides in the handle, and the crowd toss him their coppers the same as before.

Do you suppose that that Massachusetts which is now doing these things—which hesitates to crown these men, some of whose lawyers, and even judges, perchance, may be driven to take refuge in some poor quibble, that they may not wholly outrage their instinctive sense of justice—do you suppose that she is anything but base and servile? that she is the champion of liberty?

Show me a free state, and a court truly of justice, and I will fight for them, if need be; but show me Massachusetts, and I refuse her my allegiance, and express contempt for her courts.

The effect of a good government is to make life more valuable—of a bad one, to make it less valuable. We can afford that railroad and all merely material stock should lose some of its value, for that only compels us to live more simply and economically; but suppose that the value of life itself should be diminished! How can we make a less demand on man and nature, how live more economically in respect to virtue and all noble qualities, than we do? I have lived for the last month—and I think that every man in Massachusetts capable of the sentiment of patriotism must have had a similar experience—with the sense of having suffered a vast and indefinite loss. I did not know at first what ailed me. At last it occurred to me that what I had lost was a country. I had never respected the government near to which I lived, but I had foolishly thought that I might manage to live here, minding my private affairs, and forget it. For my part, my old and worthiest pursuits have lost I cannot say how much of their attraction, and I feel that my investment in life here is worth many per cent less since Massachusetts last deliberately sent back an innocent man, Anthony Burns, to slavery. I dwelt before, perhaps, in the illusion that my life passed somewhere only *between* heaven and hell, but now I cannot persuade myself that I do not dwell *wholly within* hell. The site of that political organization called Massachusetts is to me morally covered with volcanic scoriae and cinders, such as Milton describes in the infernal regions. If there is any hell more unprincipled than our rulers, and we, the ruled, I feel curious to see it. Life itself being worth less, all things with it, which minister to it, are worth less. Suppose you have a small library, with pictures to adorn the walls—a garden laid out around—and contemplate scientific and literary pursuits, &c., and discover all at once that your villa, with all its contents is located in hell, and that the justice of the peace has a cloven foot and a forked tail—do not these things suddenly lose their value in your eyes?

I feel that, to some extent, the State has fatally interfered with my lawful business. It has not only interrupted me in my passage through Court Street on errands of trade, but it has interrupted me and every man on his onward and upward path, on which he had trusted soon to leave Court Street far behind. What right had it to remind me of Court Street? I have found that hollow which even I had relied on for solid.

Nature's Purity Contrasts with Human Corruption

I am surprised to see men going about their business as if nothing had happened. I say to myself, "Unfortunates! they have not heard the news." I am surprised that the man whom I just met on horseback should be so earnest to overtake his newly bought cows running away—since all property is insecure, and if they do not run away again, they may be taken away from him when he gets them. Fool! does he not know that his seed-corn is worth less this year—that all beneficent harvests fail as you approach the empire of hell? No prudent man will build a stone house under these circumstances, or engage in any peaceful enterprise which it requires a long time to accomplish. Art is as long as ever, but life is more interrupted and less available for a man's proper pursuits. It is not an era of repose. We have used up all our inherited freedom. If we would save our lives, we must fight for them.

I walk toward one of our ponds; but what signifies the beauty of nature when men are base? We walk to lakes to see our serenity reflected in them; when we are not serene, we go not to them. Who can be serene in a country where both the rulers and the ruled are without principle? The remembrance of my country spoils my walk. My thoughts are murder to the State, and involuntarily go plotting against her.

But it chanced the other day that I scented a white water-lily, and a season I had waited for had arrived. It is the emblem of purity. It bursts up so pure and fair to the eye, and so sweet to the scent, as if to show us what purity and sweetness reside in, and can be extracted from, the slime and muck of earth. I think I have plucked the first one that has opened for a mile. What confirmation of our hopes is in the fragrance of this flower! I shall not so soon despair of the world for it, notwithstanding slavery, and the cowardice and want of principle of Northern men. It suggests what kind of laws have prevailed longest and widest, and still prevail, and that the time may come when man's deeds will smell as sweet. Such is the odor which the plant emits. If Nature can compound this fragrance still annually, I shall believe her still young and full of vigor, her integrity and genius unimpaired, and that there is virtue even in man, too, who is fitted to perceive and love it. It reminds me that Nature has been partner to no Missouri Compromise. I scent no compromise in the fragrance of the water-lily. It is not a *Nymphoea Douglasii* [a reference, apparently, to Senator Stephen Douglas]. In it, the sweet, and pure, and innocent are wholly sundered from the obscene and baleful. I do not scent in this the time-serving irresolution of a Massachusetts Governor, nor of a Boston Mayor. So behave that the odor of your actions may enhance the general sweetness of the atmosphere, that when we behold or scent a flower, we may not be reminded how inconsistent your deeds are with it; for all odor is but one form of advertisement of a moral quality, and if fair actions had not been performed, the lily would not smell sweet. The foul slime stands for the sloth and vice of man, the decay of humanity; the fragrant flower that springs from it, for the purity and courage which are immortal.

Slavery and servility have produced no sweet-scented flower annually, to charm the senses of men, for they have no real life: they are merely a decaying and a death, offensive to all healthy nostrils. We do not complain that they *live*, but that they do not get *buried*. Let the living bury them: even they are good for manure.

"The Crime Against Kansas"

Charles Sumner

Charles Sumner (1811–1874) was a Boston-born legal
scholar and U.S. senator (1851–1874) well known for his
fierce denunciations of slavery. He fought against slavery's expansion and for emancipation, becoming after the
Civil War a so-called Radical Republican advocating
harsh Reconstruction measures against the former Confederate states and pushing for the impeachment of President Andrew Johnson.

The occasion of Sumner's most famous speech "The
Crime Against Kansas" incited a single gesture of violence
that symbolized the fervent antipathy between Northern
abolitionists and Southern slaveholders. Addressing the
Senate over the course of two days in May 1856, Sumner
argued against the admission of Kansas as a slave state in
highly charged florid language. In what would turn out to
be his most rhetorically incendiary gesture, Sumner invoked Spanish writer Miguel de Cervantes's classic work
Don Quixote to castigate Senators Andrew Butler (South
Carolina) and Stephen Douglas (Illinois) as, respectively,
the delusional knight Quixote and humble flunky Sancho
Panza of slavery. Three days after Sumner concluded his
speech, South Carolina representative Preston Brooks, a
kinsman of Senator Butler, attacked Sumner with a cane
and beat him senseless, an assault from which it took
Sumner months to recuperate.

From Charles Sumner's address before the U.S. Senate, March 19 and 20, 1856.

Mr. President: You are now called to redress a great transgression. Seldom in the history of nations has such a question been presented. Tariffs, Army bills, Navy bills, Land bills, are important, and justly occupy your care; but these all belong to the course of ordinary legislation. As means and instruments only, they are necessarily subordinate to the conservation of government itself. Grant them or deny them, in greater or less degree, and you will inflict no shock. The machinery of government will continue to move. The State will not cease to exist. Far otherwise is it with the eminent question now before you, involving, as it does, Liberty in a broad territory, and also involving the peace of the whole country, with our good name in history forever more.

Take down your map, sir, and you will find that the Territory of Kansas, more than any other region, occupies the middle spot of North America, equally distant from the Atlantic on the east, and the Pacific on the west; from the frozen waters of Hudson's Bay on the north, and the tepid Gulf Stream on the south, constituting the precise territorial centre of the whole vast continent. To such advantages of situation, on the very highway between two oceans, are added a soil of unsurpassed richness, and a fascinating, undulating beauty of surface, with a healthgiving climate, calculated to nurture a powerful and generous people, worthy to be a central pivot of American institutions. A few short months only have passed since this spacious and mediterranean country was open only to the savage who ran wild in its woods and prairies; and now it has already drawn to its bosom a population of freemen larger than Athens crowded within her historic gates, when her sons, under Miltiades, won liberty for mankind on the field of Marathon; more than Sparta contained when she ruled Greece, and sent forth her devoted children, quickened by a mother's benediction, to return with their shields, or on them; more than Rome gathered on her seven hills, when, under her kings, she commenced that sovereign sway, which afterward embraced the whole earth; more than London held, when, on the fields of Crecy and Agincourt, the English banner was carried victoriously over the chivalrous hosts of France.

Against this Territory, thus fortunate in position and population, a crime has been committed, which is without example in the records of the past. Not in plundered provinces or in the cruelties of selfish governors will you find its parallel; and yet there is an ancient instance, which may show at least the path of justice. In the terrible impeachment by which the great Roman orator [Cato] has blasted through all time the name of Verres, amidst charges of robbery and sacrilege, the enormity which most aroused the indignant voice of his accuser, and which still stands forth with strongest distinctness, arresting the sympathetic indignation of all who read the story, is, that away in Sicily he had scourged a citizen of Rome that the cry, "I am a Roman citizen," had been interposed in vain against the lash of the tyrant governor. Other charges were, that he had carried away productions of art, and that he had violated the sacred shrines. It was in the presence of the Roman Senate that this arraignment proceeded; in a temple of the Forum amidst crowds such as no orator had ever before drawn together thronging the porticos and colonnades, even clinging to the housetops and neighboring slopes—and under the anxious gaze of witnesses summoned from the scene of crime. But an audience grander far, of higher dignity, of more various people, and of wider intelligence, the countless multitude of succeeding generations, in every land, where eloquence has been studied, or where the Roman name has been recognized, has listened to the accusation, and throbbed with condemnation of the criminal. Sir, speaking in an age of light, and a land of constitutional liberty, where the safeguards of elections are justly placed among the highest triumphs of civilization, I fearlessly assert that the wrongs of much abused Sicily, thus memorable in history, were small by the side of the wrongs of Kansas, where the very shrines of popular institutions, more sacred than any heathen altar, have been desecrated . . . where the ballot-box, more precious than any work, in ivory or marble, from the cunning hand of art, has been plundered . . . and where the cry, "I am an American citizen," has been interposed in vain against outrage of every kind, even upon life itself. Are you against sacrilege? I present it for your execration. Are you against robbery? I hold it up to your scorn. Are you for the protection of American citizens? I show you how their dearest rights have been cloven down, while a Tyrannical Usurpation has sought to install itself on their very necks!

But the wickedness which I now begin to expose is immeasurably aggravated by the motive which prompted it. Not in any common lust for power did this uncommon tragedy have its origin. It is the rape of a virgin Territory, compelling it to the hateful embrace of Slavery; and it may be clearly traced to a depraved longing for a new slave State, the hideous offspring of such a crime, in the hope of adding to the power of slavery in the National Government. Yes, sir, when the whole world, alike Christian and Turk, is rising up to condemn this wrong, and to make it a hissing to the nations, here in our Republic, force, aye, sir, FORCE has been openly employed in compelling Kansas to this pollution, and all for the sake of political power. There is the simple fact, which you will in vain attempt to deny, but which in itself presents an essential wickedness that makes other public crimes seem like public virtues.

But this enormity, vast beyond comparison, swells to dimensions of wickedness which the imagination toils in vain to grasp, when it is understood that for this purpose are hazarded the horrors of intestine feud not only in this distant Territory, but everywhere throughout the country. Already the muster has begun. The strife is no longer local, but national. Even now, while I speak, portents hang on all the arches of the horizon threatening to darken the broad land, which already yawns with the mutterings of civil war. The fury of the propagandists of Slavery, and the calm determination of their opponents, are now diffused from the distant Territory over widespread communities, and the whole country, in all its extent marshalling hostile divisions, and foreshadowing a strife which, unless happily averted by the triumph of Freedom, will become war fratricidal, parricidal war with an accumulated wickedness beyond the wickedness of any war in human annals; justly provoking the avenging judgment of Providence and the avenging pen of history, and constituting a strife, in the language of the ancient writer [Florus], more than foreign, more than social, more than civil; but something compounded of all these strifes, and in

itself more than war; sed potius commune quad dam ex om-
nibus, et plus quam bellum. [Translation: "Something which
shares in all the evils of war, and is more than war."]

The Nature of the Criminal

Such is the crime which you are to judge. But the criminal
also must be dragged into day, that you may see and measure
the power by which all this wrong is sustained. From no
common source could it proceed. In its perpetration was
needed a spirit of vaulting ambition which would hesitate at
nothing; a hard hood of purpose which was insensible to the
judgment of mankind; a madness for Slavery which would
disregard the Constitution, the laws, and all the great examples of our history; also a consciousness of power such as
comes from the habit of power; a combination of energies
found only in a hundred arms directed by a hundred eyes; a
control of public opinion through venal pens and a prosti-
tuted press; an ability to subsidize crowds in every vocation
of life—the politician with his local importance, the lawyer
with his subtle tongue, and even the authority of the judge on
the bench; and a familiar use of men in places high and low,
so that none, from the President to the lowest border post-
master, should decline to be its tool; all these things and more
were needed, and they were found in the slave power of our
Republic. There, sir, stands the criminal, all unmasked before
you—heartless, grasping, and tyrannical—with an audacity
beyond that of Verres, a subtlety beyond that of Machiavelli,
a meanness beyond that of Bacon, and an ability beyond that
of Hastings. Justice to Kansas can be secured only by the
prostration of this influence; for this the power behind
greater than any President which succors and sustains the
crime. Nay, the proceedings I now arraign derive their fear-
ful consequences only from this connection.

In now opening this great matter, I am not insensible to
the austere demands of the occasion; but the dependence of
the crime against Kansas upon the slave power is so peculiar
and important, that I trust to be pardoned while I impress it
with an illustration, which to some may seem trivial. It is related in Northern mythology that the god of Force, visiting

an enchanted region, was challenged by his royal entertainer to what seemed an humble feat of strength merely, sir, to lift a cat from the ground. The god smiled at the challenge, and, calmly placing his hand under the belly of the animal, with superhuman strength strove, while the back of the feline monster arched far up ward, even beyond reach, and one paw actually forsook the earth, until at last the discomfited divinity desisted; but he was little surprised at his defeat when he learned that this creature, which seemed to be a cat, and nothing more, was not merely a cat, but that it belonged to and was a part of the great Terrestrial Serpent, which, in its innumerable folds, encircled the whole globe. Even so the creature, whose paws are now fastened upon Kansas, whatever it may seem to be, constitutes in reality a part of the slave power, which, in its loathsome folds, is now coiled about the whole land. Thus do I expose the extent of the present contest, where we encounter not merely local resistance, but also the unconquered sustaining arm behind. But out of the vastness of the crime attempted, with all its woe and shame, I derive a well-founded assurance of a commensurate vastness of effort against it by the aroused masses of the country, determined not only to vindicate Right against Wrong, but to redeem the Republic from the thraldom of that Oligarchy which prompts, directs, and concentrates the distant wrong.

Such is the crime, and such the criminal, which it is my duty in this debate to expose, and, by the blessing of God, this duty shall be done completely to the end.

Champions of "The Harlot, Slavery"

But, before entering upon the argument, I must say something of a general character, particularly in response to what has fallen from Senators who have raised themselves to eminence on this floor in championship of human wrongs. I mean the Senator from South Carolina (Mr. [Andrew P.] Butler), and the Senator from Illinois (Mr. [Stephen] Douglas), who, though unlike as Don Quixote and Sancho Panza, yet, like this couple, sally forth together in the same adventure. I regret much to miss the elder Senator from his seat; but the cause, against which he has run a tilt, with such activity of animosity, demands that the opportunity of exposing him should not be lost; and it is for the cause that I speak. The Senator from South Carolina has read many books of chivalry, and believes himself a chivalrous knight, with sentiments of honor and courage. Of course he has chosen a mistress to whom he has made his vows, and who, though ugly to others, is always lovely to him; though polluted in the sight of the world, is chaste in his sight I mean the harlot, Slavery. For her, his tongue is always profuse in words. Let her be impeached in character, or any proposition made to shut her out from the extension of her wantonness, and no extravagance of manner or hardihood of assertion is then too great for this Senator. The frenzy of Don Quixote, in behalf of his wench, Dulcinea del Toboso, is all surpassed. The asserted rights of Slavery, which shock equality of all kinds, are cloaked by a fantastic claim of equality. If the slave States cannot enjoy what, in mockery of the great fathers of the Republic, he misnames equality under the Constitution in other words, the full power in the National Territories to compel fellowmen to unpaid toil, to separate husband and wife, and to sell little children at the auction block then, sir, the chivalric Senator will conduct the State of South Carolina out of the Union! Heroic knight! Exalted Senator! A second Moses come for a second exodus!

But not content with this poor menace, which we have been twice told was "measured," the Senator in the unrestrained chivalry of his nature, has undertaken to apply opprobrious words to those who differ from him on this floor. He calls them "sectional and fanatical"; and opposition to the usurpation in Kansas he denounces as "an uncalculating fanaticism." To be sure these charges lack all grace of originality, and all sentiment of truth; but the adventurous Senator does not hesitate. He is the uncompromising, unblushing representative on this floor of a flagrant sectionalism, which now domineers over the Republic, and yet with a ludicrous ignorance of his own position unable to see himself as others see him—or with an effrontery which even his white head ought not to protect from rebuke, he applies to those here who resist his sectionalism the very epithet which designates himself. The men who strive to bring back the Government to its original policy, when Freedom and not Slavery was sectional, he arraigns as sectional. This will not do. It involves too great a perversion of terms. I tell that Senator that it is to himself, and to the "organization" of which he is the "committed advocate," that this epithet belongs. I now fasten it upon them. For myself, I care little for names; but since the question has been raised here, I affirm that the Republican party of the Union is in no just sense sectional, but, more than any other party, national; and that it now goes forth to dislodge from the high places of the Government the tyrannical sectionalism of which the Senator from South Carolina is one of the maddest zealots.

As the Senator from South Carolina, is the Don Quixote, the Senator from Illinois (Mr. Douglas) is the Squire of Slavery, its very Sancho Panza, ready to do all its humiliating offices. This Senator, in his labored address, vindicating his labored report—piling one mass of elaborate error upon another mass constrained himself, as you will remember, to unfamiliar decencies of speech. Of that address I have nothing to say at this moment, though before I sit down I shall show something of its fallacies. But I go back now to an earlier occasion, when, true to his native impulses, he threw into this discussion, "for a charm of powerful trouble," personalities most discreditable to this body. I will not stop to repel the imputations which he cast upon myself; but I mention them to remind you of the "sweltered venom sleeping got," which, with other poisoned ingredients, he cast into the caldron of this debate. Of other things I speak. Standing on this floor, the Senator issued his rescript, requiring submission to the Usurped Power of Kansas; and this was accompanied by a manner—all his own—such as befits the tyrannical threat. Very well. Let the Senator try. I tell him now that he cannot enforce any such submission. The Senator, with the slave power at his back, is strong; but he is not strong enough for this purpose. He is bold. He shrinks from nothing. Like Danton, he may cry, "L'audace! L'audace! toujours L'audace!" [Such audacity! Always such audacity!] but even his audacity cannot compass this work. The Senator copies the British officer who, with boastful swagger, said that with the hilt of his sword he would cram the "stamps" down the throats of the American people, and he will meet a similar failure. He may convulse this country with a civil feud. Like the ancient madman, he may set fire to this Temple of Constitutional Liberty, grander than the Ephesian dome; but he cannot enforce obedience to that Tyrannical Usurpation.

The Senator dreams that he can subdue the North. He disclaims the open threat, but his conduct still implies it. How little that Senator knows himself or the strength of the cause which he persecutes! He is but a mortal man; against him is an immortal principle. With finite power he wrestles with the infinite, and he must fall. Against him are stronger battalions than any marshalled by mortal arm—the inborn, ineradicable, invincible sentiments of the human heart against him is nature in all her subtle forces; against him is God. Let him try to subdue these.

The Law Distorted

With regret, I come again upon the Senator from South Carolina (Mr. Butler), who, omnipresent in this debate, overflowed with rage at the simple suggestion that Kansas had applied for admission as a State and, with incoherent phrases, discharged the loose expectoration of his speech, now upon her representative, and then upon her people. There was no extravagance of the ancient parliamentary debate, which he did not repeat; nor was there any possible deviation from truth which he did not make, with so much of passion, I am glad to add, as to save him from the suspicion of intentional aberration. But the Senator touches nothing which he does not disfigure with error, sometimes of principle, sometimes of fact. He shows an incapacity of accuracy, whether in stating the Constitution, or in stating the law, whether in the details of statistics or the diversions of scholarship. He cannot open his mouth, but out there flies a blunder. . . .

But it is against the people of Kansas that the sensibilities of the Senator are particularly aroused. Coming, as he announces, "from a State" aye, sir, from South Carolina he turns with lordly disgust from this newly-formed community, which he will not recognize even as a "body politic." Pray,

sir, by what title does he indulge in this egotism? Has he read
the history of "the State" which he represents? He cannot
surely have forgotten its shameful imbecility from Slavery,
confessed throughout the Revolution, followed by its more
shameful assumptions for Slavery since. He cannot have forgotten its wretched persistence in the slave-trade as the very
apple of its eye, and the condition of its participation in the
Union. He cannot have forgotten its constitution, which is
Republican only in name, confirming power in the hands of
the few, and founding the qualifications of its legislators on
"a settled freehold estate and ten negroes." And yet the Senator, to whom that "State" has in part committed the
guardianship of its good name, instead of moving, with back-
ward treading steps, to cover its nakedness, rushes forward
in the very ecstasy of madness, to expose it by provoking a
comparison with Kansas. South Carolina is old; Kansas is
young. South Carolina counts by centuries; where Kansas
counts by years. But a beneficent example may be born in a
day; and I venture to say, that against the two centuries of the
older "State," may be already set the two years of trial,
evolving corresponding virtue, in the younger community. In
the one, is the long wail of Slavery; in the other, the hymns
of Freedom. And if we glance at special achievements, it will
be difficult to find any thing in the history of South Carolina
which presents so much of heroic spirit in an heroic cause
[as] appears in that repulse of the Missouri invaders by the
beleaguered town of Lawrence, where even the women gave
their effective efforts to Freedom. The matrons of Rome,
who poured their jewels into the treasury for the public defence the wives of Prussia, who, with delicate fingers, clothed
their defenders against French invasion the mothers of our
own Revolution, who sent forth their sons, covered with
prayers and blessings, to combat for human rights, did nothing of self-sacrifice truer than did these women on this occasion. Were the whole history of South Carolina blotted out
of existence, from its very beginning down to the day of the
last election of the Senator to his present seat on this floor,
civilization might lose—I do not say how little; but surely less
than it has already gained by the example of Kansas, in its
valiant struggle against oppression, and in the development

of a new science of emigration. Already, in Lawrence alone, there are newspapers and schools, including a High School, and throughout this infant Territory there is more mature scholarship far, in proportion to its inhabitants, than in all South Carolina. Ah, sir, I tell the Senator that Kansas, welcomed as a free State, will be a "ministering angel" to the Republic, when South Carolina, in the cloak of darkness which she hugs, "lies howling."

The Senator from Illinois (Mr. Douglas) naturally joins the Senator from South Carolina in this warfare, and gives to it the superior intensity of his nature. He thinks that the National Government has not completely proved its power, as it has never hanged a traitor but, if the occasion requires, he hopes there will be no hesitation; and this threat is directed at Kansas, and even at the friends of Kansas throughout the country. Again occurs the parallel with the struggle of our fathers, and I borrow the language of Patrick Henry, when, to the cry from the Senator, of "treason." "Treason," I reply, "if this be treason, make the most of it." Sir, it is easy to call names; but I beg to tell the Senator that if the word "traitor" is in any way applicable to those who refuse submission to a Tyrannical Usurpation, whether in Kansas or elsewhere, then must some new word, of deeper color, be invented, to designate those mad spirits who could endanger and degrade the Republic, while they betray all the cherished sentiments of the fathers and the spirit of the Constitution, in order to give new spread to Slavery. Let the Senator proceed. It will not be the first time in history, that a scaffold erected for punishment has become a pedestal of honor. Out of death comes life, and the "traitor" whom he blindly executes will live immortal in the cause.

For Humanity sweeps onward where today the martyr stands, On the morrow crouches Judas, with the silver in his hands; When the hooting mob of yesterday in silent awe return, To glean up the scattered ashes into History's golden urn.

Among these hostile Senators, there is yet another, with all the prejudices of the Senator from South Carolina, but without his generous impulses, who, on account of his character before the country, and the rancor of his opposition, deserves to be named. I mean the Senator from Virginia (Mr.

[George] Mason), who, as the author of the Fugitive Slave bill, has associated himself with a special act of inhumanity and tyranny. Of him I shall say little, for he has said little in this debate, though within that little was compressed the bitterness of a life absorbed in the support of Slavery. He holds the commission of Virginia; but he does not represent that early Virginia, so dear to our hearts, which gave to us the pen of Jefferson, by which the equality of men was declared, and the sword of Washington, by which Independence was secured; but he represents that other Virginia, from which Washington and Jefferson now avert their faces, where human beings are bred as cattle for the shambles, and where a dungeon rewards the pious matron who teaches little children to relieve their bondage by reading the Book of Life. It is proper that such a Senator, representing such a State, should rail against free Kansas.

Senators such as these are the natural enemies of Kansas, and I introduce them with reluctance, simply that the country may understand the character of the hostility which must be overcome. Arrayed with them, of course, are all who unite, under any pretext or apology, in the propagandism of human Slavery. To such, indeed, the time-honored safeguards of popular rights can be a name only, and nothing more. What are trial by jury, habeas corpus, the ballot-box, the right of petition, the liberty of Kansas, your liberty, sir, or mine, to one who lends himself, not merely to the support at home, but to the propagandism abroad, of that preposterous wrong, which denies even the right of a man to himself! Such a cause can be maintained only by a practical subversion of all rights. It is, therefore, merely according to reason that its partisans should uphold the Usurpation in Kansas.

A Duty to Oppose the Slave Oligarchy

To overthrow this Usurpation is now the special, importunate duty of Congress, admitting of no hesitation or postponement. To this end it must lift itself from the cabals of candidates, the machinations of party, and the low level of vulgar strife. It must turn from that Slave Oligarchy which now controls the Republic, and refuse to be its tool. Let its power be stretched forth toward this distant Territory, not to bind, but to unbind; not for the oppression of the weak, but for the subversion of the tyrannical; not for the prop and maintenance of a revolting Usurpation, but for the confirmation of Liberty.

"These are imperial arts and worthy thee!"

Let it now take its stand between the living and dead, and cause this plague to be stayed. All this it can do; and if the interests of Slavery did not oppose, all this it would do at once, in reverent regard for justice, law, and order, driving away all the alarms of war nor would it dare to brave the shame and punishment of this great refusal. But the slave power dares any thing; and it can be conquered only by the united masses of the people. From Congress to the People I appeal.

The contest, which, beginning in Kansas, has reached us, will soon be transferred from Congress to a broader stage, where every citizen will be not only spectator, but actor; and to their judgment I confidently appeal. To the People, now on the eve of exercising the electoral franchise, in choosing a Chief Magistrate of the Republic, I appeal, to vindicate the electoral franchise in Kansas. Let the ballot-box of the Union, with multitudinous might, protect the ballot-box in that Territory. Let the voters everywhere, while rejoicing in their own rights, help to guard the equal rights of distant fellow-citizens; that the shrines of popular institutions, now desecrated, may be sanctified anew; that the ballot-box, now plundered, may be restored; and that the cry, "I am an American citizen," may not be sent forth in vain against outrage of every kind. In just regard for free labor in that Territory, which it is sought to blast by unwelcome association with slave labor; in Christian sympathy with the slave, whom it is proposed to task and sell there; in stern condemnation of the crime which has been consummated on that beautiful soil; in rescue of fellow-citizens now subjugated to a Tyrannical Usurpation; in dutiful respect for the early fathers, whose aspirations are now ignobly thwarted; in the name of the Constitution, which has been outraged of the laws trampled down of Justice banished of Humanity degraded of Peace destroyed of Freedom crushed to earth; and, in the name of the Heavenly Father, whose service is perfect Freedom, I make this last appeal.

Final Address to the Court

John Brown

To the members of the abolitionist movement, John Brown
(1800–1859) was saint and martyr. The Connecticut-born
Brown moved to Kansas with his family in 1855, where
he was active in the often violent fight between pro- and
antislavery forces. In 1859 Brown launched a plan to establish a colony in the Virginia mountains for freed
slaves. On October 15, 1859, he and a group of followers (consisting of radical white abolitionists and free
blacks) seized the federal armory at Harpers Ferry, Virginia, in hopes of inciting a general slave rebellion, but a
Marine detachment led by Colonel Robert E. Lee over-
came the insurrectionists. Brown was found guilty of
murder, treason, and conspiracy to incite slave revolt. He
was hanged on December 2, 1859.

The Harpers Ferry raid, followed by Brown's trial
and execution, further polarized the nation. Supporters
such as Ralph Waldo Emerson and Henry David Thoreau
lauded Brown's doomed heroism in the name of emancipation, while proslavery Southerners viewed Brown as
the epitome of the rash, violent abolitionist. In his last
address to the court a month before his execution, Brown
admits only to his "design . . . to free slaves," pointedly
denying the other charges of which he was convicted. Yet
he also embraces his martyrdom, asserting the Christian
principle of loving one's neighbor as oneself as a justification for his efforts on behalf of slaves.

From John Brown's final address to the court, Virginia, November 2, 1859.

I have, may it please the court, a few words to say.

In the first place, I deny everything but what I have all along admitted: of a design on my part to free slaves. I intended certainly to have made a clean thing of that matter, as I did last winter, when I went into Missouri and there took slaves without the snapping of a gun on either side, moving them through the country, and finally leaving them in Canada. I designed to have done the same thing again on a larger scale. That was all I intended. I never did intend murder, or treason, or the destruction of property, or to excite or incite slaves to rebellion, or to make insurrection.

I have another objection, and that is that it is unjust that I should suffer such a penalty. Had I interfered in the manner which I admit, and which I admit has been fairly proved—for I admire the truthfulness and candor of the greater portion of the witnesses who have testified in this case—had I so interfered in behalf of the rich, the powerful, the intelligent, the so called great, or in the behalf of any of their friends, either father, mother, brother, sister, wife, or children, or any of that class, and suffered and sacrificed what I have in this interference, it would have been all right. Every man in this court would have deemed it an act worthy of reward rather than punishment.

This court acknowledges, too, as I suppose, the validity of the law of God. I see a book kissed, which I suppose to be the Bible, or at least the New Testament, which teaches me that all things whatsoever I would that men should do to me, I should do even so to them. It teaches me, further, to remember them that are in bonds as bound with them. I endeavored to act up to the instruction. I say I am yet too young to understand that God is any respecter of persons. I believe that to have interfered as I have done, as I have always freely admitted I have done, in behalf of his despised poor, I did not wrong but right. Now, if it is deemed necessary that I should forfeit my life for the furtherance of the ends of justice, and mingle my blood further with the blood of my children and with the blood of millions in this slave country whose rights are disregarded by wicked, cruel, and unjust enactments, I say let it be done.

Let me say one word further. I feel entirely satisfied with

the treatment I have received on my trial. Considering all the circumstances, it has been more generous than I expected. But I feel no consciousness of guilt. I have stated from the first what was my intention, and what was not. I never had any design against the liberty of any person, nor any disposition to commit treason or incite slaves to rebel or make any general insurrection. I never encouraged any man to do so, but always discouraged any idea of that kind.

Let me say, also, in regard to the statements made by some of those who were connected with me, I hear it has been stated by some of them that I have induced them to join me. But the contrary is true. I do not say this to injure them, but as regretting their weakness. Not one but joined me of his own accord, and the greater part at his own expense. A number of them I never saw, and never had a word of conversation with, till the day they came to me, and that was for the purpose I have stated.

Now I have done.

Republicans Oppose the Expansion of Slavery

Abraham Lincoln

Abraham Lincoln is widely regarded as one of the greatest U.S. presidents, having been elected at a time of unprecedented division and strife that led shortly to the Civil War. While Lincoln initially advocated a gradual abolition of slavery and at times seemed to make the preservation of the Union his chief priority, his speeches both before and after he became president reveal a profound abhorrence toward slavery.

The following speech, also known as "The Cooper Union Address," was delivered in New York in 1860 at the Cooper Institute, sponsored by the Young Men's Republican Union. Lincoln, as yet an undeclared presidential candidate, begins by assailing Illinois Senator Stephen Douglas's claim that the Constitution "forbid[s] our Federal Government to control . . . slavery in our Federal Territories." Speaking as both lawyer and historian, Lincoln meticulously considers the framers' various acts and declarations as regards slavery and the ostensible division of federal from local power. After demonstrating that the Founding Fathers endorsed neither slavery nor the relegation of matters concerning it to the states or territories, Lincoln pointedly addresses the southern condemnation of the so-called Black Republicans. He refutes the attacks on Republicans for being "sectionalist," radical, and for supposedly fomenting slave insurrections, deftly turning the criticism back on the critics. In closing, Lincoln

---

From Abraham Lincoln's speech "The Cooper Union Address," New York, New York, February 27, 1860.

makes a passionate case for the justice of the Republican cause in fighting the expansion of slavery to the territories and in opposing slavery itself on both moral and constitutional grounds.

M r. President and fellow citizens of New York:—
The facts with which I shall deal this evening are mainly old and familiar; nor is there anything new in the general use I shall make of them. If there shall be any novelty, it will be in the mode of presenting the facts, and the inferences and observations following that presentation.

In his speech last autumn, at Columbus, Ohio, as reported in "The New-York Times," Senator [Stephen] Douglas said:

"Our fathers, when they framed the Government under which we live, understood this question just as well, and even better, than we do now."

I fully indorse this, and I adopt it as a text for this discourse. I so adopt it because it furnishes a precise and an agreed starting point for a discussion between Republicans and that wing of the Democracy headed by Senator Douglas. It simply leaves the inquiry: "What was the understanding those fathers had of the question mentioned?"

What is the frame of government under which we live?

The answer must be: "The Constitution of the United States." That Constitution consists of the original, framed in 1787, (and under which the present government first went into operation,) and twelve subsequently framed amendments, the first ten of which were framed in 1789.

Who were our fathers that framed the Constitution? I suppose the "thirty-nine" who signed the original instrument may be fairly called our fathers who framed that part of the present Government. It is almost exactly true to say they framed it, and it is altogether true to say they fairly represented the opinion and sentiment of the whole nation at that time. Their names, being familiar to nearly all, and accessible to quite all, need not now be repeated.

I take these "thirty-nine," for the present, as being "our fathers who framed the Government under which we live."

What is the question which, according to the text, those fathers understood "just as well, and even better than we do now?"

It is this: Does the proper division of local from federal authority, or anything in the Constitution, forbid our *Federal Government* to control as to slavery in *our Federal Territories*?

Upon this, Senator Douglas holds the affirmative, and Republicans the negative. This affirmation and denial form an issue; and this issue—this question—is precisely what the text declares our fathers understood "better than we."

Let us now inquire whether the "thirty-nine," or any of them, ever acted upon this question; and if they did, how they acted upon it—how they expressed that better understanding?

In 1784, three years before the Constitution—the United States then owning the Northwestern Territory, and no other, the Congress of the Confederation had before them the question of prohibiting slavery in that Territory; and four of the "thirty-nine" who afterward framed the Constitution, were in that Congress, and voted on that question. Of these, Roger Sherman, Thomas Mifflin, and Hugh Williamson voted for the prohibition, thus showing that, in their understanding, no line dividing local from federal authority, nor anything else, properly forbade the Federal Government to control as to slavery in federal territory. The other of the four—James M'Henry—voted against the prohibition, showing that, for some cause, he thought it improper to vote for it.

In 1787, still before the Constitution, but while the Convention was in session framing it, and while the Northwestern Territory still was the only territory owned by the United States, the same question of prohibiting slavery in the territory again came before the Congress of the Confederation; and two more of the "thirty-nine" who afterward signed the Constitution, were in that Congress, and voted on the question. They were William Blount and William Few; and they both voted for the prohibition—thus showing that, in their understanding, no line dividing local from federal authority, nor anything else, properly forbids the Federal Government to control as to slavery in Federal territory. This time the prohibition became a law, being part of what is now well known as the Ordinance of '87.

The question of federal control of slavery in the territories, seems not to have been directly before the Convention which framed the original Constitution; and hence it is not recorded that the "thirty-nine," or any of them, while engaged on that instrument, expressed any opinion on that precise question.

Slavery and the Constitution

In 1789, by the first Congress which sat under the Constitution, an act was passed to enforce the Ordinance of '87, including the prohibition of slavery in the Northwestern Territory. The bill for this act was reported by one of the "thirty-nine," Thomas Fitzsimmons, then a member of the House of Representatives from Pennsylvania. It went through all its stages without a word of opposition, and finally passed both branches without yeas and nays, which is equivalent to a unanimous passage. In this Congress there were sixteen of the thirty-nine fathers who framed the original Constitution. They were John Langdon, Nicholas Gilman, Wm. S. Johnson, Roger Sherman, Robert Morris, Thos. Fitzsimmons, William Few, Abraham Baldwin, Rufus King, William Paterson, George Clymer, Richard Bassett, George Read, Pierce Butler, Daniel Carroll, James Madison. This shows that, in their understanding, no line dividing local from federal authority, nor anything in the Constitution, properly forbade Congress to prohibit slavery in the federal territory; else both their fidelity to correct principle, and their oath to support the Constitution, would have constrained them to oppose the prohibition.

Again, George Washington, another of the "thirty-nine," was then President of the United States, and, as such approved and signed the bill; thus completing its validity as a law, and thus showing that, in his understanding, no line dividing local from federal authority, nor anything in the Constitution, forbade the Federal Government, to control as to slavery in federal territory.

No great while after the adoption of the original Constitution, North Carolina ceded to the Federal Government the country now constituting the State of Tennessee; and a few years later Georgia ceded that which now constitutes the States of Mississippi and Alabama. In both deeds of cession it was made a condition by the ceding States that the Federal Government should not prohibit slavery in the ceded territory. Besides this, slavery was then actually in the ceded country. Under these circumstances, Congress, on taking charge of these countries, did not absolutely prohibit slavery within them. But they did interfere with it—take control of it—even there, to a certain extent. In 1798, Congress organized the Territory of Mississippi. In the act of organization, they prohibited the bringing of slaves into the Territory, from any place without the United States, by fine, and giving freedom to slaves so bought. This act passed both branches of Congress without yeas and nays. In that Congress were three of the "thirty-nine" who framed the original Constitution. They were John Langdon, George Read and Abraham Baldwin. They all, probably, voted for it. Certainly they would have placed their opposition to it upon record, if, in their understanding, any line dividing local from federal authority, or anything in the Constitution, properly forbade the Federal Government to control as to slavery in federal territory.

In 1803, the Federal Government purchased the Louisiana country. Our former territorial acquisitions came from certain of our own States; but this Louisiana country was acquired from a foreign nation. In 1804, Congress gave a territorial organization to that part of it which now constitutes the State of Louisiana. New Orleans, lying within that part, was an old and comparatively large city. There were other considerable towns and settlements, and slavery was extensively and thoroughly intermingled with the people. Congress did not, in the Territorial Act, prohibit slavery; but they did interfere with it—take control of it—in a more marked and extensive way than they did in the case of Mississippi. The substance of the provision therein made, in relation to slaves, was:

First. That no slave should be imported into the territory from foreign parts.

Second. That no slave should be carried into it who had been imported into the United States since the first day of May, 1798.

Third. That no slave should be carried into it, except by the owner, and for his own use as a settler; the penalty in all the cases being a fine upon the violator of the law, and freedom to the slave.

This act also was passed without yeas and nays. In the Congress which passed it, there were two of the "thirty-nine." They were Abraham Baldwin and Jonathan Dayton. As stated in the case of Mississippi, it is probable they both voted for it. They would not have allowed it to pass without recording their opposition to it, if, in their understanding, it violated either the line properly dividing local from federal authority, or any provision of the Constitution.

In 1819–20, came and passed the Missouri question. Many votes were taken, by yeas and nays, in both branches of Congress, upon the various phases of the general question. Two of the "thirty-nine"—Rufus King and Charles Pinckney—were members of that Congress. Mr. King steadily voted for slavery prohibition and against all compromises, while Mr. Pinckney as steadily voted against slavery prohibition and against all compromises. By this, Mr. King showed that, in his understanding, no line dividing local from federal authority, nor anything in the Constitution, was violated by Congress prohibiting slavery in federal territory; while Mr. Pinckney, by his votes, showed that, in his understanding, there was some sufficient reason for opposing such prohibition in that case.

The cases I have mentioned are the only acts of the "thirty-nine," or of any of them, upon the direct issue, which I have been able to discover.

To enumerate the persons who thus acted, as being four in 1784, two in 1787, seventeen in 1789, three in 1798, two in 1804, and two in 1819–20—there would be thirty of them. But this would be counting John Langdon, Roger Sherman, William Few, Rufus King, and George Read each twice, and Abraham Baldwin, three times. The true number of those of the "thirty-nine" whom I have shown to have acted upon the question, which, by the text, they understood better than we, is twenty-three, leaving sixteen not shown to have acted upon it in any way.

Here, then, we have twenty-three out of our thirty-nine

fathers "who framed the government under which we live," who have, upon their official responsibility and their corporal oaths, acted upon the very question which the text affirms they "understood just as well, and even better than we do now;" and twenty-one of them—a clear majority of the whole "thirty-nine"—so acting upon it as to make them guilty of gross political impropriety and willful perjury, if, in their understanding, any proper division between local and federal authority, or anything in the Constitution they had made themselves, and sworn to support, forbade the Federal Government to control as to slavery in the federal territories. Thus the twenty-one acted; and, as actions speak louder than words, so actions, under such responsibility, speak still louder.

Two of the twenty-three voted against Congressional prohibition of slavery in the federal territories, in the instances in which they acted upon the question. But for what reasons they so voted is not known. They may have done so because they thought a proper division of local from federal authority, or some provision or principle of the Constitution, stood in the way; or they may, without any such question, have voted against the prohibition, on what appeared to them to be sufficient grounds of expediency. No one who has sworn to support the Constitution can conscientiously vote for what he understands to be an unconstitutional measure, however expedient he may think it; but one may and ought to vote against a measure which he deems constitutional, if, at the same time, he deems it inexpedient. It, therefore, would be unsafe to set down even the two who voted against the prohibition, as having done so because, in their understanding, any proper division of local from federal authority, or anything in the Constitution, forbade the Federal Government to control as to slavery in federal territory.

The remaining sixteen of the "thirty-nine," so far as I have discovered, have left no record of their understanding upon the direct question of federal control of slavery in the federal territories. But there is much reason to believe that their understanding upon that question would not have appeared different from that of their twenty-three compeers, had it been manifested at all.

For the purpose of adhering rigidly to the text, I have

purposely omitted whatever understanding may have been manifested by any person, however distinguished, other than the thirty-nine fathers who framed the original Constitution; and, for the same reason, I have also omitted whatever understanding may have been manifested by any of the "thirty-nine" even, on any other phase of the general question of slavery. If we should look into their acts and declarations on those other phases, as the foreign slave trade, and the morality and policy of slavery generally, it would appear to us that on the direct question of federal control of slavery in federal territories, the sixteen, if they had acted at all, would probably have acted just as the twenty-three did. Among that sixteen were several of the most noted anti-slavery men of those times—as Dr. [Benjamin] Franklin, Alexander Hamilton and Gouverneur Morris—while there was not one now known to have been otherwise, unless it may be John Rutledge, of South Carolina.

No Division of Local from Federal Authority

The sum of the whole is, that of our thirty-nine fathers who framed the original Constitution, twenty-one—a clear majority of the whole—certainly understood that no proper division of local from federal authority, nor any part of the Constitution, forbade the Federal Government to control slavery in the federal territories; while all the rest probably had the same understanding. Such, unquestionably, was the understanding of our fathers who framed the original Constitution; and the text affirms that they understood the question "better than we."

But, so far, I have been considering the understanding of the question manifested by the framers of the original Constitution. In and by the original instrument, a mode was provided for amending it; and, as I have already stated, the present frame of "the Government under which we live" consists of that original, and twelve amendatory articles framed and adopted since. Those who now insist that federal control of slavery in federal territories violates the Constitution, point us to the provisions which they suppose it thus violates; and, as I understand, that all fix upon provisions in these amendatory articles, and not in the original instrument. The Supreme Court, in the Dred Scott case, plant themselves upon the fifth amendment, which provides that no person shall be deprived of "life, liberty or property without due process of law;" while Senator Douglas and his peculiar adherents plant themselves upon the tenth amendment, providing that "the powers not delegated to the United States by the Constitution" "are reserved to the States respectively, or to the people."

Now, it so happens that these amendments were framed by the first Congress which sat under the Constitution—the identical Congress which passed the act already mentioned, enforcing the prohibition of slavery in the Northwestern Territory. Not only was it the same Congress, but they were the identical, same individual men who, at the same session, and at the same time within the session, had under consideration, and in progress toward maturity, these Constitutional amendments, and this act prohibiting slavery in all the territory the nation then owned. The Constitutional amendments were introduced before, and passed after the act enforcing the Ordinance of '87; so that, during the whole pendency of the act to enforce the Ordinance, the Constitutional amendments were also pending.

The seventy-six members of that Congress, including sixteen of the framers of the original Constitution, as before stated, were pre-eminently our fathers who framed that part of "the Government under which we live," which is now claimed as forbidding the Federal Government to control slavery in the federal territories.

Is it not a little presumptuous in any one at this day to affirm that the two things which that Congress deliberately framed, and carried to maturity at the same time, are absolutely inconsistent with each other? And does not such affirmation become impudently absurd when coupled with the other affirmation from the same mouth, that those who did the two things, alleged to be inconsistent, understood whether they really were inconsistent better than we—better than he who affirms that they are inconsistent?

It is surely safe to assume that the thirty-nine framers of

the original Constitution, and the seventy-six members of the Congress which framed the amendments thereto, taken together, do certainly include those who may be fairly called "our fathers who framed the Government under which we live." And so assuming, I defy any man to show that any one of them ever, in his whole life, declared that, in his understanding, any proper division of local from federal authority, or any part of the Constitution, forbade the Federal Government to control as to slavery in the federal territories. I go a step further. I defy any one to show that any living man in the whole world ever did, prior to the beginning of the present century, (and I might almost say prior to the beginning of the last half of the present century,) declare that, in his understanding, any proper division of local from federal authority, or any part of the Constitution, forbade the Federal Government to control as to slavery in the federal territories. To those who now so declare, I give, not only "our fathers who framed the Government under which we live," but with them all other living men within the century in which it was framed, among whom to search, and they shall not be able to

Lincoln's speeches both before and after he became president reveal a profound abhorrence toward slavery.

find the evidence of a single man agreeing with them.

Now, and here, let me guard a little against being misunderstood. I do not mean to say we are bound to follow implicitly in whatever our fathers did. To do so, would be to discard all the lights of current experience—to reject all progress—all improvement. What I do say is, that if we would supplant the opinions and policy of our fathers in any case, we should do so upon evidence so conclusive, and argument so clear, that even their great authority, fairly considered and weighed, cannot stand; and most surely not in a case whereof we ourselves declare they understood the question better than we.

If any man at this day sincerely believes that a proper division of local from federal authority, or any part of the Constitution, forbids the Federal Government to control as to slavery in the federal territories, he is right to say so, and to enforce his position by all truthful evidence and fair argument which he can. But he has no right to mislead others, who have less access to history, and less leisure to study it, into the false belief that "our fathers who framed the Government under which we live" were of the same opinion— thus substituting falsehood and deception for truthful evidence and fair argument. If any man at this day sincerely believes "our fathers who framed the Government under which we live," used and applied principles, in other cases, which ought to have led them to understand that a proper division of local from federal authority or some part of the Constitution, forbids the Federal Government to control as to slavery in the federal territories, he is right to say so. But he should, at the same time, brave the responsibility of declaring that, in his opinion, he understands their principles better than they did themselves; and especially should he not shirk that responsibility by asserting that they "understood the question just as well, and even better, than we do now."

But enough! *Let all who believe that "our fathers, who framed the Government under which we live, understood this question just as well, and even better, than we do now," speak as they spoke, and act as they acted upon it. This is all Republicans ask—all Republicans desire—in relation to slavery. As those fathers marked it, so let it be again marked, as an evil not to be extended, but to be tolerated and protected only because of and so far as its actual presence among us makes that toleration and protection a necessity. Let all the guarantees those fathers gave it, be, not grudgingly, but fully and fairly, maintained.* For this Republicans contend, and with this, so far as I know or believe, they will be content.

An Appeal to the Southern People

And now, if they would listen—as I suppose they will not—I would address a few words to the Southern people.

I would say to them:—You consider yourselves a reasonable and a just people; and I consider that in the general qualities of reason and justice you are not inferior to any other people. Still, when you speak of us Republicans, you do so only to denounce us as reptiles, or, at the best, as no better than outlaws. You will grant a hearing to pirates or murderers, but nothing like it to "Black Republicans." In all your contentions with one another, each of you deems an unconditional condemnation of "Black Republicanism" as the first thing to be attended to. Indeed, such condemnation of us seems to be an indispensable prerequisite—license, so to speak—among you to be admitted or permitted to speak at all. Now, can you, or not, be prevailed upon to pause and to consider whether this is quite just to us, or even to yourselves? Bring forward your charges and specifications, and then be patient long enough to hear us deny or justify.

You say we are sectional. We deny it. That makes an issue; and the burden of proof is upon you. You produce your proof; and what is it? Why, that our party has no existence in your section—gets no votes in your section. The fact is substantially true; but does it prove the issue? If it does, then in case we should, without change of principle, begin to get votes in your section, we should thereby cease to be sectional. You cannot escape this conclusion; and yet, are you willing to abide by it? If you are, you will probably soon find that we have ceased to be sectional, for we shall get votes in your section this very year. You will then begin to discover, as the truth plainly is, that your proof does not touch the issue. The fact that we get no votes in your section, is a fact of your making, and not of ours. And if there be fault in that fact, that fault is primarily yours, and remains until you show that we repel you by some wrong principle or practice. If we do repel you by any wrong principle or practice, the fault is ours; but this brings you to where you ought to have started—to a discussion of the right or wrong of our principle. If our principle, put in practice, would wrong your section for the benefit of ours, or for any other object, then our principle, and we with it, are sectional, and are justly opposed and denounced as such. Meet us, then, on the question of whether our principle, put in practice, would wrong your section; and so meet it as if it were possible that something may be said on our side. Do you accept the challenge? No! Then you really believe that the principle which "our fathers who framed the Government under which we live" thought so clearly right as to adopt it, and indorse it again and again, upon their official oaths, is in fact so clearly wrong as to demand your condemnation without a moment's consideration.

Some of you delight to flaunt in our faces the warning against sectional parties given by Washington in his Farewell Address. Less than eight years before Washington gave that warning, he had, as President of the United States, approved and signed an act of Congress, enforcing the prohibition of slavery in the Northwestern Territory, which act embodied the policy of the Government upon that subject up to and at the very moment he penned that warning; and about one year after he penned it, he wrote LaFayette that he considered that prohibition a wise measure, expressing in the same connection his hope that we should at some time have a confederacy of free States.

Bearing this in mind, and seeing that sectionalism has since arisen upon this same subject, is that warning a weapon in your hands against us, or in our hands against you? Could Washington himself speak, would he cast the blame of that sectionalism upon us, who sustain his policy, or upon you who repudiate it? We respect that warning of Washington, and we commend it to you, together with his example pointing to the right application of it.

But you say you are conservative—eminently conservative —while we are revolutionary, destructive, or something of the sort. What is conservatism? Is it not adherence to the old and tried, against the new and untried? We stick to, contend for, the identical old policy on the point in controversy which was adopted by "our fathers who framed the Government under which we live;" while you with one accord reject, and scout, and spit upon that old policy, and insist upon substituting something new. True, you disagree among yourselves as to what that substitute shall be. You are divided on new propositions and plans, but you are unanimous in rejecting and denouncing the old policy of the fathers. Some of you are for reviving the foreign slave trade; some for a Congressional Slave-Code for the Territories; some for Congress forbidding the Territories to prohibit Slavery within their limits; some for maintaining Slavery in the Territories through the judiciary; some for the "gur-reat pur-rinciple" that "if one man would enslave another, no third man should object," fantastically called "Popular Sovereignty;" but never a man among you is in favor of federal prohibition of slavery in federal territories, according to the practice of "our fathers who framed the Government under which we live." Not one of all your various plans can show a precedent or an advocate in the century within which our Government originated. Consider, then, whether your claim of conservatism for yourselves, and your charge or destructiveness against us, are based on the most clear and stable foundations.

Again, you say we have made the slavery question more prominent than it formerly was. We deny it. We admit that it is more prominent, but we deny that we made it so. It was not we, but you, who discarded the old policy of the fathers. We resisted, and still resist, your innovation; and thence comes the greater prominence of the question. Would you have that question reduced to its former proportions? Go back to that old policy. What has been will be again, under the same conditions. If you would have the peace of the old times, readopt the precepts and policy of the old times.

Slave Insurrections

You charge that we stir up insurrections among your slaves. We deny it; and what is your proof? Harpers Ferry! John

Brown!! John Brown was no Republican; and you have failed to implicate a single Republican in his Harpers Ferry enterprise. If any member of our party is guilty in that matter, you know it or you do not know it. If you do know it, you are inexcusable for not designating the man and proving the fact. If you do not know it, you are inexcusable for asserting it, and especially for persisting in the assertion after you have tried and failed to make the proof. You need to be told that persisting in a charge which one does not know to be true, is simply malicious slander.

Some of you admit that no Republican designedly aided or encouraged the Harpers Ferry affair, but still insist that our doctrines and declarations necessarily lead to such results. We do not believe it. We know we hold to no doctrine, and make no declaration, which were not held to and made by "our fathers who framed the Government under which we live." You never dealt fairly by us in relation to this affair. When it occurred, some important State elections were near at hand, and you were in evident glee with the belief that, by charging the blame upon us, you could get an advantage of us in those elections. The elections came, and your expectations were not quite fulfilled. Every Republican man knew that, as to himself at least, your charge was a slander, and he was not much inclined by it to cast his vote in your favor. Republican doctrines and declarations are accompanied with a continual protest against any interference whatever with your slaves, or with you about your slaves. Surely, this does not encourage them to revolt. True, we do, in common with "our fathers, who framed the Government under which we live," declare our belief that slavery is wrong; but the slaves do not hear us declare even this. For anything we say or do, the slaves would scarcely know there is a Republican party. I believe they would not, in fact, generally know it but for your misrepresentations of us, in their hearing. In your political contests among yourselves, each faction charges the other with sympathy with Black Republicanism; and then, to give point to the charge, defines Black Republicanism to simply be insurrection, blood and thunder among the slaves.

Slave insurrections are no more common now than they were before the Republican party was organized. What induced the Southampton insurrection, twenty-eight years ago, in which, at least three times as many lives were lost as at Harpers Ferry? You can scarcely stretch your very elastic fancy to the conclusion that Southampton was "got up by Black Republicanism." In the present state of things in the United States, I do not think a general, or even a very extensive slave insurrection is possible. The indispensable concert of action cannot be attained. The slaves have no means of rapid communication; nor can incendiary freemen, black or white, supply it. The explosive materials are everywhere in parcels; but there neither are, nor can be supplied, the indispensable connecting trains.

Much is said by Southern people about the affection of slaves for their masters and mistresses; and a part of it, at least, is true. A plot for an uprising could scarcely be devised and communicated to twenty individuals before some one of them, to save the life of a favorite master or mistress, would divulge it. This is the rule; and the slave revolution in Hayti was not an exception to it, but a case occurring under peculiar circumstances. The gunpowder plot of British history, though not connected with slaves, was more in point. In that case, only about twenty were admitted to the secret; and yet one of them, in his anxiety to save a friend, betrayed the plot to that friend, and, by consequence, averted the calamity. Occasional poisonings from the kitchen, and open or stealthy assassinations in the field, and local revolts extending to a score or so, will continue to occur as the natural results of slavery; but no general insurrection of slaves, as I think, can happen in this country for a long time. Whoever much fears, or much hopes for such an event, will be alike disappointed.

In the language of Mr. [Thomas] Jefferson, uttered many years ago, "It is still in our power to direct the process of emancipation, and deportation, peaceably, and in such slow degrees, as that the evil will wear off insensibly; and their places be, *pari passu*, filled up by free white laborers. If, on the contrary, it is left to force itself on, human nature must shudder at the prospect held up."

Mr. Jefferson did not mean to say, nor do I, that the power of emancipation is in the Federal Government. He spoke of Virginia; and, as to the power of emancipation, I speak of the slaveholding States only. The Federal Government, however, as we insist, has the power of restraining the extension of the institution—the power to insure that a slave insurrection shall never occur on any American soil which is now free from slavery.

John Brown's effort was peculiar. It was not a slave insurrection. It was an attempt by white men to get up a revolt among slaves, in which the slaves refused to participate. In fact, it was so absurd that the slaves, with all their ignorance, saw plainly enough it could not succeed. That affair, in its philosophy, corresponds with the many attempts, related in history, at the assassination of kings and emperors. An enthusiast broods over the oppression of a people till he fancies himself commissioned by Heaven to liberate them. He ventures the attempt, which ends in little else than his own execution. Orsini's attempt on Louis Napoleon, and John Brown's attempt at Harpers Ferry were, in their philosophy, precisely the same. The eagerness to cast blame on old England in the one case, and on New England in the other, does not disprove the sameness of the two things.

No Constitutional Right to Slavery

And how much would it avail you, if you could, by the use of John Brown, Helper's Book [Hinton Rowan Helper's anti-slavery treatise, *The Impending Crisis of the South* (1857)], and the like, break up the Republican organization? Human action can be modified to some extent, but human nature cannot be changed. There is a judgment and a feeling against slavery in this nation, which cast at least a million and a half of votes. You cannot destroy that judgment and feeling—that sentiment—by breaking up the political organization which rallies around it. You can scarcely scatter and disperse an army which has been formed into order in the face of your heaviest fire; but if you could, how much would you gain by forcing the sentiment which created it out of the peaceful channel of the ballot-box, into some other channel? What would that other channel probably be? Would the number of John Browns be lessened or enlarged by the operation?

But you will break up the Union rather than submit to a

denial of your Constitutional rights.

That has a somewhat reckless sound; but it would be palliated, if not fully justified, were we proposing, by the mere force of numbers, to deprive you of some right, plainly written down in the Constitution. But we are proposing no such thing.

When you make these declarations, you have a specific and well-understood allusion to an assumed Constitutional right of yours, to take slaves into the federal territories, and to hold them there as property. But no such right is specifically written in the Constitution. That instrument is literally silent about any such right. We, on the contrary, deny that such a right has any existence in the Constitution, even by implication.

Your purpose, then, plainly stated, is that you will destroy the Government, unless you be allowed to construe and enforce the Constitution as you please, on all points in dispute between you and us. You will rule or ruin in all events.

This, plainly stated, is your language. Perhaps you will say the Supreme Court has decided the disputed Constitutional question in your favor. Not quite so. But waiving the lawyer's distinction between dictum and decision, the Court have decided the question for you in a sort of way. The Court have substantially said, it is your Constitutional right to take slaves into the federal territories, and to hold them there as property. When I say the decision was made in a sort of way, I mean it was made in a divided Court, by a bare majority of the Judges, and they not quite agreeing with one another in the reasons for making it; that it is so made as that its avowed supporters disagree with one another about its meaning, and that it was mainly based upon a mistaken statement of fact—the statement in the opinion that "the right of property in a slave is distinctly and expressly affirmed in the Constitution."

An inspection of the Constitution will show that the right of property in a slave is not *"distinctly* and *expressly* affirmed" in it. Bear in mind, the Judges do not pledge their judicial opinion that such right is *impliedly* affirmed in the Constitution; but they pledge their veracity that it is *"distinctly* and *expressly"* affirmed there—"distinctly," that is, not mingled with anything else—"expressly," that is, in words meaning just that, without the aid of any inference, and susceptible of no other meaning.

If they had only pledged their judicial opinion that such right is affirmed in the instrument by implication, it would be open to others to show that neither the word "slave" nor "slavery" is to be found in the Constitution, nor the word "property" even, in any connection with language alluding to the things slave, or slavery; and that wherever in that instrument the slave is alluded to, he is called a "person;"—and wherever his master's legal right in relation to him is alluded to, it is spoken of as "service or labor which may be due,"—as a debt payable in service or labor. Also, it would be open to show, by contemporaneous history, that this mode of alluding to slaves and slavery, instead of speaking of them, was employed on purpose to exclude from the Constitution the idea that there could be property in man.

To show all this, is easy and certain.

When this obvious mistake of the Judges shall be brought to their notice, is it not reasonable to expect that they will withdraw the mistaken statement, and reconsider the conclusion based upon it?

And then it is to be remembered that "our fathers, who framed the Government under which we live"—the men who made the Constitution—decided this same Constitutional question in our favor, long ago—decided it without division among themselves, when making the decision; without division among themselves about the meaning of it after it was made, and, so far as any evidence is left, without basing it upon any mistaken statement of facts.

Under all these circumstances, do you really feel yourselves justified to break up this Government unless such a court decision as yours is, shall be at once submitted to as a conclusive and final rule of political action? But you will not abide the election of a Republican president! In that supposed event, you say, you will destroy the Union; and then, you say, the great crime of having destroyed it will be upon us! That is cool. A highwayman holds a pistol to my ear, and mutters through his teeth, "Stand and deliver, or I shall kill you, and then you will be a murderer!"

To be sure, what the robber demanded of me—my money—was my own; and I had a clear right to keep it; but it was no more my own than my vote is my own; and the threat of death to me, to extort my money, and the threat of destruction to the Union, to extort my vote, can scarcely be distinguished in principle.

The Justice of the Republican Cause

A few words now to Republicans. *It is exceedingly desirable that all parts of this great Confederacy shall be at peace, and in harmony, one with another. Let us Republicans do our part to have it so. Even though much provoked, let us do nothing through passion and ill temper. Even though the southern people will not so much as listen to us, let us calmly consider their demands, and yield to them if, in our deliberate view of our duty, we possibly can.* Judging by all they say and do, and by the subject and nature of their controversy with us, let us determine, if we can, what will satisfy them.

Will they be satisfied if the Territories be unconditionally surrendered to them? We know they will not. In all their present complaints against us, the Territories are scarcely mentioned. Invasions and insurrections are the rage now. Will it satisfy them, if, in the future, we have nothing to do with invasions and insurrections? We know it will not. We so know, because we know we never had anything to do with invasions and insurrections; and yet this total abstaining does not exempt us from the charge and the denunciation.

The question recurs, what will satisfy them? Simply this: We must not only let them alone, but we must somehow, convince them that we do let them alone. This, we know by experience, is no easy task. We have been so trying to convince them from the very beginning of our organization, but with no success. In all our platforms and speeches we have constantly protested our purpose to let them alone; but this has had no tendency to convince them. Alike unavailing to convince them, is the fact that they have never detected a man of us in any attempt to disturb them.

These natural, and apparently adequate means all failing, what will convince them? This, and this only: cease to call slavery *wrong*, and join them in calling it *right*. And this must be done thoroughly—done in *acts* as well as in *words*. Silence will not be tolerated—we must place ourselves avowedly with them. Senator Douglas' new sedition law must be enacted and enforced, suppressing all declarations that slavery is wrong, whether made in politics, in presses, in pulpits, or in private. We must arrest and return their fugitive slaves with greedy pleasure. We must pull down our Free State constitutions. The whole atmosphere must be disinfected from all taint of opposition to slavery, before they will cease to believe that all their troubles proceed from us.

I am quite aware they do not state their case precisely in this way. Most of them would probably say to us, "Let us alone, do nothing to us, and say what you please about slavery." But we do let them alone—have never disturbed them—so that, after all, it is what we say, which dissatisfies them. They will continue to accuse us of doing, until we cease saying.

I am also aware they have not, as yet, in terms, demanded the overthrow of our Free-State Constitutions. Yet those Constitutions declare the wrong of slavery, with more solemn emphasis, than do all other sayings against it; and when all these other sayings shall have been silenced, the overthrow of these Constitutions will be demanded, and nothing be left to resist the demand. It is nothing to the contrary, that they do not demand the whole of this just now. Demanding what they do, and for the reason they do, they can voluntarily stop nowhere short of this consummation. Holding, as they do, that slavery is morally right, and socially elevating, they cannot cease to demand a full national recognition of it, as a legal right, and a social blessing.

Nor can we justifiably withhold this, on any ground save our conviction that slavery is wrong. If slavery is right, all words, acts, laws, and constitutions against it, are themselves wrong, and should be silenced, and swept away. If it is right, we cannot justly object to its nationality—its universality; if it is wrong, they cannot justly insist upon its extension—its enlargement. All they ask, we could readily grant, if we thought slavery right; all we ask, they could as readily grant, if they thought it wrong. Their thinking it right, and our thinking it wrong, is the precise fact upon which depends the whole controversy. Thinking it right, as they do, they are not to blame for desiring its full recognition, as being right; but, thinking it wrong, as we do, can we yield to them? Can we cast our votes with their view, and against our own? In view of our moral, social, and political responsibilities, can we do this?

Wrong as we think slavery is, we can yet afford to let it alone where it is, because that much is due to the necessity arising from its actual presence in the nation; but can we, while our votes will prevent it, allow it to spread into the National Territories, and to overrun us here in these Free States? If our sense of duty forbids this, then let us stand by our duty, fearlessly and effectively. Let us be diverted by none of those sophistical contrivances wherewith we are so industriously plied and belabored—contrivances such as groping for some middle ground between the right and the wrong, vain as the search for a man who should be neither a living man nor a dead man—such as a policy of "don't care" on a question about which all true men do care—such as Union appeals beseeching true Union men to yield to Disunionists, reversing the divine rule, and calling, not the sinners, but the righteous to repentance—such as invocations to Washington, imploring men to unsay what Washington said, and undo what Washington did.

Neither let us be slandered from our duty by false accusations against us, nor frightened from it by menaces of destruction to the Government nor of dungeons to ourselves. LET US HAVE FAITH THAT RIGHT MAKES MIGHT, AND IN THAT FAITH, LET US, TO THE END, DARE TO DO OUR DUTY AS WE UNDERSTAND IT.

"A House Divided": Civil War

Northern Agitation Endangers the Union

James Buchanan

Democrat James Buchanan (1791–1868) was the fifteenth president of the United States. Buchanan represented Pennsylvania first in the House of Representatives and then in the Senate. He then served as ambassador and secretary of state under James K. Polk before being elected president in 1856. His support of laws protecting slavery won him the backing of the South but the disapproval of abolitionists, effectively splitting the Democratic Party and enabling Lincoln's 1860 victory.

In the following excerpt from his Fourth Annual Message to Congress (December 3, 1860), Buchanan seems to assign much of the blame for the secession crisis to northern abolitionists. Their attempts to thwart the Fugitive Slave Law, their opposition to the expansion of slavery into the territories, and their incitement of slave rebellions through the incessant distribution of abolitionist propaganda have infringed on the sovereignty of the southern states and thus unsettled the stability of the entire nation. Although he would later support Lincoln during the war, in this address Buchanan makes clear his sympathy for the grievances of the slaveholding South.

From James Buchanan's speech "Fourth Annual Message to Congress," December 3, 1860.

*F*ellow-Citizens of the Senate and House of Representatives:

Throughout the year since our last meeting the country has been eminently prosperous in all its material wants. The general health has been excellent, our harvests have been abundant, and plenty smiles throughout the land. Our commerce and manufactures have been prosecuted with energy and industry, and have yielded fair and ample returns. In short, no nation in the tide of time has ever presented a spectacle of greater material prosperity than we have done until within a very recent period.

Why is it, then, that discontent now so extensively prevails, and the Union of the States, which is the source of all these blessings, is threatened with destruction?

The long-continued and intemperate interference of the Northern people with the question of slavery in the Southern States has at length produced its natural effects. The different sections of the Union are now arrayed against each other, and the time has arrived, so much dreaded by the Father of his Country, when hostile geographic parties have been formed.

I have long foreseen and often forewarned my countrymen of the now impending danger. This does not proceed solely from the claim on the part of Congress or the Territorial legislatures to exclude slavery from the Territories, nor from the efforts of different States to defeat the execution of the fugitive-slave law. All or any of these evils might have been endured by the South without danger to the Union (as others have been) in the hope that time and reflection might apply the remedy. The immediate peril arises not so much from these causes as from the fact that the incessant and violent agitation of the slavery question throughout the North for the last quarter of a century has at length produced its malign influence on the slaves and inspired them with vague notions of freedom. Hence a sense of security no longer exists around the family altar. This feeling of peace at home has given place to apprehensions of servile insurrections. Many a matron throughout the South retires at night in dread of what may befall herself and children before the morning. Should this apprehension of domestic danger, whether real or imaginary, extend and intensify itself until it shall pervade the masses of the Southern people, then disunion will become inevitable. Self-preservation is the first law of nature, and has been implanted in the heart of man by his Creator for the wisest purpose; and no political union, however fraught with blessings and benefits in all other respects, can long continue if the necessary consequence be to render the homes and firesides of nearly half the parties to it habitually and hopelessly insecure. Sooner or later the bonds of such a union must be severed. It is my conviction that this fatal period has not yet arrived, and my prayer to God is that He would preserve the Constitution and the Union throughout all generations.

But let us take warning in time and remove the cause of danger. It can not be denied that for five and twenty years the agitation at the North against slavery has been incessant. In 1835 pictorial handbills and inflammatory appeals were circulated extensively throughout the South of a character to excite the passions of the slaves, and, in the language of General Jackson, "to stimulate them to insurrection and produce all the horrors of a servile war." This agitation has ever since been continued by the public press, by the proceedings of State and county conventions and by abolition sermons and lectures. The time of Congress has been occupied in violent speeches on this never-ending subject, and appeals, in pamphlet and other forms, indorsed by distinguished names, have been sent forth from this central point and spread broadcast over the Union.

How easy it would be for the American people to settle the slavery question forever and to restore peace and harmony to this distracted country! They, and they alone, can do it. All that is necessary to accomplish the object, and all for which the slave States have ever contended, is to be let alone and permitted to manage their domestic institutions in their own way. As sovereign States, they, and they alone, are responsible before God and the world for slavery existing among them. For this the people of the North are not more responsible and have no more right to interfere than with similar institutions in Russia or in Brazil.

Southern States Have the Right to Secede

Jefferson Davis

Jefferson Davis (1808–1889) was the Confederacy's only president. A decorated hero of the Mexican-American War, Davis served as Secretary of War under President Franklin Pierce and twice served as U.S. senator from Mississippi (1847–1851; 1857–1861), emerging as a spokesperson for the interests of the slaveholding South. Davis was not first choice for president, but after Alexander H. Stephens of Georgia was rejected as too pro-Union and fellow Georgian Howell Cobb turned down the position, the provisional Congress of the Confederacy named Davis leader of the new government. (In 1862 he would win the popular vote for the presidency.) Davis was generally ineffectual as both a military and political leader. Upon the fall of the Confederacy, Davis was captured in Georgia and served two years imprisoned for treason before being released without a trial in 1867.

In Davis's farewell speech to the U.S. Senate (21 January 1861), he justifies Mississippi's decision to secede. He distinguishes secession from "nullification," the doctrine espoused by John C. Calhoun and others that holds a state's right to disregard federal law and yet remain in the Union if the law in question is deemed to be unconstitutional. Secession, rather, entails the withdrawal of a sovereign state from the Union and all its laws as well as protections. But Davis makes abundantly clear that the reason for seceding is the conflict over slavery, brought to

From Jefferson Davis's farewell to the U.S. Senate, January 21, 1861.

a critical head by the election of Abraham Lincoln. He
denies the northern contention that the Declaration of Independence mandates the equality of the races. He likens
the architects of the southern secession to their revolutionary forebears who rejected British tyranny, and proclaims no ill will against his former countrymen.

I rise, Mr. President, for the purpose of announcing to the
Senate that I have satisfactory evidence that the State of
Mississippi, by a solemn ordinance of her people, in convention assembled, has declared her separation from the
United States. Under these circumstances, of course, my functions are terminated here. It has seemed to me proper, however, that I should appear in the Senate to announce that fact
to my associates, and I will say but very little more. The occasion does not invite me to go into argument; and my physical condition would not permit me to do so, if it were otherwise; and yet it seems to become me to say something on
the part of the State I here represent on an occasion as
solemn as this.

It is known to Senators who have served with me here
that I have for many years advocated, as an essential attribute of State sovereignty, the right of a State to secede from
the Union. Therefore, if I had thought that Mississippi was
acting without sufficient provocation, or without an existing
necessity, I should still, under my theory of the Government,
because of my allegiance to the State of which I am a citizen,
have been bound by her action. I, however, may be permitted
to say that I do think she has justifiable cause, and I approve
of her act. I conferred with her people before that act was
taken, counseled them then that, if the state of things which
they apprehended should exist when their Convention met,
they should take the action which they have now adopted.

I hope none who hear me will confound this expression
of mine with the advocacy of the right of a State to remain in
the Union, and to disregard its constitutional obligation by
the nullification of the law. Such is not my theory. Nullification and secession, so often confounded, are, indeed, antag-

onistic principles. Nullification is a remedy which it is sought to apply within the Union, against the agent of the States. It is only to be justified when the agent has violated his constitutional obligations, and a State, assuming to judge for itself, denies the right of the agent thus to act, and appeals to the other states of the Union for a decision; but, when the States themselves and when the people of the States have so acted as to convince us that they will not regard our constitutional rights, then, and then for the first time, arises the doctrine of secession in its practical application.

A great man who now reposes with his fathers, and who has often been arraigned for want of fealty to the Union, advocated the doctrine of nullification because it preserved the Union. It was because of his deep-seated attachment to the Union—his determination to find some remedy for existing ills short of a severance of the ties which bound South Carolina to the other States—that Mr. [John C.] Calhoun advocated the doctrine of nullification, which he proclaimed to be peaceful, to be within the limits of State power, not to disturb the Union, but only to be a means of bringing the agent before the tribunal of the States for their judgement.

Secession belongs to a different class of remedies. It is to be justified upon the basis that the states are sovereign. There was a time when none denied it. I hope the time may come again when a better comprehension of the theory of our Government, and the inalienable rights of the people of the States, will prevent any one from denying that each State is a sovereign, and thus may reclaim the grants which it has made to any agent whomsoever.

I, therefore, say I concur in the action of the people of Mississippi, believing it to be necessary and proper, and should have been bound by their action if my belief had been otherwise; and this brings me to the important point which I wish, on this last occasion, to present to the Senate. It is by this confounding of nullification and secession that the name of a great man whose ashes now mingle with his mother earth has been invoked to justify coercion against a seceded State. The phrase, "to execute the laws," was an expression which General Jackson applied to the case of a State refusing to obey the laws while yet a member of the Union. That is not the case which is now presented. The laws are to be executed over the United States, and upon the people of the United States. They have no relation to any foreign country. It is a perversion of terms—at least, it is a great mis-apprehension of the case—which cites that expression for application to a State which has withdrawn from the Union. You may make war on a foreign state. If it be the purpose of gentlemen, they may make war against a State which has withdrawn from the Union; but there are no laws of the United States to be executed within the limits of a seceded State. A State, finding herself in the condition in which Mississippi has judged she is—in which her safety requires that she should provide for the maintenance of her rights out of the Union—surrenders all the benefits (and they are known to be many), deprives herself of the advantages (and they are known to be great), severs all the ties of affection (and they are close and enduring), which have bound her to the Union; and thus divesting herself of every benefit—taking upon herself every burden—she claims to be exempt from any power to execute the laws of the United States within her limits.

I well remember an occasion when Massachusetts was arraigned before the bar of the Senate, and when the doctrine of coercion was rife, and to be applied against her, because of the rescue of a fugitive slave in Boston. My opinion then was the same that it is now. Not in a spirit of egotism, but to show that I am not influenced in my opinions because the case is my own, I refer to that time and that occasion as containing the opinion which I then entertained, and on which my present conduct is based. I then said that if Massachusetts—following her purpose through a stated line of conduct—chose to take the last step, which separates her from the Union, it is her right to go, and I will neither vote one dollar nor one man to coerce her back; but I will say to her, Godspeed, in memory of the kind associations which once existed between her and the other States.

It has been a conviction of pressing necessity—it has been a belief that we are to be deprived in the Union of the rights which our fathers bequeathed to us—which has brought Mississippi to her present decision. She has heard proclaimed the theory that all men are created free and equal, and this made the basis of an attack upon her social institutions; and the sacred Declaration of Independence has been invoked to maintain the position of the equality of the races. That Declaration is to be construed by the circumstances and purposes for which it was made. The communities were declaring their independence; the people of those communities were asserting that no man was born—to use the language of Mr. Jefferson—booted and spurred, to ride over the rest of mankind; that men were created equal—meaning the men of the political community; that there was no divine right to rule; that no man inherited the right to govern; that there were no classes by which power and place descended to families; but that all stations were equally within the grasp of each member of the body politic. These were the great principles they announced; these were the purposes for which they made their declaration; these were the ends to which their enunciation was directed. They have no reference to the slave; else, how happened it that among the items of arraignment against George III was that he endeavored to do just what the North has been endeavoring of late to do, to stir up insurrection among our slaves? Had the Declaration announced that the negroes were free and equal, how was the prince to be arraigned for raising up insurrection among them? And how was this to be enumerated among the high crimes which caused the colonies to sever their connection with the mother-country? When our Constitution was formed, the same idea was rendered more palpable; for there we find provision made for that very class of persons as property; they were not put upon the equality of footing with white men—not even upon that of paupers and convicts; but, so far as representation was concerned, were discriminated against as a lower caste, only to be represented in the numerical proportion of three-fifths. So stands the compact which binds us together.

Then, Senators, we recur to the principles upon which our Government was founded; and when you deny them, and when you deny us the right to withdraw from a Government which, thus perverted, threatens to be destructive of our rights, we but tread in the path of our fathers when we proclaim our independence and take the hazard. This is done, not in hostility to others, not to injure any section of the country, not even for our own pecuniary benefit, but from the high and solemn motive of defending and protecting the rights we inherited, and which it is our duty to transmit unshorn to our children.

I find in myself perhaps a type of the general feeling of my constituents towards yours. I am sure I feel no hostility toward you, Senators from the North. I am sure there is not one of you, whatever sharp discussion there may have been between us, to whom I cannot now say, in the presence of my God, I wish you well; and such, I feel, is the feeling of the people whom I represent toward those whom you represent. I, therefore, feel that I but express their desire when I say I hope, and they hope, for peaceable relations with you, though we must part. They may be mutually beneficial to us in the future, as they have been in the past, if you so will it. The reverse may bring disaster on every portion of the country, and, if you will have it thus, we will invoke the God of our fathers, who delivered them from the power of the lion, to protect us from the ravages of the bear; and thus, putting our trust in God and in our firm hearts and strong arms, we will vindicate the right as best we may.

In the course of my service here, associated at different times with a variety of Senators, I see now around me some with whom I have served long; there have been points of collision, but, whatever of offense there has been to me, I leave here. I carry with me no hostile remembrance. Whatever offense I have given which has not been redressed, or for which satisfaction has not been demanded, I have, Senators, in this hour of our parting, to offer you my apology for any pain which, in the heat of discussion, I have inflicted. I go hence unencumbered by the remembrance of any injury received, and having discharged the duty of making the only reparation in my power for any injury offered.

Mr. President and Senators, having made the announcement which the occasion seemed to me to require, it only remains for me to bid you a final adieu.

The Cornerstone of the Confederacy Is Slavery

Alexander H. Stephens

Alexander Hamilton Stephens (1812–1883) was vice president of the Confederacy under Jefferson Davis. Earlier, Stephens represented Georgia in the U.S. Senate from 1836 through 1859. Briefly imprisoned after the end of the war, Stephens returned to serve in the House of Representatives in 1873. In 1882 he resigned and was elected governor of Georgia. He died a year later in Atlanta.

In this speech, delivered at the Athenaeum in Savannah, Georgia, in March 1861, Stephens makes the explicit argument that slavery is indeed the "cornerstone" of the Confederacy. After clarifying the more practical political functions of the new government, he declares as an unequivocal "physical, philosophical and moral truth" the inferiority of the Negro race and the necessity of black people's subordination to whites. Any attempts to impose equality violate natural law. In what is perhaps a gesture of tragic hubris, Stephens claims that the threat of war with the North is diminishing; however, he urges the Confederate states to cling to their rights and remain prepared for the possibility of armed conflict.

The new constitution [of the confederacy] has put at rest, *forever,* all the agitating questions relating to our peculiar institution—African slavery as it exists

From Alexander H. Stephens's address "Cornerstone Speech," Savannah, Georgia, March 21, 1861.

amongst us—the proper *status* of the negro in our form of civilization. This was the immediate cause of the late rupture and present revolution. Jefferson in his forecast, had anticipated this, as the "rock upon which the old Union would split." He was right. What was conjecture with him, is now a realized fact. But whether he fully comprehended the great truth upon which that rock *stood* and *stands,* may be doubted. The prevailing ideas entertained by him and most of the leading statesmen at the time of the formation of the old constitution, were that the enslavement of the African was in violation of the laws of nature; that it was wrong in *principle,* socially, morally, and politically. It was an evil they knew not well how to deal with, but the general opinion of the men of that day was that, somehow or other in the order of Providence, the institution would be evanescent and pass away. This idea, though not incorporated in the constitution, was the prevailing idea at that time. The constitution, it is true, secured every essential guarantee to the institution while it should last, and hence no argument can be justly urged against the constitutional guarantees thus secured, because of the common sentiment of the day. Those ideas, however, were fundamentally wrong. They rested upon the assumption of the equality of races. This was an error. It was a sandy foundation, and the government built upon it fell when the "storm came and the wind blew."

Our new government is founded upon exactly the opposite idea; its foundations are laid, its corner-stone rests upon the great truth, that the negro is not equal to the white man; that slavery—subordination to the superior race—is his natural and normal condition. [Applause.] This, our new government, is the first, in the history of the world, based upon this great physical, philosophical, and moral truth. This truth has been slow in the process of its development, like all other truths in the various departments of science. It has been so even amongst us. Many who hear me, perhaps, can recollect well, that this truth was not generally admitted, even within their day. The errors of the past generation still clung to many as late as twenty years ago. Those at the North, who still cling to these errors, with a zeal above knowledge, we justly denominate fanatics. All fanaticism springs from an aberration of the mind—from a defect in reasoning. It is a species of insanity. One of the most striking characteristics of insanity, in many instances, is forming correct conclusions from fancied or erroneous premises; so with the anti-slavery fanatics; their conclusions are right if their premises were. They assume that the negro is equal, and hence conclude that he is entitled to equal privileges and rights with the white man. If their premises were correct, their conclusions would be logical and just—but their premise being wrong, their whole argument fails. I recollect once of having heard a gentleman from one of the northern States, of great power and ability, announce in the House of Representatives, with imposing effect, that we of the South would be compelled, ultimately, to yield upon this subject of slavery, that it was as impossible to war successfully against a principle in politics, as it was in physics or mechanics. That the principle would ultimately prevail. That we, in maintaining slavery as it exists with us, were warring against a principle, a principle founded in nature, the principle of the equality of men. The reply I made to him was, that upon his own grounds, we should, ultimately, succeed, and that he and his associates, in this crusade against our institutions, would ultimately fail. The truth announced, that it was as impossible to war successfully against a principle in politics as it was in physics and mechanics, I admitted; but told him that it was he, and those acting with him, who were warring against a principle. They were attempting to make things equal which the Creator had made unequal.

In the conflict thus far, success has been on our side, complete throughout the length and breadth of the Confederate States. It is upon this, as I have stated, our social fabric is firmly planted; and I cannot permit myself to doubt the ultimate success of a full recognition of this principle throughout the civilized and enlightened world.

As I have stated, the truth of this principle may be slow in development, as all truths are and ever have been, in the various branches of science. It was so with the principles announced by Galileo—it was so with Adam Smith and his principles of political economy. It was so with Harvey, and his theory of the circulation of the blood. It is stated that not a single one of the medical profession, living at the time of the announcement of the truths made by him, admitted them. Now, they are universally acknowledged. May we not, therefore, look with confidence to the ultimate universal acknowledgment of the truths upon which our system rests? It is the first government ever instituted upon the principles in strict conformity to nature, and the ordination of Providence, in furnishing the materials of human society. Many governments have been founded upon the principle of the subordination and serfdom of certain classes of the same race; such were and are in violation of the laws of nature. Our system commits no such violation of nature's laws. With us, all of the white race, however high or low, rich or poor, are equal in the eye of the law. Not so with the negro. Subordination is his place. He, by nature, or by the curse against Canaan, is fitted for that condition which he occupies in our system. The architect, in the construction of buildings, lays the foundation with the proper material—the granite; then comes the brick or the marble. The substratum of our society is made of the material fitted by nature for it, and by experience we know that it is best, not only for the superior, but for the inferior race, that it should be so. It is, indeed, in conformity with the ordinance of the Creator. It is not for us to inquire into the wisdom of his ordinances, or to question them. For his own purposes, he has made one race to differ from another, as he has made "one star to differ from another star in glory."

The great objects of humanity are best attained when there is conformity to his laws and decrees, in the formation of governments as well as in all things else. Our confederacy is founded upon principles in strict conformity with these laws. This stone which was rejected by the first builders "is become the chief of the corner"—the real "corner-stone"—in our new edifice. [Applause.]

The Future of the Confederacy

I have been asked, what of the future? It has been apprehended by some that we would have arrayed against us the civilized world. I care not who or how many they may be against us, when we stand upon the eternal principles of truth, *if we are true to ourselves and the principles for which we contend,* we are obliged to, and must triumph. [Immense applause.]

Thousands of people who begin to understand these truths are not yet completely out of the shell; they do not see them in their length and breadth. We hear much of the civilization and christianization of the barbarous tribes of Africa. In my judgment, those ends will never be attained, but by first teaching them the lesson taught to Adam, that "in the sweat of his brow he should eat his bread," [applause,] and teaching them to work, and feed, and clothe themselves.

But to pass on: Some have propounded the inquiry whether it is practicable for us to go on with the confederacy without further accessions? Have we the means and ability to maintain nationality among the powers of the earth? On this point I would barely say, that as anxiously as we all have been, and are, for the border States, with institutions similar to ours, to join us, still we are abundantly able to maintain our position, even if they should ultimately make up their minds not to cast their destiny with us. That they ultimately will join us—be compelled to do it—is my confident belief; but we can get on very well without them, even if they should not. . . .

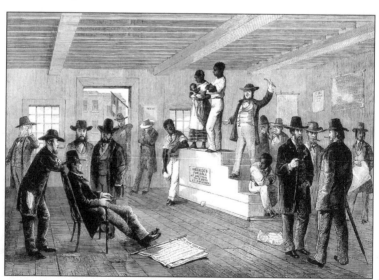

The auctioning of slaves was a common occurrence in the South, whose economy was supported by the institution of slavery.

But to return to the question of the future. What is to be the result of this revolution?

Will every thing, commenced so well, continue as it has begun? In reply to this anxious inquiry, I can only say it all depends upon ourselves. A young man starting out in life on his majority, with health, talent, and ability, under a favoring Providence, may be said to be the architect of his own fortunes. His destinies are in his own hands. He may make for himself a name, of honor or dishonor, according to his own acts. If he plants himself upon truth, integrity, honor and uprightness, with industry, patience and energy, he cannot fail of success. So it is with us. We are a young republic, just entering upon the arena of nations; we will be the architects of our own fortunes. Our destiny, under Providence, is in our own hands. With wisdom, prudence, and statesmanship on the part of our public men, and intelligence, virtue and patriotism on the part of the people, success, to the full measures of our most sanguine hopes, may be looked for. But if unwise counsels prevail—if we become divided—if schisms arise—if dissensions spring up—if factions are engendered—if party spirit, nourished by unholy personal ambition shall rear its hydra head, I have no good to prophesy for you. Without intelligence, virtue, integrity, and patriotism on the part of the people, no republic or representative government can be durable or stable.

We have intelligence, and virtue, and patriotism. All that is required is to cultivate and perpetuate these. Intelligence will not do without virtue. France was a nation of philosophers. These philosophers become Jacobins. They lacked that virtue, that devotion to moral principle, and that patriotism which is essential to good government. Organized upon principles of perfect justice and right-seeking amity and friendship with all other powers—I see no obstacle in the way of our upward and onward progress. Our growth, by accessions from other States, will depend greatly upon whether we present to the world, as I trust we shall, a better government than that to which neighboring States belong. If we do this, North Carolina, Tennessee, and Arkansas cannot hesitate long; neither can Virginia, Kentucky, and Missouri. They will necessarily gravitate to us by an imperious law. We made ample provision in our constitution for the admission of other States; it is more guarded, and wisely so, I think, than the old constitution on the same subject, but not too guarded to receive them as fast as it may be proper. Looking to the distant future, and, perhaps, not very far distant either, it is not beyond the range of possibility, and even probability, that all the great States of the north-west will gravitate this way, as well as Tennessee, Kentucky, Missouri, Arkansas, etc. Should they do so, our doors are wide enough to receive them, but not until they are ready to assimilate with us in principle.

The process of disintegration in the old Union may be expected to go on with almost absolute certainty if we pursue the right course. We are now the nucleus of a growing power which, if we are true to ourselves, our destiny, and high mission, will become the controlling power on this continent. To what extent accessions will go on in the process of time, or where it will end, the future will determine. So far as it concerns States of the old Union, this process will be upon no such principles of *reconstruction* as now spoken of, but upon *reorganization* and new assimilation. [Loud applause.] Such are some of the glimpses of the future as I catch them.

But at first we must necessarily meet with the inconveniences and difficulties and embarrassments incident to all changes of government. These will be felt in our postal affairs and changes in the channel of trade. These inconveniences, it is to be hoped, will be but temporary, and must be borne with patience and forbearance.

As to whether we shall have war with our late confederates, or whether all matters of differences between us shall be amicably settled, I can only say that the prospect for a peaceful adjustment is better, so far as I am informed, than it has been.

The prospect of war is, at least, not so threatening as it has been. The idea of coercion, shadowed forth in President Lincoln's inaugural, seems not to be followed up thus far so vigorously as was expected. Fort Sumter, it is believed, will soon be evacuated. What course will be pursued toward Fort Pickens, and the other forts on the gulf, is not so well understood. It is to be greatly desired that all of them should be surrendered. Our object is *peace*, not only with the North, but with the world. All matters relating to the public property, public liabilities of the Union when we were members of it, we are ready and willing to adjust and settle upon the principles of right, equity, and good faith. War can be of no more benefit to the North than to us. Whether the intention of evacuating Fort Sumter is to be received as an evidence of a desire for a peaceful solution of our difficulties with the United States, or the result of necessity, I will not undertake to say. I would fain hope the former. Rumors are afloat, however, that it is the result of necessity. All I can say to you, therefore, on that point is, keep your armor bright and your powder dry. [Enthusiastic cheering.]

The surest way to secure peace, is to show your ability to maintain your rights. The principles and position of the present administration of the United States—the republican party—present some puzzling questions. While it is a fixed principle with them never to allow the increase of a foot of slave territory, they seem to be equally determined not to part with an inch "of the accursed soil." Notwithstanding their clamor against the institution, they seemed to be equally opposed to getting more, or letting go what they have got. They were ready to fight on the accession of Texas, and are equally ready to fight now on her secession. Why is this? How can this strange paradox be accounted for? There seems to be but one rational solution—and that is, notwithstanding their professions of humanity, they are disinclined to give up the benefits they derive from slave labor. Their philanthropy yields to their interest. The idea of enforcing the laws, has but one object, and that is a collection of the taxes, raised by slave labor to swell the fund, necessary to meet their heavy appropriations. The spoils is what they are after—though they come from the labor of the slave. [Continued applause.] . . .

If, [said he,] we are true to ourselves, true to our cause, true to our destiny, true to our high mission, in presenting to the world the highest type of civilization ever exhibited by man—there will be found in our lexicon no such word as fail.

"The Mighty Scourge of War"

Abraham Lincoln

Lincoln delivered his Second Inaugural Address on March 4, 1865, with the end of war and Union victory in sight. Lincoln strikes a markedly providential note, characterizing the war as a playing out of God's divine plan. While positing that slavery is an evil that seemingly cried out for God's vengeance, Lincoln also makes several conciliatory gestures toward the rebel states, granting their belief in the righteousness of their cause and expressing "malice toward none" and "charity toward all." He was plainly looking ahead to reconstruction and reconciliation, which, tragically, he would not oversee due to his assassination by John Wilkes Booth just over a month later.

Fellow-Countrymen:

At this second appearing to take the oath of the Presidential office there is less occasion for an extended address than there was at the first. Then a statement somewhat in detail of a course to be pursued seemed fitting and proper. Now, at the expiration of four years, during which public declarations have been constantly called forth on every point and phase of the great contest which still absorbs the attention and engrosses the energies of the nation, little that is new could be presented. The progress of our arms, upon which all else chiefly depends, is as well known to the public as to myself, and it is, I trust, reasonably satisfactory and encouraging to all. With high hope for the future, no

From Abraham Lincoln's speech "Second Inaugural Address," Washington, D.C., March 4, 1865.

prediction in regard to it is ventured.

On the occasion corresponding to this four years ago all thoughts were anxiously directed to an impending civil war. All dreaded it, all sought to avert it. While the inaugural address was being delivered from this place, devoted altogether to saving the Union without war, urgent agents were in the city seeking to destroy it without war—seeking to dissolve the Union and divide effects by negotiation. Both parties deprecated war, but one of them would make war rather than let the nation survive, and the other would accept war rather than let it perish, and the war came.

One-eighth of the whole population were colored slaves, not distributed generally over the Union, but localized in the southern part of it. These slaves constituted a peculiar and powerful interest. All knew that this interest was somehow the cause of the war. To strengthen, perpetuate, and extend this interest was the object for which the insurgents would rend the Union even by war, while the Government claimed no right to do more than to restrict the territorial enlargement of it. Neither party expected for the war the magnitude or the duration which it has already attained. Neither anticipated that the cause of the conflict might cease with or even before the conflict itself should cease. Each looked for an easier triumph, and a result less fundamental and astounding. Both read the same Bible and pray to the same God, and each invokes His aid against the other. It may seem strange that any men should dare to ask a just God's assistance in wringing their bread from the sweat of other men's faces, but let us judge not, that we be not judged. The prayers of both could not be answered. That of neither has been answered fully. The Almighty has His own purposes. "Woe unto the world because of offenses; for it must needs be that offenses come, but woe to that man by whom the offense cometh." If we shall suppose that American slavery is one of those offenses which, in the providence of God, must needs come, but which, having continued through His appointed time, He now wills to remove, and that He gives to both North and South this terrible war as the woe due to those by whom the offense came, shall we discern therein any departure from those divine attributes which the believers in a living God always ascribe to

Him? Fondly do we hope, fervently do we pray, that this mighty scourge of war may speedily pass away. Yet, if God wills that it continue until all the wealth piled by the bondsman's two hundred and fifty years of unrequited toil shall be sunk, and until every drop of blood drawn with the lash shall be paid by another drawn with the sword, as was said three thousand years ago, so still it must be said "the judgments of the Lord are true and righteous altogether."

With malice toward none, with charity for all, with firmness in the right as God gives us to see the right, let us strive on to finish the work we are in, to bind up the nation's wounds, to care for him who shall have borne the battle and for his widow and his orphan, to do all which may achieve and cherish a just and lasting peace among ourselves and with all nations.

Emancipation
and
Reconstruction

Celebrating Liberty

William Lloyd Garrison

William Lloyd Garrison (1805–1879) was among the most eminent and outspoken figures in the abolitionist movement. As editor of the early abolitionist newspaper the *Genius of Universal Emancipation* (1829–1830), Garrison was found guilty by a Baltimore court of libeling a slave-ship owner, and unable to pay the fine, served a brief time in jail. Undaunted, Garrison launched another abolitionist newspaper, the *Liberator*, which he both published and edited. The *Liberator*, published from 1831 to 1865, was a major organ for the passionate denunciation of slavery and calls for immediate emancipation. Pro-slavery factions reviled the paper, while freed blacks in New England embraced it and Garrison. Garrison was also a founding member of the New England Anti-Slavery Society and the subsequent abolitionist organization the Friends of Universal Reform. He was friend and inspiration to such fellow soldiers in the antislavery movement as Frederick Douglass and Wendell Phillips.

In the following speech delivered in Charleston, South Carolina, five days after Robert E. Lee's surrender, Garrison reflects upon his early travails as an abolitionist, including his imprisonment in Baltimore as well as his recent triumphs. He praises President Lincoln in almost epic terms and celebrates the legislative introduction of the Thirteenth Amendment outlawing slavery. Finally, Garrison, a lightning rod for the most ardent passions of both pro- and antislavery forces for most of his adult life, strikes a patriotic note, declaring "universal emancipation" the very core of union.

From William Lloyd Garrison's speech "The Governing Passion of My Soul," Charleston, South Carolina, April 14, 1865.

My friends:

I am so unused to speaking in this place that I rise with feelings natural to a first appearance. You would scarce expect one of my age—and antecedents—to speak in public on this stage, or anywhere else in the city of Charleston, South Carolina. And yet, why should I not speak here? Why should I not speak anywhere in my native land? Why should I not have spoken here twenty years ago, or forty, as freely as any one? What crime had I committed against the laws of my country? I have loved liberty for myself, for all who are dear to me, for all who dwell on American soil, for all mankind. The head and front of my offending hath this extent, no more. Thirty years ago I put this sentiment into rhyme:—

"I am an Abolitionist;
I glory in the name;
Though now by Slavery's minions hissed,
And covered o'er with shame.
It is a spell of light and power,
The watchword of the free;
Who spurns it in the trial hour,
A craven soul is he."

I said that in the city of Boston in 1835, and I was drawn through the streets of that city by violent hands, and committed to jail in order to preserve my life. In 1865, I say it, not only with impunity, but with the approbation of all loyal hearts in the city of Charleston. Yes, we are living in altered times. To me it is something like the transition from death to life—from the cerements of the grave to the robes of heaven. In 1829 I first hoisted in the city of Baltimore the flag of immediate, unconditional, uncompensated emancipation; and they threw me into their prison for preaching such gospel truth. My reward is, that in 1865 Maryland has adopted Garrisonian Abolitionism, and accepted a constitution indorsing every principle and idea that I have advocated in behalf of the oppressed slave.

The first time I saw that noble man, Abraham Lincoln, President of the United States, at Washington,—and of one thing I feel sure, either he has become a Garrisonian Abolitionist, or I a Lincoln Emancipationist, for I know that we blend together, like kindred drops, into one, and his brave heart beats freedom everywhere,—I then said to him: "Mr. President, it is thirty-four years since I visited Baltimore; and when I went there recently to see if I could find the old Prison, and, get into my old cell again, I found that all was gone." The President answered promptly and wittily, as he is wont to make his responses: "Well, Mr. Garrison, the difference between 1830 and 1864 appears to be this, that in 1830 you could not get out, and in 1864 you could not get in." This symbolizes the revolution which has been brought about in Maryland. For if I had spoken till I was as hoarse as I am tonight against slaveholders in Baltimore, there

William Lloyd Garrison

would have been no indictment brought against me, and no prison opened to receive me.

But a broader, sublimer basis than that, the United States has at last rendered its verdict. The people, on the eighth of November last, recorded their purpose that slavery in our country should be forever abolished; and the Congress of the United States at its last session adopted, and nearly the requisite states have already voted in favor of, an amendment to the Constitution of the country, making it forever unlawful for any man to hold property in man. I thank God in view of these great changes.

Abolitionism, what is it? Liberty. What is liberty? Abolitionism. What are they both? Politically, one is the Declaration of Independence; religiously, the other is the Golden Rule of our Savior. I am here in Charleston, South Carolina. She is smitten to the dust. She has been brought down from her pride of place. The chalice was put to her lips, and she has drunk it to the dregs. I have never been her enemy, nor the enemy of the South, and in the desire to save her from this great retribution demanded in the name of the living God that every fetter should be broken, and the oppressed set free.

I have not come here with reference to any flag but that of freedom. If your Union does not symbolize universal emancipation, it brings no Union for me. If your Constitution does not guarantee freedom for all, it is not a Constitution I can ascribe to. If your flag is stained by the blood of a brother held in bondage, I repudiate it in the name of God. I came here to witness the unfurling of a flag under which every human being is to be recognized as entitled to his freedom. Therefore, with a clear conscience, without any compromise of principles, I accepted the invitation of the Government of the United States to be present and witness the ceremonies that have taken place today.

And now let me give the sentiment which has been, and ever will be, the governing passion of my soul:

"Liberty for each, for all, and forever!"

What the Black Man Wants

Frederick Douglass

In a speech delivered within days of the war's end and
Lincoln's subsequent assassination, Frederick Douglass
addresses the Massachusetts Antislavery Society on the
matter of equality before the law. Douglass recognizes
that emancipation is a hollow victory for the black man
unless accompanied by the full rights of citizenship, most
specifically suffrage. Nor does he expect black franchise
to come about as the inevitable offshoot of emancipation,
saying that "now is the time to press this right." Rather
presciently Douglass foresees the endurance of Southern
animosity toward freed slaves and the federal government, and he reminds Northern whites that their chief al-
lies in the South will be blacks. Employing touches of hu-
mor, he dismisses as a fallacy the claim that blacks are
too ignorant to vote. But in closing, when he invokes
honor and patriotism as moral mandates for black suffrage, Douglass is at his rhetorical loftiest.

I came here, as I come always to the meetings in New England, as a listener, and not as a speaker; and one of the
reasons why I have not been more frequently to the
meetings of this society, has been because of the disposition
on the part of some of my friends to call me out upon the
platform, even when they knew that there was some difference of opinion and of feeling between those who rightfully
belong to this platform and myself; and for fear of being

From Frederick Douglass's speech "The Equality of All Men Before the Law," to
the annual meeting of the Massachusetts Antislavery Society, Boston, Massachusetts, April 1865.

misconstrued, as desiring to interrupt or disturb the proceedings of these meetings, I have usually kept away, and have thus been deprived of that educating influence, which I am always free to confess is of the highest order, descending from this platform. I have felt, since I have lived out West [Douglass means west of Boston, in Rochester, NY], that in going there I parted from a great deal that was valuable; and I feel, every time I come to these meetings, that I have lost a great deal by making my home west of Boston, west of Massachusetts; for, if anywhere in the country there is to be found the highest sense of justice, or the truest demands for my race, I look for it in the East, I look for it here. The ablest discussions of the whole question of our rights occur here, and to be deprived of the privilege of listening to those discussions is a great deprivation.

I do not know, from what has been said, that there is any difference of opinion as to the duty of abolitionists, at the present moment. How can we get up any difference at this point, or any point, where we are so united, so agreed? I went especially, however, with that word of Mr. [Wendell] Phillips, which is the criticism of Gen. [Nathaniel P.] Banks and Gen. Banks' policy. I hold that that policy is our chief danger at the present moment; that it practically enslaves the Negro, and makes the Proclamation [the Emancipation Proclamation] of 1863 a mockery and delusion. What is freedom? It is the right to choose one's own employment. Certainly it means that, if it means anything; and when any individual or combination of individuals undertakes to decide for any man when he shall work, where he shall work, at what he shall work, and for what he shall work, he or they practically reduce him to slavery. [Applause.] He is a slave. That I understand Gen. Banks to do—to determine for the so-called freedman, when, and where, and at what, and for how much he shall work, when he shall be punished, and by whom punished. It is absolute slavery. It defeats the beneficent intention of the Government, if it has beneficent intentions, in regards to the freedom of our people.

I have had but one idea for the last three years to present to the American people, and the phraseology in which I clothe it is the old abolition phraseology. I am for the "immediate, unconditional, and universal" enfranchisement of the black man, in every State in the Union. [Loud applause.] Without this, his liberty is a mockery; without this, you might as well almost retain the old name of slavery for his condition; for in fact, if he is not the slave of the individual master, he is the slave of society, and holds his liberty as a privilege, not as a right. He is at the mercy of the mob, and has no means of protecting himself.

It may be objected, however, that this pressing of the Negro's right to suffrage is premature. Let us have slavery abolished, it may be said, let us have labor organized, and then, in the natural course of events, the right of suffrage will be extended to the Negro. I do not agree with this. The constitution of the human mind is such, that if it once disregards the conviction forced upon it by a revelation of truth, it requires the exercise of a higher power to produce the same conviction afterwards. The American people are now in tears. The Shenandoah has run blood—the best blood of the North. All around Richmond, the blood of New England and of the North has been shed—of your sons, your brothers and your fathers. We all feel, in the existence of this Rebellion, that judgments terrible, wide-spread, far-reaching, overwhelming, are abroad in the land; and we feel, in view of these judgments, just now, a disposition to learn righteousness. This is the hour. Our streets are in mourning, tears are falling at every fireside, and under the chastisement of this Rebellion we have almost come up to the point of conceding this great, this all-important right of suffrage. I fear that if we fail to do it now, if abolitionists fail to press it now, we may not see, for centuries to come, the same disposition that exists at this moment. [Applause.] Hence, I say, now is the time to press this right.

Why the Black Man Needs Suffrage

It may be asked, "Why do you want it? Some men have got along very well without it. Women have not this right." Shall we justify one wrong by another? This is the sufficient answer. Shall we at this moment justify the deprivation of the Negro of the right to vote, because some one else is deprived of that privilege? I hold that women, as well as men, have the right to vote [applause], and my heart and voice go with the movement to extend suffrage to woman; but that question rests upon another basis than which our right rests. We may be asked, I say, why we want it. I will tell you why we want it. We want it because it is our right, first of all. No class of men can, without insulting their own nature, be content with any deprivation of their rights. We want it again, as a means for educating our race. Men are so constituted that they derive their conviction of their own possibilities largely by the estimate formed of them by others. If nothing is expected of a people, that people will find it difficult to contradict that expectation. By depriving us of suffrage, you affirm our incapacity to form an intelligent judgment respecting public men and public measures; you declare before the world that we are unfit to exercise the elective franchise, and by this means lead us to undervalue ourselves, to put a low estimate upon ourselves, and to feel that we have no possibilities like other men. Again, I want the elective franchise, for one, as a colored man, because ours is a peculiar government, based upon a peculiar idea, and that idea is universal suffrage. If I were in a monarchial government, or an autocratic or aristocratic government, where the few bore rule and the many were subject, there would be no special stigma resting upon me, because I did not exercise the elective franchise. It would do me no great violence. Mingling with the mass I should partake of the strength of the mass; I should be supported by the mass, and I should have the same incentives to endeavor with the mass of my fellow-men; it would be no particular burden, no particular deprivation; but here where universal suffrage is the rule, where that is the fundamental idea of the Government, to rule us out is to make us an exception, to brand us with the stigma of inferiority, and to invite to our heads the missiles of those about us; therefore, I want the franchise for the black man.

There are, however, other reasons, not derived from any consideration merely of our rights, but arising out of the conditions of the South, and of the country—considerations which have already been referred to by Mr. Phillips—considerations which must arrest the attention of statesmen. I believe that when the tall heads of this Rebellion shall have been swept down, as they will be swept down, when the Davises and Toombses and Stephenses, and others who are leading this Rebellion shall have been blotted out, there will be this rank undergrowth of treason, to which reference has been made,

Frederick Douglass

growing up there, and interfering with, and thwarting the quiet operation of the Federal Government in those states. You will see those traitors, handing down, from sire to son, the same malignant spirit which they have manifested and which they are now exhibiting, with malicious hearts, broad blades, and bloody hands in the field, against our sons and brothers. That spirit will still remain; and whoever sees the Federal Government extended over those Southern States will see that Government in a strange

land, and not only in a strange land, but in an enemy's land. A post-master of the United States in the South will find himself surrounded by a hostile spirit; a collector in a Southern port will find himself surrounded by a hostile spirit; a United States marshal or United States judge will be surrounded there by a hostile element. That enmity will not die out in a year, will not die out in an age. The Federal Government will be looked upon in those States precisely as the Governments of Austria and France are looked upon in Italy at the present moment. They will endeavor to circumvent, they will endeavor to destroy, the peaceful operation of this Government. Now, where will you find the strength to counterbalance this spirit, if you do not find it in the Negroes of the South? They are your friends, and have always been your friends. They were your friends even when the Government did not regard them as such. They comprehended the genius of this war before you did. It is a significant fact, it is a marvellous fact, it seems almost to imply a direct interposition of Providence, that this war, which began in the interest of slavery on both sides, bids fair to end in the interest of liberty on both sides. [Applause.] It was begun, I say, in the interest of slavery on both sides. The South was fighting to take slavery out of the Union, and the North was fighting to keep it in the Union; the South fighting to get it beyond the limits of the United States Constitution, and the North fighting to retain it within those limits; the South fighting for new guarantees, and the North fighting for the old guarantees;—both despising the Negro, both insulting the Negro. Yet, the Negro, apparently endowed with wisdom from on high, saw more clearly the end from the beginning than we did. When [Secretary of State William H.] Seward said the status of no man in the country would be changed by the war, the Negro did not believe him. [Applause.] When our generals sent their underlings in shoulder-straps to hunt the flying Negro back from our lines into the jaws of slavery, from which he had escaped, the Negroes thought that a mistake had been made, and that the intentions of the Government had not been rightly understood by our officers in shoulder-straps, and they continued to come into our lines, threading their way through bogs and fens, over briers and thorns, fording streams, swimming rivers, bringing us tidings as to the safe path to march, and pointing out the dangers that threatened us. They are our only friends in the South, and we should be true to them in this their trial hour, and see to it that they have the elective franchise.

I know that we are inferior to you in some things—virtually inferior. We walk about you like dwarfs among giants. Our heads are scarcely seen above the great sea of humanity. The Germans are superior to us; the Irish are superior to us; the Yankees are superior to us [Laughter]; they can do what we cannot, that is, what we have not hitherto been allowed to do. But while I make this admission, I utterly deny, that we are originally, or naturally, or practically, or in any way, or in any important sense, inferior to anybody on this globe. [Loud applause.] This charge of inferiority is an old dodge. It has been made available for oppression on many occasions. It is only about six centuries since the blue-eyed and fair-haired Anglo-Saxons were considered inferior by the haughty Normans, who once trampled upon them. If you read the history of the Norman Conquest, you will find that this proud Anglo-Saxon was once looked upon as of coarser clay than his Norman master, and might be found in the highways and byways of Old England laboring with a brass collar on his neck, and the name of his master marked upon it. You were down then! [Laughter and applause.] You are up now. I am glad you are up, and I want you to be glad to help us up also. [Applause.]

The story of our inferiority is an old dodge, as I have said; for wherever men oppress their fellows, wherever they enslave them, they will endeavor to find the needed apology for such enslavement and oppression in the character of the people oppressed and enslaved. When we wanted, a few years ago, a slice of Mexico, it was hinted that the Mexicans were an inferior race, that the old Castilian blood had become so weak that it would scarcely run down hill, and that Mexico needed the long, strong and beneficent arm of the Anglo-Saxon care extended over it. We said that it was necessary to its salvation, and a part of the "manifest destiny" of this Republic, to extend our arm over that dilapidated government. So, too, when Russia wanted to take possession of a part of the Ottoman Empire, the Turks were an "inferior race." So, too, when England wants to set the heel of her power more firmly in the quivering heart of old Ireland, the Celts are an "inferior race." So, too, the Negro, when he is to be robbed of any right which is justly his, is an "inferior man." It is said that we are ignorant; I admit it. But if we know enough to be hung, we know enough to vote. If the Negro knows enough to pay taxes to support the government, he knows enough to vote; taxation and representation should go together. If he knows enough to shoulder a musket and fight for the flag, fight for the government, he knows enough to vote. If he knows as much when he is sober as an Irishman knows when drunk, he knows enough to vote, on good American principles. [Laughter and applause.]

A Sense of Honor

But I was saying that you needed a counterpoise in the persons of the slaves to the enmity that would exist at the South after the Rebellion is put down. I hold that the American people are bound, not only in self-defence, to extend this right to the freedmen of the South, but they are bound by their love of country, and by all their regard for the future safety of those Southern States, to do this—to do it as a measure essential to the preservation of peace there. But I will not dwell upon this. I put it to the American sense of honor. The honor of a nation is an important thing. It is said in the Scriptures, "What doth it profit a man if he gain the whole world, and lose his own soul?" It may be said, also, What doth it profit a nation if it gain the whole world, but lose its honor? I hold that the American government has taken upon itself a solemn obligation of honor, to see that this war—let it be long or short, let it cost much or let it cost little—that this war shall not cease until every freedman at the South has the right to vote. [Applause.] It has bound itself to it. What have you asked the black men of the South, the black men of the whole country to do? Why, you have asked them to incur the enmity of their masters, in order to befriend you and to befriend this Government. You have asked us to call down, not only upon ourselves, but upon our children's children, the deadly hate of the entire Southern people. You have called upon us to turn our backs upon our masters, to abandon their cause and espouse yours; to turn against the South and in favor of the North; to shoot down the Confederacy and uphold the flag—the American flag. You have called upon us to expose ourselves to all the subtle machinations of their malignity for all time. And now, what do you propose to do when you come to make peace? To reward your enemies, and trample in the dust your friends? Do you intend to sacrifice the very men who have come to the rescue of your banner in the South, and incurred the lasting displeasure of their masters thereby? Do you intend to sacrifice them and reward your enemies? Do you mean to give your enemies the right to vote, and take it away from your friends? Is that wise policy? Is that honorable? Could American honor withstand such a blow? I do not believe you will do it. I think you will see to it that we have the right to vote. There is something too mean in looking upon the Negro, when you are in trouble, as a citizen, and when you are free from trouble, as an alien. When this nation was in trouble, in its early struggles, it looked upon the Negro as a citizen. In 1776 he was a citizen. At the time of the formation of the Constitution the Negro had the right to vote in eleven States out of the old thirteen. In your trouble you have made us citizens. In 1812 Gen. [Andrew] Jackson addressed us as citizens—"fellow-citizens." He wanted us to fight. We were citizens then! And now, when you come to frame a conscription bill, the Negro is a citizen again. He has been a citizen just three times in the history of this government, and it has always been in time of trouble. In time of trouble we are citizens. Shall we be citizens in war, and aliens in peace? Would that be just?

I ask my friends who are apologizing for not insisting upon this right, where can the black man look, in this country, for the assertion of his right, if he may not look to the Massachusetts Anti-Slavery Society? Where under the whole heavens can he look for sympathy, in asserting this right, if he may not look to this platform? Have you lifted us up to a certain height to see that we are men, and then are any disposed to leave us there, without seeing that we are put in possession of all our rights? We look naturally to this platform for the assertion of all our rights, and for this one especially. I understand the anti-slavery societies of this country to be based on two principles,—first, the freedom of the blacks of this country; and, second, the elevation of them. Let me not be misunderstood here. I am not asking for sympathy at the hands of abolitionists, sympathy at the hands of any. I think the American people are disposed often to be generous rather than just. I look over this country at the present time, and I see Educational Societies, Sanitary Commissions, Freedmen's Associations, and the like,—all very good: but in regard to the colored people there is always more that is benevolent, I perceive, than just, manifested towards us. What I ask for the Negro is not benevolence, not pity, not sympathy, but simply justice. [Applause.] The American people have always been anxious to know what they shall do with us. Gen. Banks was distressed with solicitude as to what he should do with the Negro. Everybody has asked the question, and they learned to ask it early of the abolitionists, "What shall we do with the Negro?" I have had but one answer from the beginning. Do nothing with us! Your doing with us has already played the mischief with us. Do nothing with us! If the apples will not remain on the tree of their own strength, if they are wormeaten at the core, if they are early ripe and disposed to fall, let them fall! I am not for tying or fastening them on the tree in any way, except by nature's plan, and if they will not stay there, let them fall. And if the Negro cannot stand on his own legs, let him fall also. All I ask is, give him a chance to stand on his own legs! Let him alone! If you see him on his way to school, let him alone, don't disturb him! If you see him going to the dinner table at a hotel, let him go! If you see him going to the ballot-box, let him alone, don't disturb him! [Applause.] If you see him going into a work-shop, just let him alone,—your interference is doing him a positive injury. Gen. Banks' "preparation" is of a piece with this attempt to prop up the Negro. Let him fall if he cannot stand alone! If the Negro cannot live by the line of eternal justice, so beautifully pictured to you in the illustration used by Mr. Phillips, the fault will not be yours, it will be his who made the Negro, and established that line for his government. [Applause.] Let him live or die by that. If you will only untie his hands, and give him a chance, I think he will live. He will work as readily for himself as the white man. A great many delusions have been swept away by this war. One was, that the Negro would not work; he has proved his ability to work. Another was, that the Negro would not fight; that he possessed only the most sheepish attributes of humanity; was a perfect lamb, or an "Uncle Tom;" disposed to take off his coat whenever required, fold his hands, and be whipped by anybody who wanted to whip him. But the war has proved that there is a great deal of human nature in the Negro, and that "he will fight," as Mr. Quincy, our President, said, in earlier days than these, "when there is reasonable probability of his whipping anybody." [Laughter and applause.]

Black Americans Should Have Voting Rights

J. Mercer Langston

Educator, lawyer, and political figure, John Mercer
Langston (1829–1897) was the first African American
elected to public office. He was highly influential in shap-
ing the Republican Party's position on the abolition of
slavery. Born free and orphaned at an early age, Langston
grew up to earn both a bachelor's and master's degrees
from Oberlin College. He began to speak publicly for the
abolitionist cause and organizing black political clubs
across the United States. During the Civil War he led the
western recruitment of black soldiers. After the war he
fought for the rights of black Americans both as a law pro-
fessor at Howard University and elected congressman from
Virginia. Twice his name was raised as a possible candidate
for the Republican nomination for vice president.

In his address "on behalf of the colored people of
Missouri," delivered in January 1866, Langston calls for
voting rights for freed slaves, careful to distinguish the
matter of suffrage from the more volatile question of
"social equality." He reminds the Missouri Representatives, to whom he is speaking, of blacks' loyalty to the
Union and heroic service in the colored troops during the
war. Blacks have thus earned the full citizenship that the
right to vote entails.

From J. Mercer Langston's speech "Equality Before the Law," to the Hall of Representatives, Columbia, Missouri, January 9, 1866.

To every true, honest, and liberty-loving citizen of Missouri do the colored men of your redeemed Commonwealth appeal for sympathy and aid in securing those political rights and privileges which belong to us as free men.

Out of the fierce conflict which has just closed between an advanced civilization and a relic of barbarism, we at length have been released from chains, lashes, bloodhounds, and slave-marts; and to us has a "freedom at large" been ordained. For this, in behalf of our long-oppressed race, do we thank God, and now ask that this liberty shall be secured and consecrated by those guarantees and privileges which are enjoyed by every other American citizen, and which can only be found in the exercise of the right of suffrage.

Deprived of this, we are forced to pay taxes without representation; to submit, without appeal, to laws however offensive, without a single voice in framing them; to bear arms without the right to say whether against friend or foe—against loyalty or disloyalty. Without suffrage we are forced in strict subjection to a Government whose councils are to us foreign, and are called by our own countrymen to witness a violence upon the primary principle of a republican government as gross and outrageous as that which justly stirred patriot Americans to throw overboard the tea from English bottoms in a Boston harbor, and to wage the war for independence.

Let a consistent support be given to this principle of government, founded only "on the consent of the governed"—to this keystone in the arch of American liberty—and our full rights as freemen are secured.

Our demands are not excessive.

We ask not for social equality with the white man, as is often claimed by the shallow demagogue; for a law higher than human must forever govern social relations.

We ask only that privilege which is now given to the very poorest and meanest of white men who come to the ballot-box.

We demand this as those who are native-born citizens of this State, and have never known other allegiance than to its authority and to these United States.

We demand this in the names of those whose bitter toil has enriched our State and brought wealth to its homes.

We demand this as those who have ever cheerfully sustained law and order, and who have, within our means, zealously promoted education and morality.

We demand this as those who have been true and loyal to our Government from its foundation to the present, and who have never deserted its interests while even in the midst of treason and under subjection to its most violent enemies.

We demand this in the honored name of the nine thousand colored troops who, with the first opportunity, enlisted under the banner of Missouri and bared their breasts to the remorseless storm of treason, and by hundreds went down to death in the conflict; while the franchised rebel, the cowardly conservative—the now bitterest enemies of our right to suffrage—remained in quiet at home, safe, and fattened on the fruits of our sacrifice, toil, and blood.

In the names of the heroic dead who, from Missouri's colored troops, were left on the battle-field of Oxford—in the campaign against Mobile—in the battle at Blakely—at the fierce engagement on the Rio Grande—and who along every line of skirmish were like brutes shot down by savage rebels—do We appeal for the simple privilege of expressing by ballot our choice of rulers for this Government which our brothers so gallantly served; and ask that hereafter we may aid loyalty in suppressing any future attempts at its overthrow.

We make this demand as one of right, if not of expediency, and are unwilling to believe that a powerful, rating people, strengthened by new victories with the aid of our hands, could be less magnanimous in purpose and in action, less consistent with the true theory of a sound democracy, than to concede to us our claims. We believe that with expediency even our demands are not at war, but that with right does public policy strike hands and invite our votes, as it did our muskets, to the maintenance of authority over the disorganizing elements which attend a returning peace.

We have too much faith in the permanency of this Government to believe that the extension of the elective franchise to a few loyal black men could unsettle its foundations or violate a single declaration of its rights.

If our demands were not clothed with justice, we, whose very flesh still wears the scars of slavery, could hardly claim for ourselves that privilege which, enjoyed in the past by our late masters, enabled them to make cringing subjects of us all.

But we are no longer cowed beneath the name of chattels and of brutes, but we own ourselves, our families, and our homes; and as men demand that this freedom shall bear the spirit as well as the form—that we shall not be mocked with palsied hands and made helpless in our own defense—that the skeleton of liberty may be clothed with flesh and blood in order that we ourselves may resist the tyranny of the "unfriendly legislation" of our late masters and their sympathizers, who for four years past have been fighting to enslave our bodies and souls.

Among those who just now manifest so much solicitude and sympathy in our behalf, and who are so anxious to do for us our voting, to perform all our legislation, and to accept all our political responsibilities, do we chiefly discover the very men whose votes once made us slaves and chattels, and robbed the chastity of our homes, when we had no friend to counsel or law to protect us from their vandal hands and black hell-born codes.

If we are to be nursed and strengthened into manhood solely at the hands of others, we ask, in the name of God, that it be done by our friends and not by our enemies.

The Full Rights of Citizenship

But we seek not to impose our tutelage or our cares upon others; we ask the privilege of being no longer a burden on the body politic, and that no longer we be made the subject of endless discussion and legislation, but are willing to carry these responsibilities ourselves in common with every other citizen.

With President Johnson do we claim that "loyal men, whether white or black, shall control our destinies." We ask that the "two streams of loyal blood which it took to conquer one, mad with treason," shall not be separated at the ballot-box—that he who can be trusted with an army musket, which makes victory and protects the Nation, shall also be intrusted with the right to express a preference for his rulers and his laws.

We are told that we are weak; hence we ask for those rights which make free men strong, and are ever deemed essential to the white man's confidence and courage.

We are told that we are ignorant; hence we ask for those lessons of experience in governing ourselves which, also, are ever deemed essential to the white man's advancement.

We are told that we are poor; hence we ask that by our own votes we may encourage our own industry, may make corporations for our capital, may charter our enterprises and give laws to our commerce, and, with the white man, be permitted to illustrate the axiomatic truth "that no man is so reliable as he who is intrusted with the welfare of his country," and is ever "more responsible when he goes to the ballot-box," as declared by Andrew Johnson.

We ask for a citizenship based upon a principle so broad and solid that upon it black men, white men, and every American born can equally, safely, and eternally stand.

We ask that the organic law of our State shall give to suffrage irrevocable guarantees that shall know of no distinction at the polls on account of color.

If these guarantees are still to be denied, and hereafter color is to mark the line which shall be drawn about the ballot-box, we ask for statutes that shall clearly define the

The fight for black suffrage continued after the end of the war.

castes and shades of complexion which shall be permitted within or expelled from its royal precincts.

If wealth is to guard the portals of a free suffrage, we ask that our acquirements be respected and admitted to equal representation.

If intelligence shall prescribe the limit, we ask for an impartial discrimination which shall affect white as well as black; and submit that the entire ignorance and stupidity of the people should not by any presumption be wholly charged to the account of ourselves.

To such a universal test of intelligence we are willing to submit our claims to suffrage, and believe that it would promote a most healthy spirit of emulation and prove the greatest educator of the masses.

Our asserted ignorance is not a condition from choice or disposition, as is now everywhere made evident in the zealous efforts of our people to educate themselves and their children, but arises from the black-code legislation of our illiterate, franchised masters.

We ask that colored loyalty, industry, and intelligence shall receive as full rights, guarantees, and privileges as those accorded to white treason, arrogance, and indolence.

That tendency towards an enlarged freedom which distinguishes our age; which in England bears the name of Reform; in Ireland the title of Fenianism; in Europe the name of Progress; and in our Government the name of Radicalism; impresses us with the firm conviction that our claims to universal suffrage will, with no long delay, be considered in the light of reason and sound policy, and decided by the rule of pure and speedy justice.

To the advancement of our completed rights we are most earnestly committed, and shall not cease our work while a single vestige of the old slave power lingers about the black man.

To the end that our people may have an opportunity to publicly express their views upon this most important theme—destined to be the greatest before this Republic—and also that we may vindicate ourselves against the false impressions and perverse misrepresentations of our enemies, we, the undersigned, were, by a mass meeting of our people held in St. Louis on the second day of the present month, designated as a State Executive Committee, for the purpose of more efficiently promoting our object, and were directed to call a series of mass meetings to be held throughout the State, to be addressed by distinguished speakers of our own color, from abroad and at home; and to these occasions do we most cordially invite all persons, without distinction of color, to patiently hear our claims, and, if convinced that they are founded on justice, to accept our appeal.

It is also proposed that this committee procure and distribute printed addresses, and other documents in the interest of the great cause, throughout the State.

To successfully carry on this work, no inconsiderable expense will be incurred; and we most earnestly call upon all our friends for material aid, and direct that contributions of money be sent to Col. Francis Roberson, Chairman of Special Finance Committee, Post-office box 3,187, St. Louis, Mo.

Let the task before us find earnest hearts, untiring hands, and strong faith, leaving the issue to that sure sense of right to which our Government will, at no distant day, give full heed and obedience; and, in the meantime, let our trust be confided in Him whose just Providence has wrested the lash from our taskmasters, and, through our great and good Lincoln, given to our oppressed people a universal emancipation.

Celebrating the End of Slavery

Robert G. Ingersoll

Robert Green Ingersoll (1833–1899) was known as the greatest orator of his day, a progressive reformer on issues including slavery, women's rights, and religion. His free-thinking positions earned him the nickname "the Great Agnostic," as well as the admiration of such intellectuals as Ralph Waldo Emerson and Mark Twain. His lectures were enormously popular throughout the United States, holding audiences rapt for as long as four hours. An ardent Republican, Ingersoll was also a Civil War hero and a highly successful lawyer, although he is best remembered for his passionate, intellectually rigorous speeches.

In his address "to the colored people" at Galesburg, Illinois, in 1867, Ingersoll decries the destructiveness of slavery and celebrates the courage of both British and American abolitionists. He especially lauds John Brown, echoing the sentiments of many of his fellow northern reformers. He exhorts freed slaves to carry forth the spirit of progress and liberty rather than emulate the "villainy" imposed on them by whites.

Fellow-Citizens: Slavery has in a thousand forms existed in all ages, and among all people. It is as old as theft and robbery.

Every nation has enslaved its own people, and sold its own flesh and blood. Most of the white race are in slavery to-day. It has often been said that any man who ought to be free,

From Robert G. Ingersoll's speech "An Address Delivered to the Colored People," Galesburg, Illinois, 1867.

will be. The men who say this should remember that their own ancestors were once cringing, frightened, helpless slaves.

When they became sufficiently educated to cease enslaving their own people, they then enslaved the first race they could conquer. If they differed in religion, they enslaved them. If they differed in color, that was sufficient. If they differed even in language, it was enough. If they were captured, they then pretended that having spared their lives, they had the right to enslave them. This argument was worthless. If they were captured, then there was no necessity for killing them. If there was no necessity for killing them, then they had no right to kill them. If they had no right to kill them, then they had no right to enslave them under the pretence that they had saved their lives.

Every excuse that the ingenuity of avarice could devise was believed to be a complete justification, and the great argument of slave-holders in all countries has been that slavery is a divine institution, and thus stealing human beings has always been fortified with a "Thus saith the Lord."

Slavery has been upheld by law and religion in every country. The word Liberty is not in any creed in the world. Slavery is right according to the law of man, shouted the judge. It is right according to the law of God, shouted the priest. Thus sustained by what they were pleased to call the law of God and man, slave-holders never voluntarily freed the slaves, with the exception of the Quakers. The institution has in all ages been clung to with the tenacity of death; clung to until it sapped and destroyed the foundations of society; clung to until all law became violence; clung to until virtue was a thing only of history; clung to until industry folded its arms—until commerce reefed every sail—until the fields were desolate and the cities silent, except where the poor free asked for bread, and the slave for mercy; clung to until the slave forging the sword of civil war from his fetters drenched the land in the master's blood. Civil war has been the great liberator of the world.

Slavery has destroyed every nation that has gone down to death. It caused the last vestige of Grecian civilization to disappear forever, and it caused Rome to fall with a crash that shook the world. After the disappearance of slavery in its grossest forms in Europe, Gonzales [presumably Antam Gonzales, Portuguese sea-captain who was the first European to kidnap Africans into slavery in 1441] pointed out to his countrymen, the Portuguese, the immense profits that they could make by stealing Africans, and thus commenced the modern slave trade—that aggregation of all horror—that infinite of all cruelty, prosecuted only by demons, and defended only by fiends. And yet the slave trade has been defended and sustained by every civilized nation, and by each and all has been baptized "Legitimate commerce," in the Father, the Son and the Holy Ghost.

It was even justified upon the ground that it tended to Christianize the negro.

It was of the poor hypocrites who had used this argument that [the poet John Greenleaf] Whittier said,

> "They bade the slave-ship speed from coast to coast,
> Fanned by the wings of the Holy Ghost."

Backed and supported by such Christian and humane arguments slavery was planted upon our soil in 1620, and from that day to this it has been the cause of all our woes, of all the bloodshed—of all the heart-burnings—hatred and horrors of more than two hundred years, and yet we hated to part with the beloved institution. Like Pharaoh we would not let the people go. He was afflicted with vermin, with frogs—with water turned to blood—with several kinds of lice, and yet would not let the people go. We were afflicted with worse than all these combined—the Northern Democracy—before we became grand enough to say, "Slavery shall be eradicated from the soil of the Republic." When we reached this sublime moral height we were successful. The Rebellion was crushed and liberty established.

A majority of the civilized world is for freedom—nearly all the Christian denominations are for liberty. The world has changed—the people are nobler, better and purer than ever.

The Pioneers of Freedom

Every great movement must be led by heroic and self-sacrificing pioneers. In England, in Christian England, the

soul of the abolition cause was Thomas Clarkson. To the
great cause of human freedom he devoted his life. He won
over the eloquent and glorious Wilberforce, the great Pitt, the
magnificent orator, Burke, and that far-seeing and humane
statesman, Charles James Fox [British Abolitionists].

In 1788 a resolution was introduced in the House of
Commons declaring that the slave trade ought to be abolished. It was defeated. Learned lords opposed it. They said
that too much capital was invested by British merchants in
the slave trade. That if it was abolished the ships would rot
at the wharves, and that English commerce would be swept
from the seas. Sanctified Bishops—lords spiritual—thought
the scheme fanatical, and various resolutions to the same effect were defeated.

The struggle lasted twenty years, and yet during all those
years in which England refused to abolish the hellish trade,
that nation had the impudence to send missionaries all over
the world to make converts to a religion that in their opinion, at least, allowed man to steal his brother man—that allowed one Christian to rob another of his wife, his child, and
of that greatest of all blessings—his liberty. It was not until
the year 1808 that England was grand and just enough to
abolish the slave trade, and not until 1833 that slavery was
abolished in all her colonies.

The name of Thomas Clarkson should be remembered
and honored through all coming time by every black man,
and by every white man who loves liberty and hates cruelty
and injustice.

Clarkson, Wilberforce, Pitt, Fox, Burke, were the Titans
that swept the accursed slaver from that high-way—the sea.

In St. Domingo the pioneers were Oge and Chevannes;
they headed a revolt; they were unsuccessful, but they roused
the slaves to resistance. They were captured, tried, con-
demned and executed. They were made to ask forgiveness of
God, and of the King, for having attempted to give freedom
to their own flesh and blood. They were broken alive on the
wheel, and left to die of hunger and pain. The blood of these
martyrs became the seed of liberty; and afterwards in the
midnight assault, in the massacre and pillage, the infuriated
slaves shouted their names as their battle cry, until Toussaint,

the greatest of the blacks, gave freedom to them all.

In the United States, among the Revolutionary fathers, such men as John Adams, and his son John Quincy—such men as [Benjamin] Franklin and John Jay were opposed to the institution of slavery. Thomas Jefferson said, speaking of the slaves, "When the measure of their tears shall be full—when their groans shall have involved heaven itself in darkness—doubtless a God of justice will awaken to their distress, and by diffusing light and liberality among their oppressors, or at length by his exterminating thunder manifest his attention to the things of this world, and that they are not left to the guidance of a blind fatality."

Thomas Paine said, "No man can be happy surrounded by those whose happiness he has destroyed." And a more self-evident proposition was never uttered.

These and many more Revolutionary heroes were opposed to slavery and did what they could to prevent the establishment and spread of this most wicked and terrible of all institutions.

You owe gratitude to those who were for liberty as a principle and not from mere necessity. You should remember with more than gratitude that firm, consistent and faithful friend of your downtrodden race, [William] Lloyd Garrison. He has devoted his life to your cause. Many years ago in Boston he commenced the publication of a paper devoted to liberty. Poor and despised—friendless and almost alone, he persevered in that grandest and holiest of all possible undertakings. He never stopped, nor stayed, nor paused until the chain was broken and the last slave could lift his toil-worn face to heaven with the light of freedom shining down upon him, and Say, I AM A FREE MAN.

You should not forget that noble philanthropist, Wendell Phillips, and your most teamed and eloquent defender, Charles Sumner.

But the real pioneer in America was old John Brown. Moved not by prejudice, not by love of his blood, or his color, but by an infinite love of Liberty, of Right, of justice, almost single-handed, he attacked the monster, with thirty million people against him. His head was wrong. He miscalculated his forces; but his heart was right. He struck the sublimest blow of the age for freedom. It was said of him that he stepped from the gallows to the throne of God. It was said that he had made the scaffold to Liberty what Christ had made the cross to Christianity. The sublime Victor Hugo declared that John Brown was greater than Washington, and that his name would live forever.

I say, that no man can be greater than the man who bravely and heroically sacrifices his life for the good of others. No man can be greater than the one who meets death face to face, and yet will not shrink from what he believes to be his highest duty. If the black people want a patron saint, let them take the brave old John Brown. And as the gentleman who preceded me said, at all your meetings, never separate until you have sung the grand song,

> "John Brown's body lies mouldering in the grave,
> But his soul goes marching on."

You do not, in my opinion, owe a great debt of gratitude to many of the white people.

War and Liberty

Only a few years ago both parties agreed to carry out the Fugitive Slave Law. If a woman ninety-nine one-hundredths white had fled from slavery—had traveled through forests, crossed rivers, and through countless sufferings had got within one step of Canada—of free soil—with the light of the North star shining in her eyes, and her babe pressed to her withered breast, both parties agreed to clutch her and hand her back to the dominion of the hound and lash. Both parties, as parties, were willing to do this when the Rebellion commenced.

The truth is, we had to give you your liberty. There came a time in the history of the war when, defeated at the ballot box and in the field—when driven to the shattered gates of eternal chaos, we were forced to make you free, and on the first day of January, 1863, the justice so long delayed was done, and four million of people were lifted from the condition of beasts of burden to the sublime heights of freedom. [Abraham] Lincoln, the immortal, issued, and the men of the North sustained the great proclamation.

The courageous and sometimes daring acts of abolitionists helped many slaves find their way to freedom.

As in the war there came a time when we were forced to make you free, so in the history of reconstruction came a time when we were forced to make you citizens; when we were forced to say that you should vote, and that you should have and exercise all the rights that we claim for ourselves.

And to-day I am in favor of giving you every right that I claim for myself.

In reconstructing the Southern States, we could take our choice, either give the ballot to the negro, or allow the rebels to rule. We preferred loyal blacks to disloyal whites, because we believed liberty safer in the hands of its friends than in those of its foes.

We must be for freedom everywhere. Freedom is progress—slavery is desolation, cruelty and want.

Freedom invents—slavery forgets. The problem of the slave is to do the least work in the longest space of time. The problem of freemen is to do the greatest amount of work in the shortest space of time. The freeman, working for wife and children, gets his head and his hands in partnership.

Freedom has invented every useful machine, from the lowest to the highest, from the simplest to the most complex. Freedom believes in education—the salvation of slavery is ignorance.

The South always dreaded the alphabet. They looked upon each letter as an abolitionist, and well they might. With a scent keener than their own blood-hounds they detected everything that could, directly or indirectly, interfere with slavery. They knew that when slaves begin to think, masters begin to tremble. They knew that free thought would destroy them; that discussion could not be endured; that a free press would liberate every slave; and so they mobbed free thought, and put an end to free discussion and abolished a free press, and in fact did all the mean and infamous things they could, that slavery might live, and that liberty might perish from among men.

You are now citizens of many of the States, and in time you will be of all. I am astonished when I think how long it took to abolish the slave, how long it took to abolish slavery in this country. I am also astonished to think that a few years ago magnificent steamers went down the Mississippi freighted with your fathers, mothers, brothers, and sisters, and may be some of you, bound like criminals, separated from wives, from husbands, every human feeling laughed at and outraged, sold like beasts, carried away from homes to work for another, receiving for pay only the marks of the lash upon the naked back. I am astonished at these things. I hate to think that all this was done under the Constitution of the United States, under the flag of my country, under the wings of the eagle.

The flag was not then what it is now. It was a mere rag in comparison. The eagle was a buzzard; and the Constitution sanctioned the greatest crime of the world.

I wonder that you—the black people—have forgotten all this. I wonder that you ask a white man to address you on this occasion, when the history of your connection with the white race is written in your blood and tears—is still upon your flesh, put there by the branding-iron and the lash.

I feel like asking your forgiveness for the wrongs that my race has inflicted upon yours. If, in the future, the wheel of fortune should take a turn, and you should in any country have white men in your power, I pray you not to execute the villainy we have taught you.

One word in conclusion. You have your liberty—use it to

benefit your race. Educate yourselves, educate your children, send teachers to the South. Let your brethren there be educated. Let them know something of art and science. Improve yourselves, stand by each other, and above all be in favor of liberty the world over.

The time is coming when you will be allowed to be good and useful citizens of the Great Republic. This is your country as much as it is mine. You have the same rights here that I have—the same interest that I have. The avenues of distinction will be open to you and your children. Great advances have been made. The rebels are now opposed to slavery—the Democratic party is opposed to slavery, as they say. There is going to be no war of races. Both parties want your votes in the South, and there will be just enough negroes without principle to join the rebels to make them think they will get more, and so the rebels will treat the negroes well. And the Republicans will be sure to treat them well in order to prevent any more joining the rebels.

The great problem is solved. Liberty has solved it—and there will be no more slavery. On the old flag, on every fold and on every star will be liberty for all, equality before the law. The grand people are marching forward, and they will not pause until the earth is without a chain, and without a throne.

Equality for Blacks, Equality for Women

Sojourner Truth

The first annual meeting of the American Equal Rights Association convened in New York City in May 1867. The association's stated aim was "to secure Equal Rights to all American Citizens, especially the Right of Suffrage, irrespective of race, color or sex." Subject to sometimes heated debate was the matter of whether women's right to vote should be linked with the suffrage of black men.

Participating along with such prominent American reformers as Elizabeth Cady Stanton, Lucretia Mott, and Henry Ward Beecher was Sojourner Truth (1797–1883), former slave and noted abolitionist and women's suffragist. Here, Truth argues for women's rights along with rights for freed slaves; like many in the antislavery movement, Truth viewed universal suffrage as a cause that united the interests of blacks and women. Truth sees the enfranchisement of black males as an historically apt occasion for the extension of equal rights to women.

My friends, I am rejoiced that you are glad, but I don't know how you will feel when I get through. I come from another field—the country of the slave. They have got their liberty—so much good luck to have slavery partly destroyed; not entirely. I want it root and branch destroyed. Then we will all be free indeed. I feel that if I have to answer for the deeds done in my body just as much as a man, I have a right to have just as much as a man.

From Sojourner Truth's address to the American Equal Rights Association, New York, New York, May 9, 1867.

There is a great stir about colored men getting their rights, but not a word about the colored women; and if colored men get their rights, and not colored women theirs, you see the colored men will be masters over the women, and it will be just as bad as it was before. So I am for keeping the thing going while things are stirring; because if we wait till it is still, it will take a great while to got it going again. White women are a great deal smarter, and know more than colored women, while colored women do not know scarcely anything. They go out washing, which is about as high as a colored woman gets, and their men go about idle, strutting up and down; and when the women come home, they ask for their money and take it all, and then scold because there is no food. I want you to consider on that, chil'n. I call you chil'n; you are somebody's chil'n and I am old enough to be mother of all that is here. I want women to have their rights. In the courts women have no right, no voice; nobody speaks for them. I wish woman to have her voice there among the pettifoggers. If it is not a fit place for women, it is unfit for men to be there.

I am above eighty years old; it is about time for me to be going. I have been forty years a slave and forty years free, and would be here forty years more to have equal rights for all. I suppose I am kept here because something remains for me to do, I suppose I am yet to help to break the chain. I have done a great deal of work; as much as a man, but did not get so much pay. I used to work in the field and bind grain, keeping up with the cradler; but men doing no more, got twice as much pay; so with the German women. They work in the field and do as much work, but do not got the pay. We do as much, we eat as much, we want as much. I suppose I am about the only colored woman that goes about to speak for the rights of the colored women. I want to keep the thing stirring, now that the ice is cracked. What we want is a little money. You men know that you get as much again as women when you write, or for what you do. When we get our rights we shall not have to come to you for money, for then we shall have money enough in our own pockets; and may be you will ask us for money. But help us now until we get it. It is a good consolation to know that when we have got this battle once fought we shall not be coming to you any more. You have been having our rights so long, that you think, like a slave-holder, that you own us. I know that it is hard for one who has held the reins for so long to give up; it cuts like a knife. It will feel all the better when it closes up again. I have been in Washington about three years, seeing about these colored people. Now colored men have the right to vote. There ought to be equal rights now more than ever, since colored people have got their freedom. I am going to talk several times while I am here; so now I will do a little singing. I have not heard any singing since I came here.

Accordingly, suiting the action to the word, Sojourner sang, "We are going home." "There, children," said she, "in heaven we shall rest from all our labors; first do all we have to do here. There I am determined to go, not to stop short of that beautiful place, and I do not mean to stop till I get there, and meet you there, too."

Against Black Suffrage

A.G. Thurman

Allen Granberry Thurman (1813–1895), Democrat, served Ohio as representative and senator on both the state and federal level from 1845 through 1881. He ran unsuccessful campaigns for governor in 1867 and for vice president in 1882. A key issue of the 1867 gubernatorial race in Ohio was black suffrage. Running against pro-suffrage Republican candidate Rutherford B. Hayes, Thurman represented the Democratic position that opposed Negro enfranchisement.

In the following speech Thurman asserts that the Constitution has been repeatedly violated over the past six years by the abolitionist Republicans and Union army. Radical Republicans caused the war, prolonged the war, and in a new affront to the battered nation, now propose to bestow the right to vote on blacks while denying the franchise of former slaveholders. Thurman argues that emancipation in the Caribbean and Canada have yielded disastrous social consequences, and goes on to cite even Lincoln as opposing social equality between the races. Thurman calls for "peaceable separation" of blacks and whites. His speech remains a telling reminder that racism was neither limited to the South nor ended at Appomattox.

Thirty-three years ago, and in this County, I made my first political speech. I was then a beardless youth, not entitled to vote. What I then said has long since passed

From A.G. Thurman's speech "First Gun of the Campaign," Waverly, Ohio, August 5, 1867.

from my recollection; but the kindness with which I was received and listened to, I can never forget. Most of those who then heard me have passed away from earth, and I now stand in the presence of a new generation. But I feel that I am now, as I was then, surrounded by friends, and that the same kindness that was bestowed upon me by the fathers, will be shown to me by their sons.

What a change these thirty-three years have produced! When I spoke to your fathers, we were by far the freest people in the world—now, absolute despotism prevails over one-third of the Republic. Then, the Constitution of our country was regarded as only less sacred than Holy Writ—now, outside the Democratic party, there is none so poor as do it reverence. Then, the great principles of American liberty were universally cherished—now, they are openly scoffed at and trodden under foot. Then, a violation of the constitutional safeguards of public and individual freedom was a thing unknown—now, they have been violated so often that their very existence is scarcely acknowledged.

Then, we were the least indebted country on the globe—our national debt being less than six millions—now, we owe more than any other equal number of mankind, and our public debt exceeds $3,000,000,000.

Then, we were the lightest taxed people in the world—now, no other nation groans under a burden of taxation equal to ours.

Then, we had a currency of gold and silver or their equivalent—now, we have rags, and only rags.

Then the balance of trade with other countries was nearly equal—now, it is against us to the extent of more than a hundred million of dollars a year. Then, twenty-five millions of dollars per annum covered our expenses of government and the interest on the public debt—now, we pay nearly six hundred millions, and are, nevertheless, running further into debt every day.

In short, we then had a Constitutional Government, administered upon Democratic principles, by a Democratic administration—now, we have an Abolition Government, administered upon Abolition principles, by a fragment of a Congress and five military dictators.

My friends, there was a time, less than thirty three years ago, when to love and obey the Constitution was regarded as the highest characteristic of a patriot—now, to even mention it with respect is to bring down upon your head the appellation of traitor. Have you considered what this change portends? Have you reflected upon the fact that, aside from your strong arms, the only guarantees you have of life, liberty and property are contained in your Constitutions?

What is it that secures your lives from being taken at the mere will of a despot? The life of a subject can be thus taken in Turkey or Russia, and why not here? Because your Constitutions forbid it. What is it that secures your persons from imprisonment at the pleasure of a dictator? There is no such security in very many countries—why is there here? Because your Constitutions forbid it.

What is it that secures you in the acquisition, enjoyment and disposition of property? In a large part of the globe there is no such security—why is there here? Because your Constitutions declare it.

What is it that secures the minority from being trampled upon by the majority? There is no such security where there are no restrictions upon power; then, why is there here? Because your Constitutions forbid it.

He, then, who undermines the respect of the people for their Constitutions, undermines their security for life, liberty and property. He who treats the words constitutionalist and traitor as synonyms, as meaning the same thing, is himself a traitor or a fool. Understand me, my friends. I do not say that any Constitution can, of itself, secure the people from oppression. We have ample proof of this in the history of the last six years. There never have been Constitutions that guaranteed the rights of man more plainly than do ours, and there have never been Constitutions more shamefully violated. Our Federal Constitution provides that the Congress shall be composed of Senators and Representatives from all the States; and yet ten States are deprived of any representation, and two others are partially deprived. It provides that no bill shall become a law without the President's approval unless passed by two-thirds of each branch of the Congress; and yet, by disfranchising twelve States, a fragmentary and unconstitutional body, self-styled a Congress, nullifies the veto and enacts whatever it sees fit to call by the name of laws. It provides for a Supreme Court of the last resort, and yet the will of a Brigadier General is made paramount to its solemn and most thoroughly-considered decisions. It declares that the right of trial by jury shall be inviolate, and yet men, and women, too, have been sent to the scaffold and to death, by sentence of military commissions, and that, too, when the civil courts were open, and peace everywhere prevailed. It declares that no person shall be deprived of life, liberty or property, without due process of law; and yet, without process of any kind, without even the sentence of a military commission, "organized to convict," thousands of American citizens, females as well as males, have been plundered and imprisoned, and some of them slain by the Government or its agents; and this, too, where the courts were in the unobstructed exercise of their functions.

It forbids the making of any law prohibiting the free exercise of religion; and yet, preachers have been silenced, and even imprisoned, for teaching Christ's Sermon on the Mount.

It guarantees freedom of speech and of the press; and yet, banishment or imprisonment, or both, have followed the exercise of this right; while press after press has been silenced by the orders of government, or the instigated violence of mobs.

Indeed, it is but truth to assert that there is scarcely a provision of the Constitution that has not, within the last six years, been shamelessly and needlessly trampled under foot, and that is not, at this day, yet more shamelessly and needlessly violated. In the face of these facts, it is apparent that no Constitution can, of itself, protect the people.

To produce that effect, it must have the constant affection and support of the masses; and just in the proportion that this affection and support are necessary to its efficacy, just in the same proportion is the merit of obeying and teaching obedience to its commands, and the crime of violating its provisions and weakening its hold upon the popular mind.

And here, my friends, we find a broad line of distinction between the Democratic and Radical parties. The Democratic party is, and ever has been, a Constitution-loving party; and so was the old Whig party until the mass of it became disorganized by the poison of Abolitionism, and it became changed from a great National and Union-preserving party into a great Sectional and Union-destroying organization. But the Radical party, or at least its leaders, have no respect for anything but their own ungoverned will, and their own insatiate lust for power and plunder. From the day that that miserable faction, whose oracles had for twenty odd years denounced the Constitution as "a covenant with death and a league with hell," and who had strained every nerve to bring about a dissolution of the Union—from the moment, I say, that these enemies of our Government obtained the ascendancy and imposed their will upon our rulers, this country has seen little less than woe.

It was owing to the machinations of this faction that disunion and civil war were not peaceably averted; it was to their machinations that we owe the prolongation of the war two years more than it otherwise would have lasted; and it is owing to them that the Union was not completely restored as soon as peace was achieved; and they are the men, who, with diabolical ingenuity, add every day some new element of discord to aggravate our unsettled and dangerous condition, and to menace us with a future of anarchy or despotism.

They overwhelmed with abuse and ridicule every man who, before the war, sought to preserve the Union by peaceful means; they hunted down, as far as they were able, every general of the war, however meritorious, who refused to become their servile partizan; they deprived McClellan of his command, because, after South Mountain and Antietam battles, it was plain that peace could speedily be obtained on the basis of the Constitution and Union of our fathers, and because he was in favor of thus obtaining it; they converted the war from what the President and Congress at the outset declared it to be—a war to preserve the Union and the Constitution—into a war for the enfranchisement of negroes and the perpetuation of the power of a party; they denounced Sherman as a traitor because he granted terms of surrender to Johnston which, if carried out in their letter and spirit, would have given us a restored Union and a peaceful country in less than a month. They alternately coax or abuse Grant, as their hopes of being able to use him for their purposes rise or fall. They threaten the President of their own choice with impeachment because he hesitates to become the President of a party instead of being the President of the Republic.

They reject by the hundred the most gallant and meritorious officers and soldiers, when nominated for office, if they refuse to keep step to Radical music. They use every art, resort to every device, pull every string, invent or repeat every falsehood that can in any way serve to excite and maintain angry passions and prejudices among the people, and prevent their ever again becoming one people in feeling as well as in interest.

But not content with all this, they now demand that the white race, to whom this country owes all its greatness, all its free institutions, and all of liberty and civil government that is left in it, shall become subordinate to the negro. I say subordinate, for is it not subordination when white men are disfranchised and black men set to rule over them; and is it not undeniable that for every negro the Radicals propose to enfranchise, they demand the disfranchisement of more than two white men?

And do not suppose that this concerns the South alone. We have the proposition right before us here in Ohio to confer the votes on seven or eight thousand blacks and mulattoes, and to take it way from about three times as many white soldiers. But this is a mere drop in the bucket compared to the proposition to make voters out of all the negroes of the South and non-voters out of a majority of the white men there. If that be done, the negro-voters will outnumber the white voters in nearly or quite every Southern State; and their votes may make your Presidents and Vice Presidents for half a century to come.

For that result is what a considerable body of voters, voting solidly one way, though a minority, can generally effect. It is the old problem of a balance of power party that gives success to whatever side it goes with and controls its principles and governs its measures.

It was thus that the Abolitionists got control of the Whig party, destroyed its organization, and built upon its ruins a great and triumphant sectional party. And so, if the Radical plans of suffrage be carried out, the negroes of the South will become the balance of power, and destroying the present so-called Republican organization, will bring into existence a yet more radical party—a white man disfranchising, property confiscating, social equality, miscegenation party—that will rule this country until the consequences of the experiment shall become too grievous to be borne, and the people shall rise in their strength and throw off the degrading and disgusting yoke. Negro dominion first, and negro extinction finally must, it seems to me, be the inevitable result of the experiment if tried.

The Destructive Consequences of Black Suffrage

The latter is horrible to contemplate, and the former is full of horrors also. For what has been the result of political and social equality among different and greatly dissimilar races in the same country? Look at the South American republics, look at Mexico—nay, look at Hayti, where even the blacks and mulattoes, though closely related, have been compelled to separate, the former occupying one part and the latter another part of the island, because they cannot live together in peace. In all those countries what have we seen but alternations of anarchy and despotism for the last thirty years? No stable government, no advance in civilization, no increase in wealth, no security for life, liberty or property; but everywhere burnings, plunderings, murders, insurrections, proscriptions and confiscations. Shall we, my friends, bring upon one-third of our country a similar fate?

Shall we make a Mexico of the land that gave birth to Washington and Jefferson, to Marion and Rutledge, to Jackson and Clay? Shall we make the descendants of the men of '76 slaves of slaves—never to be freed from thraldom, except through the ordeal of anarchy? Shall we blindly and stupidly, for the gratification of revenge or the prolongation of the power of a party, entail such calamities upon our common country? I trust not, I believe not—for I have not yet lost my ancient confidence in the integrity and wisdom of the people. Just as firmly as I believe that the negro is not capable of self-government—and in the light of science, history and experience I certainly do believe that—just so firmly do I believe that the white race is thus capable; and, if this be so, I cannot expect it to surrender its power, or share it with those whom God, for His own wise purposes, has made inferior and incapable.

If there be any who think that the illustrations I have given are of little value, because the whites of Mexico and South America are chiefly of Spanish descent, and the inhabitants of Indian blood there outnumber all others, let him turn his eyes to Jamaica, where, under the most favorable circumstances that could be imagined, the experiment has been tried of social and political equality between our Anglo-Saxon race and the negro.

The British Parliament not only emancipated the slaves of that island, but it conferred upon them an absolute equality of rights, political as well as civil, with the whites. The right to vote, to sit on juries, to hold office, were all granted, as well as the right to freedom and to acquire, hold and dispose of property. Not only this, but immense sums have been expended, partly by the government and partly by philanthropists, to educate and Christianize the blacks, and to procure for them farms sufficient for their decent support. And now what is the result?

A plain and undeniable failure. The production of the Island is not one-third what it formerly was, society everywhere fearfully demoralized, a negro insurrection occurring last year and put down with great destruction of life, and, at length, the British Parliament compelled to supersede, for the present at least, and perhaps forever, the local government, and take the rule into its own hands. Such are the fruits of nearly thirty years' experience of white and negro equality in the fairest and most fertile island of the globe. And this state of things is not accidental or spasmodic. The decay and demoralization have gone on increasing from year to year, ever since the inauguration of negro equality. Years after the adoption of that policy, the American and Foreign Anti-Slavery Society, in its annual report of 1853, felt compelled to admit that "a nation of slaves cannot at once be converted into a nation of intelligent, industrious and moral freemen;" and that "it is not too much, even now, to say of the people of Jamaica, that their condition is exceedingly degraded, their morals wofully corrupt." About the same time, the *London Times* thus forcibly and truthfully described the situation:

"The negro has not acquired, with his freedom, any habits of industry or morality. His independence is but little better than that of an uncaptured brute. Having accepted few of the restraints of civilization, he is amenable to few of its necessities; and the wants of his nature are so easily satisfied, that at the current rate of wages he is called upon for nothing but fitful or desultory exertion. The blacks, therefore, instead of becoming intelligent husbandmen, have become vagrants and squatters, and it is now apprehended that with the failure of cultivation in the island will come the failure of its resources for instructing or controlling its population. So imminent does this consummation appear, that memorials have been signed by classes of colonial society hitherto standing aloof from politics, and not only the bench and the bar, but the Bishops, clergy and ministers of all denominations in the island, without exception, have recorded their conviction that, in the absence of timely relief, the religious and educational institutions of the island must be abandoned, and the masses of the population retrograde to barbarism.". . .

The *American Missionary,* a religious periodical, and the organ of the American Missionary Association, in its number for July, 1855, contained the following:

"From the number of churches and chapels in the island, Jamaica ought certainly to be called a christian land. The people may be called a church-going people. There are chapels and places of worship enough at least in this part of the island, to supply the people if every station of our mission were given up; and there is no lack of ministers and preachers. As far as I am acquainted, almost the entire adult population profess to have a hope of eternal life, and I think the larger part are connected with churches. In view of such facts some have been led to say. 'The spiritual condition of the population is very satisfactory.' But there is another class of facts that is perfectly astounding. With this array of the externals of religion, one broad, deep wave of moral death rolls over the land. A man may be a drunkard, a liar, a sabbath-breaker, a profane man, a fornicator, an adulterer and such like—and be known to be such—and go to chapel and hold up his head there, and feel no disgrace from these things, because they are so common as to create a public sentiment in his favor. He may go to the communion table, and cherish a hope of heaven, and not have his hope disturbed. I might tell of persons guilty of some if not all these things, ministering in holy things."

I close the proofs of the state of things in Jamaica by the following very clear statement of a correspondent of the *Boston Post,* written last June; and I pray you to note the similarity of the practices of the English and American Abolitionists, and to ask yourselves whether the same causes that produced the negro insurrection in Jamaica may not, if allowed to exist, produce like insurrections here:

"I notice in your issue a day or two since an article which censures Gov. Eyre, of Jamaica, for his vigorous measures in suppressing the late insurrection. It is not strange to me that the American press is greatly in error upon this subject, as all intelligence has reached this country through English Liberal papers. As I know you desire to arrive at the plain truth upon all subjects, allow me to give you what I believe to be a truthful presentation of facts connected with the Jamaica insurrection, gathered from personal observation on the Island at the close of the outbreak.

"In no country of the world has more money been spent and greater efforts been made for the moral, intellectual and material improvement of the negro than in Jamaica. Soon after emancipation the right of elective franchise was given to the black man. He was allowed to hold any office of trust which was at the disposal of the people. A free school system was devised and established, with a free college or institute, where the higher classics, the sciences and mechanic arts were taught. Benevolent persons in England made large endowments of professorships in these institutions, which were and are filled by eminent men of the old country. The churches of England and Scotland were supported by Government in the most liberal manner, and the Missionary Societies of the Methodist Episcopal and Baptist denominations in Europe extended their work there until the 'meeting house' was as common, and the sound of the 'church-going bell' as frequent as in the most favored portions of our own New England. Thus all which an enlightened nation could do for the prosperity, the intellectual improvement and the morality of the black man had been done—enough, one would certainly suppose, to raise a community of whites to a most prosperous state. Combined with this were the advantages of a wonderfully productive soil and a salubrious climate. The practical question for Americans to know at this juncture is, what have been the results of all these efforts?

"After emancipation, the negroes remained on the old plantations. But Liberalists from England began to teach them that they should break loose from their old masters and settle on the Government lands or become tenants of the landholders. This fatal step they took. The negro, finding himself free from restraint, gave up work. He retained only sufficient vigor to plant the few yams necessary to support life or to pick the abundant fruit of the tropics; his clothing was of the poorest kind, and in most cases was never removed from his person until it fell off; this neglect brought on loathsome disease which the foresight of a master had formerly provided against; he removed his children from school, and his religion degenerated into the most revolting sensualism.

"The effect upon the master was that his revenues were cut off for want of laborers; his rich valleys of sugar cane gave place to underbrush; his coffee and allspice groves ran up to timber; his smiling hill sides of bananas and oranges were overgrown by the invasive mango tree; his castle wasted in decay; his plantation, which had yielded him thousands of pounds per annum, was worth only a few hundred dollars, and the noble families of England which had courted alliances with the princely planters of Jamaica, now turned from him in disdain. Could his misfortune and that of the negro be greater?

"The sequel will show. The negro enthusiasts of England would not allow that this degeneracy arose from any characteristics of the black man, but from the domineering spirit of the white. They therefore sent to the Island party delegates to direct the negro vote, place Radicals in power, and destroy the influence of the white element. They chose among the Islanders a brown man named Gordon notorious for questionable principles, and several negro preachers, natives of the

Barbadoes, who had influence among the blacks. These told the negroes that the Queen designed the Island to be a black colony, that the whites were usurpers, and that the Crown secretly favored a movement to throw the power into the hands of her black subjects."

The Freed Black in Canada

So much for negro equality in Jamaica. Let us now turn to Canada. You have all heard of the under ground railroad and how thousands of negroes were run off upon it to Canada, and there settled in the enjoyment of all the privileges of the whites—the right to vote included. Well, how did the experiment work? Let the Canada officials and people answer. It would take a volume to contain all their testimony on the subject. A few brief extracts must suffice for the present. I read first from the charge of the presiding Judge of the quarter sessions court of the Amherstburg District to the grand jury. The Judge said:

"Having disposed of the law relating to these offenses I arrive at a very painful part of my observations, in once more calling the particular attention of the grand jury, as well as the public at large, to the remarkable and appalling circumstance that among a population of near 20,000 souls, inhabiting this District, the greater portion of the crime perpetuated therein should be committed by less than 2,000 refugees from a life of abject slavery, to a land of liberty, protection and comfort,—and from whom, therefore, if there be such generous feelings as thankfulness and gratitude, a far different line of conduct might reasonably be expected. I allude to the alarming increase of crime still perpetrated by the colored settlers, and who, in spite of the late numerous, harrowing, convicted examples, unhappily furnish the whole of the offenses now likely to be brought before you."

I read from the address of a public meeting held at Chatham, August 18th, 1849, to the people of Canada:

"Canadians: The hour has arrived when we should arouse from our lethargy; when we should gather ourselves together in our might, and resist the onward progress of an evil which threatens to entail upon future generations a thou-

sand curses. Now is the day. A few short years will put it beyond our power. Thousands and tens of thousands of American negroes with the aid of the abolition societies in the
States, and with the countenance given them by our philanthropic institutions, will continue to pour into Canada, if resistance is not offered. Many of you who live at a distance
from this frontier, have no conception either of the number
or the character of these emigrants, or of their poisonous effect upon the moral and social habits of a community. You
listen with active sympathy to everything narrated of the sufferings of the poor African; your feelings are enlisted and
your purse strings unloosened, and this often by the hypocritical declamation of some self-styled philanthropist. Under
such influences many of you, in our large cities and towns,
form yourselves into societies, and, without reflection, you
supply funds for the support of schemes prejudicial to the
best interests of our country. Against such proceedings, and
especially against any and every attempt to settle any town-
ship in this District with negroes, we solemnly protest, and
we call upon our countrymen in all parts of the Province, to
assist in our opposition."

The apprehensions expressed in this address were more
than realized. I find in the debates of the Canadian Parliament of 1857 the following description of Canadian negroes,
by a member, Col. Prince, who knew them well, and who had
at first encouraged their immigration, but had been forced by
experience to change his opinion. He said:

"The blacks were a worthless, useless, thriftless set of
beings—they were too indolent, lazy and ignorant to work,
too proud to be taught; and not only that, if the criminal cal-
endars of the country were examined, it would be found that
they were a majority of the criminals. They were so de-
testable that unless some method were adopted of preventing
their influx into this country by the 'under ground railroad,'
the people of the West would be obliged to drive them out by
open violence."

In November, 1859, the grand jury of Essex county made
a presentment to the court on the subject of the evils resulting from the negro settlements in that county, in which the
opinion was expressed that unless some measure was taken

by the Government to protect the whites and their property, persons of capital would be driven from the country.

In remarking upon this presentment, the Judge observed that "he was not surprised at finding prejudice existing against them (the negroes) among the respectable portion of the people, for they were indolent, shiftless and dishonest, and un-worthy of the sympathy that some mistaken parties extended to them; they would not work when opportunity was pre-sented, but preferred subsisting by thieving from respectable farmers and begging from those benevolently inclined."

Lincoln and Dennison Opposed Equality

I have thought fit to produce these proofs, (not one out of a hundred that might be produced,) notwithstanding their in-convenient length, because some of them may be new to you, and because experience is of far more value than mere opin-ion. That there may be exaggerated expressions in some of them is very possible; but, that they are in the main correct, would seem to be undeniable; and they certainly show that the Canadian and Jamaica attempts at negro and white equality, like every such effort elsewhere, have proved miser-able failures. But if there be any here who prefer the opinions of eminent men, and who, as is very likely the case, attach more weight to the judgment of gentlemen of the Republican party than they do to mine, I invite their attention, first to what was said by Mr. Lincoln in one of his celebrated debates with Senator Douglas, in Illinois, and which I take from the copy of his speech revised by himself. He said:

"I will say, then, that I am not, nor never have been, in favor of bringing about, in any way, the social and political equality of the white and black races; that I am not, nor never have been, in favor of making voters or jurors of ne-groes, nor of qualifying them to hold office or intermarrying with the white people, and I will say in addition to this, that there is a physical difference between the white and black races which, I believe, will forever forbid the two races living together on terms of social and political equality. And inas-much as they cannot so live, while they do remain together there must be the position of superior and inferior, and I, as much as any other man, am in favor of having the superior position assigned to the white man."

I next call to the stand your late distinguished Governor, Mr. [William] Dennison, and I read from his official annual message of January, 1862, to the Ohio Legislature. He said:

"An act of immediate general emancipation, throwing four millions of the colored caste loose on society, North and South, would leave them more enslaved than they are now. Without the intelligence, power and means of a master of the superior race, to support them in the competition of that race in the business of life, they would perish. The North rejecting them, as it has done in many States, and might do in many others, the four millions let loose in the South, would encounter a war of castes, a war of EXTERMINATION."

Lastly I produce our present able and learned Governor, Gen. Cox. You all remember that in 1865, certain Oberlin people wrote to the General asking for his opinion in respect to negro Suffrage. He replied at great length and with great frankness, and it is but just to say that his letter bears internal evidence that he had given the subject great consideration. I read from it as follows:

"You, judging from this distance, say, 'Deliver the four millions of freed people into the hands of their former oppressors, now embittered by their defeat, and they will make their condition worse than before.' I, starting from the same principles, and after four years of close and thoughtful observation of the races where they are, say I am unwillingly forced to the conviction that the effect of the war has not been simply to 'embitter' their relations, but to develop a rooted antagonism which makes their permanent fusion in one political community AN ABSOLUTE IMPOSSIBILITY. The sole difference between us then, is in the degree of hostility we find existing between the races, and its probable permanence. You assume that the extension of the right of suffrage to the blacks, leaving them intermixed with the whites, will cure all the trouble. I believe that it would rather be like the decisions in that outer darkness of which Milton speaks, where—

"'Chaos umpire sits,
And by decision more embroils the fray.'"

Yet, as I affirm with you that the rights to life and liberty are inalienable, and more than admit the danger of leaving a laboring class at the entire mercy of those who formerly owned them as slaves, you will say I am bound to furnish some solution of the problem which shall not deny the right or incur the peril. So I am, and the only real solution which I can see is THE PEACEABLE SEPARATION OF THE RACES. . . .

Black Suffrage Will Mean National Ruin

Great as would be the evils of negro Suffrage in Ohio, much as it would tend to bring into our State an every-way undesirable population, yet the question whether we shall let negroes vote here, is of itself, insignificant compared with that greater question whether we shall surrender the whole South to negro rule, to ruin and to anarchy, and thereby not only destroy that fair section of the Republic, but bring upon the North also untold calamities. Apart from these considerations, the reasons for refusing the vote to negroes in our State are abundant and convincing, but when we regard the proposition as we should regard it, as a part of a great scheme of national ruin, the objections become perfectly overwhelming.

Look at the causes of the present depression of business in the North, and especially in the Northwest, and do you not find prominent among them the impoverished and distracted condition or the South, once our best and most profitable market, and which under good and constitutional government would be so again. Shall this state of things be perpetuated, and we remain deprived of our best customers, that the inordinate ambition of party leaders, and the insatiate cupidity of public plunderers may be gratified?

Shall we continue to maintain freedmen's bureaus and reconstruction officials at a greater annual cost than the entire yearly expenditures of the Government under the administration of Andrew Jackson?

Shall we continue to pay over $250,000,000 a year for the support of an army, which never before in a time of peace cost us over $16,000,000, in order to disfranchise white men and enfranchise negroes? Shall we perpetuate war taxes, long after war has ceased, and pay a heavy tribute upon all we eat, all we drink, all we wear, all we own and all we earn, to support a horde of officeholders and agents whose chief employment is to violate the Constitution and promote the schemes of Radical politicians? Shall we continue to employ all the powers of Government, and powers never delegated to it, nay, powers expressly denied to it by the Constitution, and, in addition, take from the people all that an inexorable tax gatherer can safely lay his hands upon, not to foster, not to promote, not to build up the welfare and union of our country, but to yet further impoverish, yet further destroy, yet further distract and divide it?

These are the questions we have to answer and upon the answer that shall be given to them depends the destiny of the Republic. If this state of things is to continue, if the South is to remain not only impoverished but almost in a state of starvation, if nearly the whole burthen of taxation is thus to be thrown upon the North because the South has nothing to contribute; if, instead of reducing the expenses of Government we are to go on increasing them; if instead of lessening officeholders we are to go on multiplying them; if, instead of husbanding our resources we are to go on squandering them; if, instead of realizing income from our public lands we are to go on giving them away, how, let me ask, are the taxes to be paid, how is the public debt to escape repudiation? And if we continue to disregard the Constitution, if we continue the overthrow of civil government and the existence of military rule, if we prolong the disruption of the Union, and solidify instead of dissipating sectional dislikes, how, let me ask, are civil liberty and the Republic to be preserved?

No, my friends, it is by no such malignant and destructive policy as this, that true peace and union are to be restored, and this country made, what it might and should become, the glory of mankind.

I appeal to you, then, to rally to the rescue before it is too late. Let not the fairest inheritance of liberty and prosperity that man ever enjoyed, be wrested from you. Let not despair enter your souls and make you believe that because much has been lost nothing can be saved. All is not lost. There is yet hope for the future if the people will shake off their lethargy, and rising in their might, resolve to be once more prosperous and free.

Appendix of Biographies

John Brown

John Brown, whose name came to be synonymous with radical abolitionism, was born in Torrington, Connecticut, in 1800, and grew up in Hudson, Ohio. His maternal history was clouded by mental illness, leading many historians to conjecture that Brown too may have suffered from a species of the same insanity that claimed his mother's life when he was eight. During his childhood Brown received little formal education; as an adult, he worked first as a tanner, then later as a surveyor, farmer, and shepherd. Largely itinerant, Brown and six of his adult sons found their way in the mid-1850s to Osawatomie, Kansas, where they became embroiled in the often violent conflict over slavery. Brown was a lifelong abolitionist, although his embrace of armed resistance to slavery and its advocates coincided with his move to what came to be known as "Bleeding Kansas." In retaliation for the proslavery attack on Lawrence, Kansas, Brown and a small band of followers, including four of his sons, murdered five proslavery men in Pottawatomie Creek. Brown's heroic stature in the antislavery movement swelled, despite the fact that many prominent abolitionists such as Frederick Douglass and William Lloyd Garrison disavowed violent resistance.

Brown's unsuccessful raid on the federal armory at Harpers Ferry, Virginia, in 1859 served to seal both his death warrant and his legendary status as a fearless zealot in the as yet undeclared war against slavery. Brown's hopes that the raid would incite a widespread slave rebellion and the eventual establishment of a free black colony in the Virginia mountains seem quixotic if indubitably sincere. After a largely pro forma trial for treason Brown was executed by hanging on December 2, 1859. Lionized by Emerson and Thoreau and reviled by proslavery southerners, John Brown remains to this day the embodiment of the abolitionist true believer.

William Wells Brown

William Wells Brown was among the nation's most eminent African American abolitionists, a powerful orator, writer, and literary talent. Born in Lexington, Kentucky, circa 1814, Brown escaped slavery around the age of twenty. As a steamboat worker on Lake Erie, he aided many fugitive slaves in their flight to Canada. Brown became active in the abolitionist movement in 1836, upon his move to Buffalo, New York, attending antislavery meetings, housing visiting lecturers, visiting Haiti and Cuba as possible destinations for black emigrants. Brown's reputation as an effective speaker against slavery grew along with his activism. By 1844 he was addressing the annual meeting of the American Antislavery Society in New York City; in 1847 Brown was hired to lecture for the Massachusetts Antislavery Society. His autobiography appeared at the end of 1847, and was met with success.

Two years later Brown embarked on a British lecture tour. He was well received by the British abolitionist community, and did not return to the United States until 1854. During his six years abroad, he wrote his novel *Clotel* and began another work, *St. Domingo*. Brown settled in the Boston area, but continued to travel and lecture on slavery. His literary output swelled to include travel narratives, song compilations, a play, and a three-volume work on black history. He finished his last work, *My Southern Home: Or, the South and Its People,* in 1880, four years before his death.

James Buchanan

James Buchanan, fifteenth president of the United States, was born near Mercersburg, Pennsylvania, in 1791. He began his political career as a Federalist, serving in the legislature of his home state, but after his election to the U.S. House of Representatives (1821–1831), he switched party affiliation and became a Democrat. After two years as American ambassador to Russia, Pennsylvanian Buchanan was elected to the U.S. Senate in 1834, serving nine years. In 1845 President James Polk named Buchanan secretary of state; on the conclusion of Polk's term, Buchanan retired briefly before accepting a two-year ambassadorship to Great Britain (1854–1856). Buchanan's conciliatory attitude toward the South and the interests of slaveholders helped him win the presidency in 1856. He supported proslavery positions in the dispute over Kansas's status, the stringent measures mandated by the Fugitive Slave Law, and the *Dred Scott* decision. If his motive was the preservation of the Union by appeasing the South, his actions had the opposite effect, driving a wedge between pro- and (moderately) antislavery Democrats that enabled Lincoln's fateful presidential victory in 1860. Buchanan left office with the nation in the midst of the secession crisis, retiring to his estate in Pennsylvania. He stood firmly behind Lincoln in the war, and outlived his successor by three years, dying in 1868.

John C. Calhoun

John Caldwell Calhoun, statesman from South Carolina, twice served as U.S. vice president, first under John Quincy Adams (1825–1829), then under Andrew Jackson (1829–1832). Although he began his political career as a nationalist, Calhoun came to be known as a fierce defender of states' rights. He became identified with the doctrine of nullification, which held that a sovereign state had the right to nullify federal authority when the former deemed a law illegitimate. Nullification would also form the basis for the southern defense of slavery and its extension into the territories.

Born in 1782 in Abbeville District, South Carolina, Calhoun began his lengthy career in national politics in 1811. As a strong advocate of the War of 1812 Calhoun was known in Congress as a "war hawk"; fittingly, he served as secretary of war from 1817–1825. During his second term as vice president, Calhoun had a falling-out with President Jackson over the tariff issue; he resigned in 1832 and assumed a vacant South Carolina senatorial seat, from which he continued to promote his doctrine of nullification. When a compromise on the tariff matter was reached through the efforts of Senator Henry Clay of Kentucky, Calhoun refocused his political energies on legislation to counter the surging antislavery sentiment in the North. As secretary of state under President Zachary Taylor (1844), Calhoun oversaw the treaty for the annexation of Texas, which preserved the balance of slave states and free states in the Union by establishing the legality of slavery in Texas. He reentered the Senate, where he served until his death in 1850.

Jefferson Davis

Jefferson Davis was the first and only president of the Confederacy. Widely unpopular among his constituents during the Civil War for his somewhat dictatorial management of the government and his rigidity as a military leader, Davis came to be revered by many white southerners for his embodiment of their principles and dignity in defeat. Even after the war ended, Davis continued to defend the Confederate cause and the doctrine of states' rights.

Davis was born in 1808, in Christian County, Kentucky, and moved with his family to Wilkinson County, Mississippi, when he was an infant. Davis entered the U.S. Military Academy at West Point at sixteen, from where he began a distinguished army career, participating in successful campaigns against the Indians, including the Black Hawk War. After resigning from the military in 1835, Davis married Sarah Taylor, daughter of his commander Col. Zachary Taylor, who would eventually be elected U.S. president.

The coupled settled in Mississippi, at Davis's cotton plantation Brierfield, but both soon fell gravely ill from fever, Sarah Davis succumbing and Davis requiring a full year of recuperation. On his recovery he undertook the serious study of history, politics, and the Constitution, while overseeing his prospering plantation. He remarried, and with his second wife, Varina, started a family that would include six children.

Davis entered political life in 1845, elected as a Democrat to the U.S. House of Representatives, then resigned a year later to serve as a colonel in the Mexican War. His bravery in the Battles of Monterrey and Buena Vista earned him renown, and in 1847 the governor of Mississippi appointed him to fill out the term of a vacant U.S. Senate seat. Davis was elected to the seat the next year, and again in 1850, distinguishing himself as a strict constitutionalist, a follower of South Carolina senator John C. Calhoun's doctrine of states' rights, and an opponent of any measure designed to limit slavery. He opposed the Compromise of 1850, and resigned his Senate seat to run, unsuccessfully, for governor of Mississippi as a states' rights Democrat.

In 1853 Davis left his plantation once again to serve as President Franklin Pierce's secretary of war. At the conclusion of his largely effective tenure, he was reelected U.S. senator in 1857. Again, Davis vigorously espoused states' rights and the constitutional protection of slavery, though he now stopped short of advocating secession. Upon Lincoln's election Mississippi seceded from the Union, and Davis resigned from the Senate. He did not seek the presidency of the fledgling Confederacy; rather, he believed he would best serve heading its army. However, he was selected as provisional president at the Confederate convention in Montgomery, Alabama, taking the oath of office on February 18, 1861. A popular vote the next year confirmed his presidency.

Davis was a generally ineffectual wartime president, frequently at odds with his congress and military leaders. Imprisoned and charged with treason shortly after Lee's surrender at Appomattox, Davis was incarcerated for two years at Fort Monroe but ultimately released without a trial. Much of the former Confederacy embraced him for his travails, revering him as a kind of elder statesman who had suffered for a doomed cause. Davis retired to his home in Biloxi, Mississippi; in 1881, he published his work *The Rise and Fall of the Confederate Government*. He died on December 6, 1889. To this day seven southern states observe his birthday, June 3, as a legal holiday.

Frederick Douglass

Frederick Douglass was the most prominent African American of his time, an abolitionist, author, and orator of uncommon eloquence. An ally of William Lloyd Garrison (with whom he later broke), Elizabeth Cady Stanton, William Wells Brown, and other leaders in the antislavery movement, Douglass also advised President Lincoln on the recruitment and treatment of black soldiers in the Civil War. He saw emancipation as only the first step toward complete social equality, and dedicated himself to the cause of universal suffrage for women as well as blacks.

Born a slave in 1817 in Tuckahoe, Maryland, Douglass was separated at a young age from his mother, a slave named Harriet Bailey. Shuttled from one owner to another, Douglass was taught to read and write by the northern-born wife, Sophie, of his master Hugh Auld. On discovering that Sophie was secretly (and in defiance of state law) tutoring the youth, Auld forced his wife to stop, but the experience whet young Douglass's appetite for learning. Several owners later, in September 1838, Douglass made a successful escape to New York City and embarked upon his life as a free man (though technically a fugitive) and abolitionist. Through the Underground Railroad, Douglass successfully arranged for the escape of his sweetheart, Anna Murray, whom he then married.

The couple moved to New Bedford, Massachusetts, where Douglass joined the American Antislavery Society and was soon a featured lecturer known for his forceful, rhetorically sophisticated orations. Encouraged by a group of Harvard students who had heard him speak, Douglass published his first autobiography, *The Narrative of the Life of Frederick Douglass*, in 1845. But because of his status as a fugitive slave, the appearance of the book forced Douglass to temporarily immigrate to England, where he lectured against slavery for two years. He raised enough money to buy his own freedom, returned to the United States, and relocated his family to Rochester, New York. Douglass founded an abolitionist newspaper, the *North Star*, which reflected his chief philosophical difference with fellow antislavery publisher Garrison, who disdained political activism over the cause. While Douglass disagreed equally with Henry Hyde Garnet's call for armed rebellion, he had also come to believe that direct political engagement was necessary to achieve emancipation.

John Brown himself had sought Douglass's support for his ill-fated raid on the federal armory at Harpers Ferry in 1859. Douglass recognized the plan as dangerous and unfeasible, but lest he be unjustly implicated, he fled to Great Britain again for a brief period. By the time the Civil War erupted, Douglass was back in the United States, soon lobbying for soldiers' rights as well as emancipation. After the war's end he worked for the passage of the Fifteenth Amendment and started another newspaper out of Washington, D.C., the *New National Era*. From 1877 to around 1893 Douglass served in a variety of official posts, including U.S. marshal and recorder for the District of Columbia, and in Haiti and Santo Domingo, respectively, consul general and chargé d'affaires. He resigned both diplomatic appointments on learning that corrupt American business interests were exploiting his position to gain advantage with the Haitian government. He died in February 1895 in Washington, D.C., leaving a legacy of courage, commitment, and political activism that would inspire generations of civil rights workers.

Henry Highland Garnet

Presbyterian minister and leading antislavery lecturer Henry Highland Garnet was born into slavery in 1815, in New Market, Maryland. At age nine Garnet and his parents escaped to Pennsylvania. He graduated from Oneida Institute (NY) in 1840, and became a Presbyterian clergyman in Troy, New York. His eloquence as an orator earned him prominence in the antislavery movement, although his controversial 1843 speech, which called on slaves to fight their captors to the death, if necessary, resulted in his expulsion from the Antislavery Society.

Garnet remained active in the struggle for emancipation and black rights. During the Civil War he demanded that black soldiers be allowed to serve in the Union army; in 1864 he was named pastor of a Washington, D.C., Presbyterian church and became the first black American to deliver a sermon before the U.S. House of Representatives. After the war he worked for the Freedmen's Bureau on behalf of newly freed slaves. He also served as president of Avery College in Pittsburgh; two months before his death in 1882, Garnet was appointed U.S. minister to Liberia.

William Lloyd Garrison

Along with Frederick Douglass and John Brown, William Lloyd Garrison was among the most prominent abolitionists of his times. He was also one of the most controversial, reviled as a propagandist and agitator by proslavery interests and on occasion divisive even among fellow abolitionists. Garrison called for the immediate emancipation of slaves, yet eschewed political activism or armed resistance. In the inaugural editorial of his influential abolitionist newspaper, the *Liberator*, Garrison proudly disdained moderation when it came to the struggle against slavery, yet he remained firm in his conviction that emancipation ought to be achieved via moral suasion rather than coercion. Though critical of organized politics, Garrison came to admire Abraham Lincoln by the end of the Civil War.

Garrison was born in 1805 in Newburyport, Massachusetts; by the age of thirteen he had already embarked on a career in journalism, serving as an apprentice to a local editor. His opposition to slavery was evident as early as 1826, when he proclaimed it a "curse" in his short-lived newspaper the *Free Press*. John Greenleaf Whittier, poet and equally ardent abolitionist, was a frequent contributor to the paper. Ultimately Garrison went to Baltimore to coedit an abolitionist newspaper, the *Genius of Universal Emancipation*, with Benjamin Lundy. Convicted of libel for calling the owner of a slave ship a thief and murderer, Garrison served seven weeks of a six-month jail sentence before antislavery sympathizers paid his fine.

It would not be Garrison's last brush with the law. He returned to Boston and on January 1, 1831, the first issue of the *Liberator* appeared. South Carolina made distribution of the *Liberator* a punishable crime, and the Georgia state legislature offered a $5,000 bounty for Garrison's arrest. Undaunted, by year's end Garrison was cofounding the New England Anti-Slavery Society, which became one of the most important abolitionist organizations in the North. In 1833 he helped form the American Anti-Slavery Society. Garrison's abolitionist activities rankled proslavery northerners, who sought to reap the reward offered by Georgia by capturing him and sending him south to face trial. Garrison evaded his would-be apprehenders by sailing to England for an international abolitionist convention. Upon his 1835 homecoming to Boston, Garrison was greeted by a mob who forced a rope around his neck and dragged him through the streets. Ostensibly "for his own good," Garrison was jailed for disturbing the peace.

By 1841 the abolitionist movement, riven by disagreements over gradual versus immediate emancipation, political involvement versus detachment, and the role of women, was splintering into several competing, smaller groups. Garrison threw his lot with the Friends of Universal Reform, which he cofounded with Bronson Alcott, Maria Chapman, Abby Kelley-Foster, and Oliver Johnson, fellow progressives likewise committed to women's suffrage, temperance, and pacifism. He continued to publish the *Liberator*, and to lecture against slavery; in 1854 he publicly burned a copy of the Constitution, to great applause, in protest of the return of runaway slave Anthony Burns to his Virginia owner. By the war's end Garrison was generally hailed as a patriot and hero. With the abolition of slavery finally a reality, he stopped publishing the *Liberator* in 1865, but continued to publicly advocate women's rights and temperance until his death in 1879.

Angelina and Sarah Grimké

Born on November 26, 1805, in Charleston, South Carolina, Angelina Grimké was the daughter of a slaveholding judge. She shared with her sister Sarah a lifelong aversion to slavery, and both sisters became active in the abolitionist and women's rights movements. In 1829 Angelina Grimké joined Sarah in Philadelphia, and became a member of the Society of Friends (Quakers). In 1836 Angelina's pamphlet, *An Appeal to the Christian Women of the South* (followed the next year by Sarah's *Epistle to the Clergy of the Southern States*) exhorted southern women to free their slaves and denounce slavery. Proslavery southerners retaliated by burning the Grimké pamphlets and warning the sisters not to return to the South.

The Grimkés were the first women to address the Antislavery Society in New York, and their activism as abolitionists raised questions in the North as to the propriety of women's assuming so public a role in the fight against slavery. Indeed, the Grimkés saw the struggle for equal rights as pertinent to the cause of women as well as of slaves. In 1838 Angelina Grimké married fellow abolitionist Theodore Weld; with Sarah, the Welds founded progressive schools first in New Jersey and then in New York.

Angelina's public life continued throughout the Civil War, during which she spoke and wrote in support of President Lincoln, and until her death in 1879. In 1870 the Grimké sisters led forty women in casting symbolic ballots in Massachusetts to underscore the inequity of denying female suffrage.

Robert G. Ingersoll

Robert Green Ingersoll was the preeminent public speaker of his time, known and sometimes reviled for his progressive social views on slavery, women's rights, and religion. Ingersoll was also an accomplished attorney and Civil War hero, a Renaissance man admired by Mark Twain and Thomas Edison. He was born in Dresden, New York, on August 11, 1833, and lived most of his life in Illinois, New York, and Washington, D.C.

It has been estimated that more Americans heard Ingersoll speak than any other public figure until the advent of technologically driven media. Ingersoll addressed his rapt audiences, sometimes as large as twenty thousand people, for as long as four hours, expounding on ethical, religious, and political issues. His attacks on religious orthodoxy, including his rejection of the notion of hell, earned him the epithet "the Great Agnostic," and by his own admission restricted any aspirations he may have had to national office. (He served only as Illinois attorney general, an appointed office.) Nonetheless, Ingersoll was an ardent Republican who campaigned tirelessly for the party's candidates. His 1876 speech nominating James G. Blaine for the Republican presidential ticket is considered a high point in American political oratory.

As a lawyer, Ingersoll also litigated a number of nationally prominent cases, including the Star Route trial (over political corruption in the U.S. Post Office) and the Reynolds blasphemy trial, which, though he lost, effectively ended the prosecution of blasphemy in America. As a colonel in the Union army, Ingersoll fought at the Battle of Shiloh and was captured by Gen. Nathaniel Bedford Forrest. Ingersoll died in 1899 in Dobbs Ferry, New York.

J. Mercer Langston

In 1855, John Mercer Langston became the first African American elected to public office, in his case the relatively unassuming position of town clerk in Ohio. But Langston's career as an educator, progressive political activist, and public official was second to only Frederick Douglass's in distinction among black Americans in the nineteenth century. Twice Langston was suggested as a vice presidential candidate on the Republican slate. He was born free in Louisa County, Virginia, the son of a plantation owner and his emancipated slave, in 1829, and orphaned five years later. Langston started Oberlin College at age fourteen, where he earned bachelor's and master's degrees in theology and law. He entered public life while still a youth, addressing the first national black convention in 1848. In addition to his town clerkship, Langston worked tirelessly for the abolition of slavery and for black political rights. He was a committed Republican greatly responsible for persuading the fledgling party to fully embrace the cause of emancipation. During the Civil War, Langston recruited blacks for the Union army and fought for the equal treatment of the enlistees.

After the war, Langston served as inspector general of the Freedmen's Bureau (1868) before accepting the positions of dean and vice president of newly formed Howard University, where he also helped establish a law school. In 1877 he was appointed a U.S. diplomat to Haiti, serving eight years. In 1888 he ran successfully for Congress in Virginia, but his legal battle over electoral fraud kept him from assuming his seat for a year and a half, and he ended up serving only the last three months of his term. (He was not re-elected.) Undaunted in his commitment to black equality, Langston published his autobiography, *From the Virginia Plantation to the National Capital,* in 1894. He died three years later, in 1897, in Washington, D.C.

Abraham Lincoln

Perhaps more than any other U.S. president, Abraham Lincoln has been the subject of countless biographies, historical studies, and even psychoanalytic discussion. While it is occasionally difficult to separate fact from legend and speculation where Lincoln is concerned, there can be little argument that he presided over the nation during a period of unparalleled domestic crisis. Noted for his power and eloquence as a public speaker, lionized for his Emancipation Proclamation, and all but deified after his violent death, Lincoln was at heart a pragmatist as well as a patriot, a politician who valued compromise but also recognized its ultimate ineffectuality. Although personally opposed to slavery, Lincoln believed it was protected by the Constitution in the states where it already existed; however, he sought unequivocally to prohibit its expansion into the territories. He strove to preserve the Union, but once war erupted, he was committed to fighting for a wholesale northern victory, as his appointments of Gens. William Sherman and Ulysses S. Grant demonstrate. His Emancipation Proclamation of 1862 was carefully timed to maximize its detrimental impact on the South, and, as has been noted, only freed slaves in the Confederate states. Yet Lincoln also supported the Thirteenth Amendment against such Democrats as his 1864 presidential opponent George B. McClellan, who argued for restoring all 1860 rights to reconstructed southern states. He insisted repeatedly that the cause of the Civil War was preserving the Union and not abolishing slavery, yet in what is arguably his most famous speech, the Gettysburg Address, he asserted as a fundamental American principle the notion that "all men are created equal."

Lincoln was indeed born in a log cabin, on February 12, 1809, in Hardin County, Kentucky. His father, Thomas Lincoln, was a carpenter and farmer by trade; both of Lincoln's parents had minimal formal education. Thomas and Nancy Lincoln did, however, belong to a Baptist church that decried the immorality of slavery, likely accounting for Lincoln's later observation that he could recall no time in his life when he had not regarded slavery as abhorrent.

In 1816 the Lincoln family moved to a farm near Pigeon Creek, Indiana; Nancy Hanks Lincoln died two years later after drinking contaminated milk. Occupied with assisting his father with the duties of farming and hunting that sustained the family, Lincoln attended school only sporadically. Thomas Lincoln remarried in 1819, and although Abraham would eventually become estranged from his father, he grew fond of his stepmother, Sarah, to whom he often referred as his mother. In 1830 the Lincolns resettled in Illinois.

As a young adult, Lincoln made two trips by flatboat to New Orleans, which may have enabled him to see firsthand the effects of slavery and thus cement his aversion to human bondage. In New Salem, Illinois, he oversaw a mill and general store, and participated in the local debate team. After a brief stint in the military, during which he was elected captain but saw no active duty, Lincoln entered public life, running unsuccessfully for the Illinois legislature in 1832 as a Whig. He was elected to that body two years later, and served four consecutive terms. As early as 1837 he was publicly voicing his opposition to slavery. During his tenure in the state legislature, Lincoln also studied law and passed the Illinois bar, going into practice with one of his Whig mentors, John Todd Stuart. In 1842 he married genteel, Kentucky-born Mary Todd.

Lincoln was elected to the U.S. House of Representatives in 1847, where he served one term. He viewed the Mexican War as unconstitutional and registered his opposition to the expansion of slavery by supporting the failed Wilmot Proviso, but apparently uninspired by a career in national politics, returned to Springfield and his private law practice in 1849. The Kansas-Nebraska Act of 1854 reignited his political passions; unswayed by Illinois senator Stephen Douglas's arguments for "popular sovereignty," Lincoln viewed the act's passage as both unconstitutional and immoral. In 1855 Lincoln sought the Whig nomination in the U.S. Senate race, which he failed to win. A year later he joined the fledgling Republican Party, and in 1858 accepted its nomination to challenge Douglas for his senatorial seat. Although Lincoln lost to Douglas, his powerful performance in their famed series of debates established him on the national political landscape. He won the Republican presidential nomination over the party's initial favorite, William Henry Seward, in 1860, and with the opposition splintered among Democrats Douglas and John C. Breckinridge and Constitutional Union candidate John Bell, Lincoln won the general election. Seven southern states responded by seceding between the months of Lincoln's election and inauguration.

As a wartime president, Lincoln came under criticism for suspending the writ of habeas corpus and differing with his generals over matters of military strategy. But both his cabinet and his military appointments included Democrats and Republicans, and Lincoln adopted a less active role in directing the armed forces after his reelection in 1864. Perhaps most importantly, his Emancipation Proclamation, his decision to allow black soldiers to serve in the military (January 1863), and his support of the Thirteenth Amendment underscored to the fragmented nation that there would be no turning back on the issue of slavery. While to radical abolitionists Lincoln was (at least at the beginning of his presidency) too conciliatory and to slavery's defenders he was too extremist, the nation's sixteenth president indisputably shaped the course of race relations in America. Five days after Lee's surrender to Grant at Appomattox, actor John Wilkes Booth, a southern sympathizer and racist, shot Lincoln at Washington's Ford Theater, where the president and his wife had gone to enjoy a play. Lincoln died the next morning, on April 15, 1865.

George McDuffie

George McDuffie, Democrat, served South Carolina as representative and senator. He was born in Columbia County, Georgia, in 1790, but he attended school and college in South Carolina. McDuffie served in the state House of Representatives from 1818 to 1819 before moving on to the U.S. Congress in 1821, where he chaired the Ways and Means Committee for three terms. He left Congress in 1834 to serve as South Carolina governor for two years. He was appointed U.S. senator from South Carolina in 1842 to fill a vacancy, won election, and served until 1846, when he resigned. He died in South Carolina in March 1851.

During his tenure in the U.S. Congress, McDuffie represented southern interests in vigorously fighting the Tariff Acts of 1828 and 1832, supporting Senator John C. Calhoun's advocacy of South Carolina's right to nullify the federally backed tariffs. Like Calhoun, McDuffie also viewed the preservation of slavery as key to southern prosperity and to "natural" social hierarchy. In many ways McDuffie's views are representative of the antebellum proslavery position held by southern politicians, for whom moral and economic arguments in defense of the institution were commonly entwined.

Alexander H. Stephens

Vice president of the Confederacy, Alexander Hamilton Stephens was born on February 11, 1812, near Crawfordville, Georgia. He served in the Georgia state legislature as representative and senator from 1836 to 1842, when he was elected to the U.S. House of Representatives. Stephens remained in Congress until 1859. At the Georgia state secession convention of 1861, Stephens was elected to the Confederate Congress, and shortly thereafter named vice president of the provisional government. (Like Confederate president Jefferson Davis, Stephens was subsequently elected in 1862.) Stephens headed the failed peace delegation at Hampton Roads, Virginia, in February 1865. After the war he was imprisoned for five months at Fort Warren in Boston, Massachusetts. In 1866 he was elected as a Democrat to the U.S. Senate, but as Georgia had yet to be readmitted to the Union in terms of representation, Stephens was denied his seat. He did return to the House of Representatives in 1873, where he served for nine years. He was elected governor of Georgia in 1882, but died on March 4, 1883.

Despite Stephens's straightforward declaration in his famous 1861 speech that slavery was the "cornerstone" of the Confederacy, he was before the secession crisis a fairly staunch, if proslavery, Unionist. In the 1860 presidential contest he supported Stephen Douglas, a Democrat conciliatory to the interests of both North and South. He did not actively seek the vice presidency of the Confederacy, and once elected, opposed many of Jefferson Davis's more ineffectual policies, although to little avail. After being denied his U.S. Senate seat in 1866, Stephens wrote and published a two-volume defense of the Confederacy, *A Constitutional View of the Late War Between the States* (1868–1870). Like many proslavery southerners and even Free-Soil northerners, Stephens preferred to cast the conflict in legalistic rather than moral terms, a dispute over property rights rather than human rights.

Charles Sumner

Born in Boston, Massachusetts, in 1811, Charles Sumner was a Harvard-educated lawyer, U.S. Senator, and fierce opponent of slavery. He is perhaps best known for his "The Crime Against Kansas" speech, which lasted two days and resulted in his caning attack by Representative Preston Brooks, nephew of South Carolina senator Andrew Butler, whom Brooks believed Sumner had maligned. Sumner began his political career as an antislavery Whig opposed to the annexation of Texas, but left the party in 1848 to support Martin Van Buren's unsuccessful Free-Soil Party bid for the presidency. In 1851 Daniel Webster's appointment as secretary of state led a Democratic–Free-Soil coalition in the Massachusetts legislature to pick Sumner to fill Webster's seat in the U.S. Senate.

As a senator, Sumner argued before and throughout the Civil War for the emancipation of slaves, and in 1864 introduced the

Thirteenth Amendment to the Senate. A so-called Radical Republican, he was integral to the creation of the Freedmen's Bureau, and a sharp critic of the Reconstruction policies of President Andrew Johnson, whose impeachment Sumner wholly supported. Sumner also called for the prohibition of racial discrimination in public places, and for the legitimacy of financial claims against the British for supplying the Confederacy with ships during the war. In 1872 he supported Horace Greeley, presidential candidate of the Liberal Republican–Democratic coalition; the same coalition nominated Sumner for governor of Massachusetts, but he declined due to poor health. Sumner died in Washington, D.C., in 1874.

Henry David Thoreau

Henry David Thoreau is one of the major figures of American literature, a poet, essayist, and social philosopher whose ideas about nature and political conscience continue to influence thinkers 150 years after his death. His work *Walden* (1854) has inspired generations of environmentalists, and his essay "On the Duty of Civil Disobedience" (1849), which put forth the notion of "passive resistance," helped shape the political activism of Mohandas Gandhi and Martin Luther King Jr., among others. Born in Concord, Massachusetts, in 1817, Thoreau was thoroughly a son of New England. He graduated from Harvard in 1837, and initially taught school. Deeply influenced by the Transcendentalist movement and its proponents Ralph Waldo Emerson, Bronson Alcott, and Orestes Brownson, Thoreau incorporated their ideas about nature, ethics, and spiritual development into his teaching as well as his writing. He grew close to Emerson, to whose Transcendentalist literary journal, the *Dial*, Thoreau occasionally contributed.

He constructed a small dwelling on Walden Pond on Emerson's land, where he resided sporadically from 1845 through 1847. During this period Thoreau refused to pay a poll tax in protest of the war with Mexico; out of this experience he wrote his famous essay on civil disobedience. His opposition to slavery intensified with the enactment of the Fugitive Slave Law of 1850, but his position was also a logical extension of his views on the supremacy of individual conscience over socially constructed laws. In his later years he suffered from tuberculosis, and died in 1862, largely unknown beyond his immediate contemporaries in the "*Dial* circle." Much of his work was published posthumously, but not until the twentieth century was Thoreau granted the status of American literary giant.

A.G. Thurman

Allen Granberry Thurman, Democrat, was an Ohio lawyer, representative, and senator. Born in Lynchburg, Virginia, in 1813, Thurman moved with his parents to Chillicothe, Ohio, in 1819. He served in the House of Representatives from 1845 to 1847, as an associate justice of the Ohio Supreme Court (1851–1854), and as chief justice from 1854 to 1856. As judge, Thurman was fondly known to many as "the old Roman." His 1867 bid for the governorship of Ohio against Republican Rutherford B. Hayes failed, but the next year Thurman was elected to the U.S. Senate, where he served from 1869 to 1881. After losing his Senate seat in 1881, Thurman was named to the American international monetary committee in Paris by President James Garfield. In 1888 he ran for vice president on the Democratic ticket headed by Grover Cleveland; the Democrats won the popular vote, but lost the electoral count, and thus the election. Thurman retired from public life; he died in 1895 in Columbus, Ohio.

On key issues affecting antebellum and Reconstruction America, Thurman was by and large conservative and racist. He supported the Wilmot Proviso, believing the settlement of Mexican territories and the West was best limited to white settlers. He was critical of Lincoln's wartime policies and of the emancipation of slaves; while he supported the war, Thurman advocated political compromise with the South and a peaceful resolution to the conflict. His major campaign issue in the 1867 gubernatorial race against Hayes was the denial of black male suffrage, and when he was elected to the Senate the following year, he vigorously opposed Republican Reconstruction policies.

Sojourner Truth

Preacher, abolitionist, and suffragist, Sojourner Truth was born a slave in 1797 in Ulster County, New York. Known to her fellow slaves and a succession of masters as "Isabella," Truth escaped to freedom in 1827, assisted by abolitionists. She documented the travails of her enslavement, including numerous rapes and the selling of most of the thirteen children to whom she gave birth, in her *Narrative of Sojourner Truth* (1850). Unable to read or write, Truth dictated her memoirs to a neighbor, Olive Gilbert.

In 1843 she changed her name to Sojourner Truth, and embarked upon public life, traveling throughout New England preaching about Jesus, the evils of slavery, and women's right to suffrage. In 1851 she delivered her most famous speech, "Ain't I a Woman?", at a women's rights convention in Akron, Ohio, in response to a male heckler. Her suffering and courage as a female slave testified to the fact that women were not inherently frail creatures incapable of the full rights of citizenship.

During the Civil War, Truth visited Union troops and assisted refugee slaves in Washington, D.C. After the war she strove fruitlessly to persuade Congress to grant freed slaves land in unclaimed regions of the West. She died on November 26, 1883, in Battle Creek, Michigan.

Daniel Webster

Daniel Webster was born in Salisbury, New Hampshire, on January 18, 1782, a farmer's son who became one of the most noted statesmen and orators of his time. After graduating from Dartmouth College in 1801, Webster went on to study and practice law. In 1812 he was elected to the House of Representatives as a Federalist opposed to the War of 1812; there he furthered his reputation as a fierce nationalist and formidable lawyer. Webster left Congress four years later, settling in Boston and devoting his energies to successfully arguing a number of key constitutional cases before the U.S. Supreme Court.

Webster returned to represent Boston in the House in 1823; four years later Massachusetts elected him U.S. senator. He supported the high tariff bill of 1828, spurring a sectional dispute with southern senators led by John C. Calhoun of South Carolina, who argued a state's right to nullify a law perceived as unjust. Webster's skills as a lawyer and orator helped defeat South Carolina's attempt at nullification.

Webster's ambitions lay toward the presidency. He launched his first bid in 1836 as one of three Whig candidates, but carried only his adopted home state of Massachusetts. In 1841 he was appointed secretary of state by President William Henry Harrison; upon the president's death and succession by John Tyler, all the Whig cabinet members resigned except for Webster, who stayed through 1843 to forge the Webster–Ashburton Treaty (1842), which resolved a boundary dispute between Maine and Canada. He was named secretary of state again by President Millard Fillmore in 1850, the same year Webster delivered his renowned 7th of March speech defending the Compromise of 1850. The stringent new Fugitive Slave Law was a means, Webster argued, justified by the overarching end of preserving the Union. As secretary of state he oversaw the implementation and enforcement of the law, incurring the enmity of abolitionists and many of his fellow Whigs. He died on October 24, 1852.

For Further Research

HERBERT APTHEKER, *American Negro Slave Revolts*. New York: International, 1965.

HENRIETTA BUCKMASTER, *Flight to Freedom: The Story of the Underground Railroad*. New York: Dell, 1972.

WILLIAM CHEEK AND AIMEE LEE CHEEK, *John Mercer Langston and the Fight for Black Freedom, 1829–65*. Urbana: University of Illinois Press, 1989.

DAVID BRION DAVIS, *The Problem of Slavery in Western Culture*. New York: Oxford University Press, 1988.

CARL DEGLER, *The Other South*. New York: Harper & Row, 1974.

DAVID HERBERT DONALD, *Charles Sumner and the Coming of the Civil War.* Chicago: University of Chicago Press, 1960.

MARTIN DUBERMAN, ED., *The Antislavery Vanguard*. Princeton, NJ: Princeton University Press, 1965.

DWIGHT LOWELL DUMOND, *Antislavery: The Crusade for Freedom in America*. Ann Arbor: University of Michigan Press, 1961.

STANLEY ELKINS, *Slavery: A Problem in American Institutional Life*. Chicago: University of Chicago Press, 1976.

ENA L. FARLEY, *The Underside of Reconstruction New York: The Struggle over the Issue of Black Equality*. New York: Garland, 1993.

DONALD E. FEHRENBACH, *Prelude to Greatness*. Palo Alto, CA: Stanford University Press, 1962.

LOUIS FILLER, *The Crusade Against Slavery, 1830–1860*. New York: Harper & Brothers, 1960.

ERIC FONER, *Free Soil, Free Labor, Free Men*. New York: Oxford University Press, 1970.

PHILLIP S. FONER, *Frederick Douglass*. New York: Citadel, 1964.

ELIZABETH FOX-GENOVESE, *Within the Plantation: Black and White Women of the Old South*. Chapel Hill: University of North Carolina Press, 1988.

JOHN HOPE FRANKLIN, *From Slavery to Freedom*. New York: Knopf, 1979.

———, *Reconstruction: After the Civil War*. Chicago: University of Chicago Press, 1961.

WILLIAM FREEHLING, *Road to Disunion*. New York: Oxford University Press, 1990.

EUGENE GENOVESE, *The World the Slaveholders Made: Two Essays in Interpretation*. New York: Pantheon, 1969.

STANLEY HARROLD, *The Abolitionists and the South, 1831–1861*. Lexington: University Press of Kentucky, 1995.

MICHAEL HOLT, *The Political Crisis of the 1850s*. New York: Wiley, 1978.

JAMES OLIVER HORTON, *Free People of Color: Inside the African American Community*. Washington: Smithsonian Institution Press, 1993.

WINTHROP D. JORDAN, *White over Black: American Attitudes Toward the Negro, 1550–1812*. Chapel Hill: University of North Carolina Press, 1968.

AILEEN KRADITOR, *Means and Ends in American Abolitionism*. New York: Ivan Dee, 1989.

DAN LACY, *The Abolitionists*. New York: McGraw-Hill, 1978.

GERDA LERNER, *The Grimke Sisters from South Carolina*. Tel Aviv: Schocken, 1967.

STEPHEN R. LILLEY, *Fighters Against American Slavery*. San Diego: Lucent, 1998.

LEON LITWACK, *Been in the Storm So Long*. New York: Random House, 1980.

HENRY MAYER, *All on Fire: William Lloyd Garrison and the Abolition of Slavery*. New York: St. Martin's, 1998.

DANIEL J. MCINERNEY, *The Fortunate Heirs of Freedom: Abolition & Republican Thought*. Lincoln: University of Nebraska Press, 1994.

AUGUST MEIER AND ELLIOTT RUDWICK, *From Plantation to Ghetto*. New York: Hill & Wang, 1976.

EDMUND MORGAN, *American Slavery, American Freedom*. New York: Norton, 1975.

RUSSELL NYE, *Fettered Freedom: Civil Liberties and the Slave Controversy, 1830–1860*. East Lansing: Michigan State University Press, 1964.

JAMES OAKES, *The Ruling Race: A History of American Slaveholders*. New York: Knopf, 1982.

————, *Slavery and Freedom: An Interpretation of the Old South*. New York: Knopf, 1990.

STEPHEN B. OATES, *With Malice Toward None*. New York: New American Library, 1981.

WILLIAM S. PARSONS AND MARGARET DREW, *The African Meeting House in Boston: A Sourcebook*. Boston: Museum of Afro-American History, 1992.

JANE AND WILLIAM PEASE, *They Who Would Be Free: Blacks' Search for Freedom, 1830–1861*. New York: Atheneum, 1974.

DAVID M. POTTER, *The Impending Crisis, 1848–1861*. New York: Harper & Row, 1976.

BENJAMIN QUARLES, *Black Abolitionists*. New York: Oxford University Press, 1969.

WILLIE LEE ROSE, *Slavery and Freedom*. New York: Oxford University Press, 1982.

SHIRLEY SAMUELS, ED., *The Culture of Sentiment: Race, Gender, and Sentimentality in Nineteenth-Century America*. New York: Oxford University Press, 1992.

RICHARD SEWELL, *Ballots for Freedom: Anti-Slavery Politics, 1837–1861*. New York: Oxford University Press, 1976.

KENNETH M. STAMP, *The Peculiar Institution: Slavery in the Ante-Bellum South*. New York: Vintage Books, 1956.

JAMES B. STEWART, *Holy Warriors*. New York: Hill & Wang, 1976.

STERLING STUCKEY, *Slave Culture*. New York: Oxford University Press, 1987.

LARRY TISE, *Proslavery: A History of the Defense of Slavery in America, 1701–1840*. Athens: University of Georgia Press, 1987.

WENDY HAMAND VENET, *Neither Ballots nor Bullets: Women Abolitionists and the Civil War*. Charlottesville: University Press of Virginia, 1991.

C. VANN WOODWARD, *American Counterpoint*. Boston: Little, Brown, 1971.

JEAN FAGAN YELLIN AND JOHN C. VAN HORNE, EDS., *The Abolitionist Sisterhood: Women's Political Culture in Antebellum America*. Ithaca, NY: Cornell University Press, 1994.

Document Collections and Other Primary Sources

American Memory: Historical Collections for the National Digital Library, Library of Congress, Washington, DC, www.memory.loc.gov/ammem/amhome.html.

The American Passages: A History of the United States. Textbook and website published by Harcourt College Publishers, www.azimuth.harcourtcollege.com/history/ ayers/MainAP/welcome.html.

ROY P. BASLER, ED., *The Collected Works of Abraham Lincoln*. Springfield, IL: Abraham Lincoln Association, 1953.

JOHN BROWN, "Speech and Sentence of Brown," *The Life, Trial and Execution of Capt. John Brown: Being a Full Account of the Attempted Insurrection at Harpers Ferry, Va*. New York: Robert M. De Witt, 1859.

LARRY CEPLAIR, ED., *The Public Years of Sarah and Angelina Grimké: Selected Writings 1835–1839.* New York: Columbia University Press, 1989.

RICHARD K. CRALLÉ, ED., *The Works of John C. Calhoun.* Vol. 6. Columbia, SC: A.S. Johnston, 1851.

Documenting the American South, electronic archive of Southern history, literature, and culture, University of North Carolina Press, Chapel Hill, www.metalab.unc.edu/docsouth.

Douglass Archives of American Public Address, electronic archive of Northwestern University Press, Evanston, IL, 2000, www.pubweb.northwestern.edu/~doetting/douglass.htm.

Electronic Oberlin Group, Oberlin Through History (Langston), Oberlin College Archives, www.oberlin.edu/~EOG.

SUZANNE PULLON FITCH AND ROSEANN M. MANDZIUK, *Sojourner Truth as Orator: Wit, Story, and Song.* Great American Orators, No. 25 (ISSN: 0898-8277). Westport, CT: Greenwood, 1997.

From Slavery to Freedom: The African American Pamphlet Collection. Washington, DC: Library of Congress, Rare Book and Special Collections, 2000.

PHILIP S. FONER, ED., *Frederick Douglass: Selected Speeches and Writings.* Library of Black America. New York: Da Capo, 1992.

Furman University, Nineteenth-Century Documents Project, www.furman.edu/~benson/docs.

Robert Green Ingersoll, *Complete Lectures of Col. Robert G. Ingersoll.* Chicago: Regan, 1928.

DEIRDRE MULLANE, ED., *Crossing the Danger Water: Three Hundred Years of African-American Writing.* New York: Anchor, published by Doubleday, a division of Bantam Doubleday, 1993.

C. PETER RIPLEY ET AL., EDS., *The Black Abolitionist Papers: Vol. I: The British Isles, 1830–1865*. Chapel Hill: University of North Carolina Press, 1985.

NANCY L. ROSENBLUM, ED., *Henry David Thoreau: Political Writings*. Cambridge Texts in the History of Political Thought. Cambridge, England: Cambridge University Press, 1996.

Daniel Webster: Dartmouth's Favorite Son, Daniel Webster Archives, Speeches and Orations, www.dartmouth.edu/~dwebster/archive.html.

Index